MAX

MAX

The Life and Music of
Peter Maxwell Davies

MIKE SEABROOK

VICTOR GOLLANCZ

LONDON

First published in Great Britain 1994
by Victor Gollancz
A Cassell imprint
Villiers House, 41/47 Strand, London WC2N 5JE

A catalogue record for this book is
available from the British Library.

ISBN 0 575 05672 X

Typeset at The Spartan Press Ltd,
Lymington, Hants
Printed in Great Britain by
Mackays of Chatham plc, Chatham, Kent

For Judy Arnold, with sincere thanks
for indispensable help, ungrudgingly given,
for generous hospitality
and for making me laugh.

S M T

And for Perviz. As always. Of course.

Contents

List of Illustrations

Joyce Palin, aged about fourteen (*Carl Cloud*)

Eric Guest, aged eighteen

The Manchester Group, 1956

Max and the original Fires of London

Max and the crew of *Taverner*, Covent Garden, 1983 (*Frank Herrmann/© Sunday Times*)

The Fires, second generation (*Martin Haswell/© Bath Festival Society*)

A scene from *The Lighthouse* (*Alex 'Tug' Wilson*)

With George Mackay Brown (*Gunnie Moberg*)

Outside the renovated and habitable Bunertoon (*Gunnie Moberg*)

In the kitchen at Bunertoon, with the monster gramophone (*Ros Drinkwater/© Sunday Times*)

Aboard Stevie's ferry, the *Scapa Ranger* (*Gunnie Moberg*)

Max and his parents outside Buckingham Palace after his award of the CBE, 1981 (*Judy Arnold*)

With his neighbour, ally and friend, David Hutchinson (Hutch), Rackwick, 1993 (*Gunnie Moberg*)

Children of North Walls School performing *Songs of Hoy*, Hoy, 1992 (*Gunnie Moberg*)

Class of 1993: with the young composers of the Hoy Summer School (*Ken Pirie*)

With György Pauk and the RPO rehearsing the Violin Concerto (*Hanya Chlala*)

Max at his desk in Bunertoon, looking out over the Pentland Firth (*Ros Drinkwater/© Sunday Times*)

Preface

The twentieth century has seen an ever-widening gulf between creative artists and the public. The result of this has been that the great majority of music lovers have tended to dismiss modern music as impenetrable, on the principle that 'I can't understand all that spiky modern stuff, all plinks and plonks and dripping taps.' This is true even now, when mysticist or minimalist composers such as Gorecki and John Tavener have reached lofty positions in the popular music charts.

This book was written on the premise that there is much contemporary music that needs hold no fears for anyone willing to listen to it with open ears and an open mind; and that this certainly applies to the music of Peter Maxwell Davies. It was written also, however, in the realistic acceptance that contemporary music, even the most accessible, does make certain demands on the listener that are not made by the music of, say, Mendelssohn or Tchaikovsky, or even by music of such acknowledged and extreme complexity and difficulty as the late quartets of Beethoven.

It is, therefore – in addition to being the life story of an interesting man – an attempt to offer the newcomer to Max's music a simple kind of map or guidebook, pointing out some of the more obvious landmarks and attractions, with the expectation that the traveller, once his appetite is whetted, his confidence boosted, will sally out in search of more without being daunted by the various obstacles to the full enjoyment of new music.

The book does not include a bibliography. There are very few books on Max and his music. The only approach to a full study of his music is *Peter Maxwell Davies*, by Paul Griffiths, published by Robson Books in 1982. This is a valuable and reliable study, which gives a great deal of insight into the music and the composer's intentions, circumstances and state of mind when he was composing it. It includes a lot of material contributed directly by Max himself, in addition to Griffiths's own analysis and exegesis, which are highly perceptive. It is thus a highly authoritative book, despite its brevity. But it is, of course, a long way out of date now. There is also *Peter Maxwell Davies: a Bio-Bibliography*, by Carolyn Smith, published by the Greenwood Press in the USA, which attempts the monumental task of listing and annotating every printed utterance of and about Max. Otherwise there is only a German study, *Peter Maxwell Davies: Ein Komponistenporträt* (Boosey & Hawkes, Bonn, 1983).

Other than these, the literature for anyone seriously interested consists mainly of articles, of varying degrees of erudition, in Boosey & Hawkes's quarterly magazine on contemporary music, *Tempo*. This scholarly periodical has carried many articles on Max and his music over the last thirty years. Many of these were reissued in collected form in 1979, in a 104-page booklet, *Peter Maxwell Davies: Studies from Two Decades*. Back numbers of most of the issues containing articles can be obtained on application to Boosey & Hawkes's London office.

The discography includes only CDs available at the time of going to press, or already scheduled for release. Max's music is well represented in the current record catalogues. His new works are now appearing on CD (from Collins Classics) very soon after their premieres, and older pieces are increasingly being recorded, often in definitive versions directed by Max himself. And although a good many works recorded in the past on LP are no longer available, anyone looking for such recordings will find that the specialist record dealers who stock such collectors' items maintain excellent catalogues.

Many people helped to make this book possible, giving freely of their time, which was usually scant and precious in proportion, taking me into their homes, giving generous hospitality and patiently answering huge numbers of questions. A few whom I was unable to meet in person kindly made tapes or corresponded with me at length; and a few interviews with Judy Arnold were recorded. I am most grateful to them all. In alphabetical order, they are:

Anne Adams of the BBC, Tim Anger, John Barnett, Archie and Elizabeth Bevan, Sir Harrison and Lady Sheila Birtwistle, Alan Booth, George Mackay Brown, John Carewe, James Clark, Jeff and Avril Clark, Nicholas Cleobury, Edward Cone, William Conway, Eona Craig of the Scottish Chamber Orchestra, Duncan Druce, John Drummond, Paul Findlay, Sir William Glock, Trevor Green, Lady Hilary Groves, Eric Guest, Alan Hacker, John and Rosemary Harbison, Håkan Hardenberger, Christine Herkes of the Scottish Chamber Orchestra, Trevor Hill, Louise Honeyman, Elgar Howarth, Richard and Glenys Hughes, David Hutchinson, Joyce Palin Jackson, Sylvia Junge, David Keeble, Ian Kellam, Milein Cosman Keller, Gerard McBurney, Michael McCarthy, Donald MacDonald, Kathy MacDowell, Neil Mackie, Ian Maclay, Neil Martin, Murray Melvin, Kris Misselbrook, Donald Mitchell, Gunnie Moberg, James Murdoch,

Mike Newman of the BBC, Bayan Northcott, György Pauk, Andrew Porter, Stephen Pruslin, Philip Reed, Jack, Dorothy and Lucy Rendall, Ian Ritchie, Eric Roseberry, The Hon. Sir Steven Runciman, Ken Russell, Derek Saul, John Steer, Isaac Stern and his personal assistant, Jacques E. Boubli, Michael Storrs, Randolph Stow, Amanda Tenneson of the BBC, Mary Thomas, Pat Tidswell, Michael Tumelty and the editor of the *Glasgow Herald*. Bob and Barbara Tyldesley, Les and Roger Walden, Judith Weir, David William, David Wilson, David Wilson-Johnson.

I owe a special debt of thanks to Roger Holmes, whose help, including with the illustrations, was invaluable, and far beyond the call of duty.

The staff of the Scottish Chamber Orchestra, the BBC Philharmonic Orchestra, and the BBC in Manchester in general, were tireless, patient and unendingly helpful, especially in unearthing photographs. I am grateful to all three bodies, as well as to the individual members of their staffs included in the list above.

Alan Booth and Anne Finerty were generous and helpful at all times, and I am grateful to both of them and to all at Collins Classics. Emma Kerr and Nicole Rochman at Boosey & Hawkes, Rhiannon Mathias at Chester Music and Sally Groves and Ulrike Muller at Schott & Co. Ltd all spent large amounts of their time to make and provide me with tapes of Max's works that are not yet available in commercial recordings. I am most grateful to them all and to their companies for their generosity.

This is a biography of a musician by a non-musician. For the passages of musical description scattered throughout the book I have drawn on the notes by Paul Griffiths for the various brochures published by Max's manager, Judy Arnold, and I am very grateful to him for his generous permission to borrow, paraphrase and quote directly from his work.

I should add that I have borrowed only descriptive material and other matters of fact – it enabled me to avoid the fairly pointless task of having to think up an alternative way, personal to me, of saying, 'This piece has four movements, allegro, presto, largo and rondo, and is scored for cathedral organ, ear trumpet and Jew's harp.' Where Mr Griffiths's kind co-operation became especially important, indeed essential, was when I had to make mention of works that I had not, despite the valiant efforts of Max's publishers, been able to hear for myself. However, where I have ventured beyond mere factual description, analysis of the works is entirely my own.

Because of the relative frequency of such musical references, and because of their brevity – often an attribution would be longer than a passage used in this way – I have not attributed these references to their sources, but with Mr Griffiths's agreement have acknowledged them in general here. Otherwise, direct quotations have been attributed in the text, except in a few cases where an attribution might have caused embarrassment, or where the source of the quotation asked directly not to be named.

Special thanks are due to Judy Arnold herself. Without her help and support, unstintingly, unfailingly and always cheerfully given, her efficiency, her awesome energy and her huge enthusiasm, this book would have been, quite simply, impossible. The dedication reflects my gratitude to her, in which I should wish her husband Michael to take his full and rightful share.

The other person to whom special thanks are due, for generous hospitality, for splendid conversation and, most of all, for endless inspiration, is, of course, Max himself.

My mother-in-law, Mrs Nergis Pavri, both put me up and put up with me throughout my two long visits to Britain to research this book. Such heroism deserves profound thanks, and she has it. Thanks also to all at the Crown Hotel, Stromness, and at Monroe's Hotel, Manchester, for making my first stays in two such very different towns so pleasant.

Finally, my debt to my wife Perviz is, as always, enormous. In particular, she compiled the index, which alone would merit gratitude enough. In general, since her contribution was far greater than a few words here can begin to convey, it is best to say simply that without her I could scarcely function at all, and leave it at that.

1 ~ *Father of the Man*

'It was thrilling for me to live with him, even as a little baby.' The words were said by Mrs Hilda Davies, in an interview recorded in her eightieth year, a few months before her final illness, and she was speaking of her son.

It is not the rarest thing in the world for a mother to enthuse over her son, especially, perhaps, an only son. But in this case both the warmth of tone and the wording are uncommon, conveying a depth of sincerity that removes the remark from the commonplace, and suggesting that the son was indeed something out of the ordinary.

He was given the Christian names Peter Maxwell, he was to become Sir Peter, and from earliest infancy he has always been known to his friends as, simply, 'Max'. No one knows why the first given name was always dropped in favour of the second, but it has always been so, and remains so to this day.

He was born – at home, as was very common in those days – on 8 September 1934, in Holly Street, Salford, Lancashire, and spent the first few years of his life living there, above the newsagent's shop owned by his mother's parents. Salford was at that time a smallish industrial city destined to perpetual junior status in a binary system with its far greater partner, Manchester. It was a major centre of the cotton industry, and had extensive docks. With the death of both and the creation of metropolitan counties under the Maud Report of 1974, Salford has become one part of the vastly populated, amorphous, sprawling entity known as Greater Manchester.

Max's parents were conventional working-class people, from conventional families. Relations between both parents and their families were friendly, and the marriage was, both then and to the end of their lives, more than conventionally happy and stable. It does not appear that it was an unequal partnership in terms of giving: husband and wife liked and respected each other. This was obvious in the interview from which the words opening this chapter were taken: they interrupted each other cheerfully and without any resentment, and spoke throughout in the tones of two people who had grown old happy, comfortable and secure in each other's company.

Tom Davies was born on 6 September 1901, and was thus two days past his thirty-third birthday when Max was born. He was employed at Thornton's, a local firm manufacturing high-precision optical instruments. Although by the time of Max's arrival he had become a foreman, Tom Davies was himself an exceptionally skilled instrument-maker. One childhood friend of Max's remembers watching Tom in the garden, very carefully gathering spiders' webs, explaining that he would use the extremely fine, delicate gossamer filaments to make the cross-hairs for theodolites, telescopic sights and other such instruments.

His wife, Hilda, was born three years later in 1904, one of a family of five daughters, all of them vivacious and high-spirited, and all blessed with considerable good looks. By the time she was twelve Hilda was a pupil-teacher at her school – a common arrangement in those days – and had already been offered the chance to train as a fully fledged schoolteacher; but the gods were against it, and she never took up the opportunity.

There is evidence of considerable artistic and creative ability on both sides of the family; but of musical talent there is no sign at all. Several members of both families played the piano well enough for family sing-songs – a popular form of family entertainment in those pre-television days – and Max's father sang for a time in a male-voice choir. Max's mother had no musical abilities at all, but she was quite clearly highly intelligent, and she had a fondness, and a considerable talent, for painting. Had she been born only a generation later, when higher education was much more readily available to the children of the poor and the less well-off, she would, without much doubt, have gone on to university, and who knows where after that. As it was, she accepted her lot as a housewife and poured her abundant energy into it, as people of her generation tended to do; nor, as far as can be ascertained, did she suffer much unhappiness or frustration from doing so.

There is no doubt that Max was wanted, and that he was much loved when he arrived. Both his parents gave him a great deal of affection, probably more openly than was often the case in those less demonstrative times. His own verdict is that they were 'very solicitous and caring. I was quite spoilt, really.' Although they were outwardly fairly conventional, Tom and Hilda Davies were clearly unusually enlightened and tolerant people, who gave their son a great deal of freedom, in particular the freedom to be his own man, to think, speak and behave in his own way. Younger readers may wonder why such a thing should be thought worthy of mention; but the fact is that until well after the Second World War such tolerance of children, such respect for their individuality and their opinions, was by no means the rule, but on the contrary rather unusual, almost a sign of bohemianism. The ancient maxim that 'children should be seen and not heard' still held to an extent that today's children may find difficult to credit.

That said, Max's infancy was conventional enough. He was a lively, healthy child, with a vivid imagination, which showed itself in his play. He had a vast and complicated railway system, wholly imaginary, that covered the whole of the garden – his mother remembered walking across the grass on one occasion to hang out some washing, and being admonished by Max: 'You've just walked all over my station.'

He enjoyed the privilege of all children lucky enough to have fathers skilled with their hands: Tom Davies made wonderful toys for his son. There was a beautifully made wooden train with metal signals, and a stage with lights and curtains, for which his mother made the sets and painted figures. Max and his friends would write their own plays, manipulating the characters and doing the voices themselves. He also played all the pretend games that all children play: he would dash round the garden on all fours, being a dog, lifting his leg against the rose bushes for authentic effect; and a great friend of his youth claims that the reason why Max never did any singing was because he ruined his voice in childhood, doing spirited and ear-splitting imitations of dogs and air-raid sirens. He also kept a diary in a private language of his own invention – something he still does to this day.

Two things were certainly apparent in the young Max from very early on: the intense, searchlight gaze of his striking blue eyes, which have been remarked on throughout his life by people meeting him for the first time; and his personality, which was attractive, perhaps indeed magnetic (though one feels somewhat shy of the word, in view of the kind of people to whom it is usually applied). He was a dominant character from early childhood. The other children of the neighbourhood tended to converge on his house and play round it, whether Max joined them or not. It was usually 'not', because he never showed any great interest in street games, and none at all in ball games and other sports – unusual in an era when Stanley Matthews, Denis Compton, Len Hutton and their contemporaries were every boy's heroes, and football and cricket were genuinely mass entertainments, drawing crowds several times the size of the biggest attendances today.

Two things happened when Max was four that were to have a profound influence on him: one unobtrusive and general, but lifelong, and the other instantaneous and dramatic, but also lifelong. First, after a couple of moves of house the family left Salford and moved into a new house in Wyville Drive, Swinton (as it happens, Max did not take part in the actual move: he was in hospital, having his tonsils out); and, second, his parents took him to a performance of *The Gondoliers*.

The move to the new address provided Max with something whose importance can hardly be over-estimated: it gave him a happy place that would always be home, to which he could always retire when he felt hurt or weary, where he knew he was loved without qualification, and where he always felt comfortable and at his ease. 'Home is the place where, when you have to go there, they have to take you in', said Robert Frost; so it was for Max, except that there was no 'have to' about it, on either side.

The fateful performance of *The Gondoliers* was at Salford Central Mission, and it proved to be what Max calls 'a great ear-opener'. In the first place it imbued him with what has turned out to be a lifelong fondness for Gilbert and Sullivan – a rare diversion into lighter music for Max, whose tastes otherwise tend to be serious, or highbrow, if the word can be used without any of the undertones of affectation normally associated with it. But the visit had other, far more momentous consequences: it was, in effect, the light on Max's personal road to Damascus. The morning after the performance Max's parents were astonished to discover that he could sing all the songs from the opera. It was the first real sign of his extraordinary musical sense, and as from that amateur and probably undistinguished performance of *The Gondoliers* there was never any doubt in Max's mind about what he was going to do with his life: he knew he was going to be not just a musician, but a composer.

When he was five he started attending the local primary school, Moorside Council School. He hated it, and remembers it both vividly and bitterly. The headmaster was a bully and a tyrant, and his wife, who took the scholarship class of the brightest pupils, was worse. These two and their staff regularly and routinely beat the children with a stick for all manner of offences: Max recalls that the pupils often went home with sore hands. All tests carried a pass-mark of 85 per cent; failure to reach this standard was rewarded, needless to say, with beating. He claims to have learned little from his years at this school, except perhaps some lessons in the art of survival.

During his years there he began taking piano lessons. The first suggestion that he should have music lessons came from an elderly woman whom he used to meet on his jaunts as a child. She somehow discovered that he was unusually interested in music, and offered to buy him a violin. He thanked her politely, but declined the offer, saying, 'I'd rather listen'. In the end it was another boy's beginning piano lessons that spurred him on to do the same.

His first teacher was a Miss Sally Jones, of Manchester Road, Swinton. She was unqualified, and taught by taking her pupil through a series of elementary exercises, which were supposed to constitute a beginner's course of several months. But Max, unknown to her, and even, largely, to himself, was an extremely unusual beginner. He had gone through the exercises in less than two weeks, during the course of which he had incidentally worked out the keys and the relationships between them, by ear. For some time he did not dare to tell Miss Jones of his progress, fearing, we may presume, that she would never believe he had achieved such a thing but rather assume that he had skimped the exercises, and dismiss him as lacking in interest.

It was not long, though, before Miss Jones came to his home to inform his parents that there was nothing more she could do for him, and that he ought to have a qualified teacher. In a short while he was installed as a pupil of a Mrs Dick, who was indeed qualified, and took him steadily through examination pieces. Over a period he went through a number of teachers, who would pass him on to someone more advanced when they found that they had nothing more to teach him. Only one of them was particularly memorable: one elderly lady kept a jar containing a set of gallstones – presumably her own – on her mantelpiece. Max was obsessed by these gallstones, and as a result the old lady would allow him to examine them as a reward for good work in a piano lesson.

With or without the incentive of the gallstones he ascended rapidly through the grades of piano proficiency, gaining Grade Eight without any difficulty; but it was, he recalls, deadly dull, tedious stuff. He was, however, doing other things which were much more interesting: within a few months of starting to learn the piano, he was already composing small pieces of his own for the instrument; this only confirmed the belief that he had held since the fateful Gilbert and Sullivan performance, that the writing of music was his destiny.

It hardly needs pointing out that many children, perhaps almost all, go through one or more stages of feeling sure they are bound for greatness: it usually takes the form of a certainty that they are destined to play for England at football or cricket, or some other such pure fantasy. A few entertain the same strength of feelings for less commonplace ambitions; but very few indeed simply *know*, from this early an age, exactly what they are going to do, and go on to put it precisely into practice. Max was one of this tiny minority, and the fact says a lot about both his clarity of vision and his tenacity of purpose. But, as he emphasizes himself, it also says a lot about the strength and security of his family home and background: they simply could not have been better, he declares. At the same time, he admits that he was powerfully conscious, throughout his childhood and youth, not just of being an only child, but also of being one of a kind, *sui generis*. Even at the age of eight or nine he had developed a liking for long, solitary walks, a passion which has remained with him all his life. It was natural and necessary for someone to whom thinking was an integral part of life; but it also emphasized his otherness.

It was not at all surprising that a child so musically gifted should need a piano of his own, and this Max certainly did within a short while of starting his first lessons. He got it when he was eight. His father's parents had a Binns Bros piano which they had bought some time early in the 1920s. It had cost £55 – an enormous sum then – and they had purchased it on the instalment system, with every member of the family putting in sixpence, a shilling or, for the wealthiest members of the family, even two shillings, a week. The piano had been at Tom's parents' house ever since; but in 1942, when Max was eight, it was brought to Swinton for his exclusive use, and there it remained, for as long as the family lived in the house.

The boy's gifts were not restricted to music. He was formidably bright in general, and showed it by taking, and passing, the eleven-plus examination a year early, thus earning an early escape from Moorside School and its brutal personnel. He gained a place at a nearby grammar school, Leigh Boys' GS – and quickly found that in some respects things were not a great deal better. But at least there was rather less beating, and for that alone he was profoundly thankful.

While Max was still at Moorside, of course, the Second World War had started. One stick of bombs fell close to his home during the air raids on Manchester. One bomb demolished the house next door, blowing out a couple of windows in the Davies' house, and another made a huge crater in a garden about 30 yards away. But the way in which the war most affected Max personally was that his father had to live away from home, in Burnt Oak in the semi-industrial suburbs of north London. There he was employed on work connected with the war – no one knows quite what he was doing, but it involved the disposal or distribution of boots and other war equipment. Max and his mother stayed in Swinton, and travelled to London to see him as often as they could.

In his first year or so at Leigh Max was happy enough: the absence of constant physical assault was one reason for this, as already mentioned. Another was that he was able to keep himself comfortably at the top of his classes without too much effort. He had a particular facility for languages, which was to prove very useful later on; but Eric Guest, his closest friend from his days at Leigh, puts it quite unequivocally: Max, he says, was *always* top of the form, in *everything*. It might be thought that this would have ensured him a place in the best books of the headmaster and staff, but it was not so. This was partly the consequence of certain aspects of Max's character; but it was also very largely to do with that of the headmaster, Bill Major.

Major was an odd mixture. He was a Quaker and something of a philanthropist: he was a wealthy man, and left three of the biggest youth hostels in the Lake District to the YHA in his will. He was capable of kindness, being especially indulgent towards those of his pupils with a scientific bias: he took the Sixth Form scientists himself for mathematics. Yet he was equally capable of the most mean-minded behaviour. Among his petty vices he was a glutton and a bully; he sulked if he did not get his own way (although that might be thought of as something of an occupational hazard for schoolmasters), and he was not above trying to steal the credit for other people's achievements. Partly because of the less-than-sympathetic side of his nature, and partly because of his fondness for eating two breakfasts (one at his lodgings and one at school) and two teas every day, his nickname was 'Pig'.

Max and his headmaster never hit it off at all. This was partly, Eric Guest is sure, because very soon after Max arrived at the school Major saw how bright and successful he was, and privately reserved him for a science scholarship to Cambridge – in other words, he marked him out for one of his own special elite corps of high-flying scientists, and determined that Max should bring glory to the school by that route.

Max, of course, was by this time utterly set on a career as a composer and musician, and so declined to accept the role set aside for him; Major never forgave him for refusing to allow his will to be subordinated to that of his headmaster. He was also entirely out of sympathy with Max's own ambitions: when the boy informed him that he wished to take music in the School Certificate examinations, Major retorted, 'No. This is not a girls' school.'

Max's response to this was to write privately to the examining board, and, eventually, to sit a Lancashire County Council scholarship in music. He passed it triumphantly, thus winning a scholarship place at the Royal Manchester College of Music in what amounted to open defiance of his headmaster. Amidst general rejoicing among Max's friends the only cracked note was Major himself. Presumably making the best of a bad job, or a virtue of necessity, he made an unctuous reference to this very considerable achievement in his speech-day oration the following day, implying that great credit for it was due to his and his staff's sterling efforts and encouragement on Max's behalf. It was for this, more than anything else, that he incurred Max's implacable contempt.

The fact is that Major did his best to obstruct Max's musical education and progress all along his journey through the school: he refused to buy or supply books, and generally took every possible opportunity to ridicule and belittle the boy and his vocation – for Max's need and determination to write music amounted to nothing less, even at this early stage in his life. Major was an unpleasant man, who made use of his petty authority to augment opportunities for unpleasantness.

It is more than likely that his hostile feelings towards his pupil were aggravated by several other factors to do with Max himself. First, there is no doubt that he was considerably more intelligent than many, perhaps all, of the staff of the school, including Major himself. This situation is bound to occur from time to time in any school, and it need not necessarily be a source of problems. On the other hand, it is a situation in which it is essential that the members of staff involved are exceptionally mature, level-headed and self-confident. An insecure master, faced with a pupil who he knows is considerably brighter and quicker on the uptake than he is, is dangerously likely to make a frightful hash of dealing with such a potential cause of embarrassment and friction. If the pupil in question also possesses a powerful, dominant personality, the risks are that much greater.

Max most certainly fitted his half of this; whether Major did so also is a matter for speculation, but Eric Guest believes it was a contributory factor in the troubled relationship between the two. He is also an authoritative witness to the fact that Max certainly was brighter than most of the staff, including the headmaster. Guest and Max knew each other from the age of eleven, and they were best friends from thirteen onwards. That friendship has lasted to the present day, so Eric Guest is Max's longest-standing friend, as well as having been among his very closest. It is noteworthy that in almost fifty years of close friendship, Max and Guest have scarcely ever talked about music: Guest, indeed, is certain that part of the bond between the two of them has always been that he is Max's one non-musical friend – not that he has no appreciation of music, but he has no professional association or technical interest in it. After university Guest went on to spend his entire working life as a master at his own old school, and he declares freely that among the many things Max was responsible for teaching him while they were schoolboys together was 'the secret of how to cope with pupils who were cleverer than I was'. Max never knew at the time that he was teaching Guest this extremely important lesson.

Even a personality as durable as Max's needs respite from conflict.

Fortunately for him not all the staff of the school were hostile, so he was able to have more normal relationships with some of them. One of them, a Miss Clough, 'a dear old soul', according to Eric Guest, even did her best to encourage him with his musical development. It was with the other boys, however, that he was really comfortable and at ease. Yet even this, in its own way, may well have been yet another contributory cause of friction between him and his headmaster.

A boy like Max would have been as conspicuous as a peacock among his dowdy hens in any assembly of boys. At Leigh he was certainly visible. Everyone knew Max, and everyone thought of him as being . . . 'just different'. They did not, says Guest, think of using the word 'eccentric': he was just different. At a time when rigorously short hair was the norm, Max was the first boy to appear wearing his hair long, anticipating the 1960s by well over a decade. His stand against the headmaster was bound, of course, to make him something of a popular hero, as he demonstrated in spectacular style on one occasion.

It was the custom at the school to celebrate the end of each term with a concert, and naturally Max was expected to take part, notwithstanding the despised and lowly status of music in official quarters. The programme included Gilbert and Sullivan, for which Max would act as répétiteur and, on the night, piano accompanist. Eric Guest always sang in the performance, and Max would always borrow his score. When he returned it Guest would find it liberally embellished throughout with obscene comments on the performers and their efforts.

Four members of the staff made up a string quartet. And Max would play a selection of his own choice on the piano. On the occasion in question, when it came to Max's turn to play his first selection, he announced, deadpan and without a tremor in his voice, 'The first piece I shall play is called "Funeral March for a Pig" . . . in B Major.' (It will be remembered that the headmaster's nickname was 'Pig', and that his forename was Bill.) It was, Max commented innocently afterwards, a rare example in music of a funeral march in a major key. At all events it received the biggest roar of applause ever heard at an end-of-term concert.

In general, the boys accepted Max as different. They also recognized that he was bright far beyond the ordinary: when it was his turn to read a lesson in morning assembly he chose an extract from the Indian poet Rabindranath Tagore. Most of all, though, they respected him for his highly developed sense of rugged integrity. He was passionately concerned with fair play. So are most boys. Unlike most boys, though, Max would unhesitatingly take risks that he certainly did not have to take in order to see justice done, in particular between boys and masters, where there was a natural imbalance between the two sides. As an example, in rehearsals for the annual Gilbert and Sullivan concert, the master in charge, who was also the producer and director, got carried away and began picking on the deputy pianist, a junior pupil. Max, who was about sixteen at the time, peremptorily halted the rehearsal and told the master, civilly but in the most unequivocal terms, that he was not to talk to the other boy in such a way, and that he, Max, would continue to hold up the rehearsal until the master accepted the fact. He won his point.

He was certainly not a barrack-room lawyer, Guest says; but he was never picked on or bullied himself, nor was anyone else in his company – they would be regarded as under his protection. He was also possessed of a rare intuition and sensitivity for a schoolboy, displayed in an incident that has stayed with Eric Guest as one of the most vivid and poignant memories of Max in his schooldays.

Guest was in a different form from Max. One day there was a knock on the classroom door while a lesson was in progress. It was Max, anxious to deliver a message to Guest that he had to talk to him, urgently, at the first opportunity. Guest duly met up with him in the next break, greatly curious to know what Max could possibly need to talk about that was so important that it merited his interrupting a lesson in this way. 'Well,' he demanded, 'what's it all about?'.

'I feel *awful*,' began Max. 'I've done something absolutely dreadful.'

Still more puzzled, Guest asked for details. 'Well,' Max went on, 'you know ——', and he mentioned a boy who was desperately keen to achieve first place in the form ratings in his speciality, languages. 'Of course,' replied Guest. 'What about him?'

'Well,' said Max, 'you know how anxious he is to come top in languages? And you know he's been working his guts out all this year to do so?' It was common knowledge that the boy in question was passionately keen to do very well, but that he was the steady, hard-grafting kind rather than the negligent genius who finds it all easy. Guest nodded. 'Well,' said Max, visibly in great distress, 'you know how easily languages come to me?' Guest did – Max learned languages without apparent effort. 'Well,' he went on, 'I've beaten him.'

That was all. Discuss it round in circles as they did, there was nothing that could be done to undo the facts. But it was, Guest says, typical of the youthful Max that he should have had enough imagination to be vividly conscious of the wound he had inflicted on another boy. The facts that he had inflicted it unwittingly and that he had as much right as the other boy, or anyone else, to come top in languages, were neither here nor there: he *ought* to have realized what his coming top would do;

and no, he *hadn't* got as much right as the other boy to come top, because it mattered to the other boy, and it didn't to him.

(As an unhappy postscript to this episode, the other boy went on to Cambridge, and there, in despair over his degree, which he felt certain he had failed, he killed himself. He was posthumously awarded a highly satisfactory Upper Second. It looks very much as if Max sensed, or perhaps intuited, a flaw in the boy's nature years before it destroyed him.)

Max's relationships with the other boys, then, were uniformly cordial. It is certain, however, that he did play up the staff at times. Guest thinks this was a mixture of sheer bloody-mindedness and a clear consciousness of being brighter and sharper-witted than they were. This was not likely to assist smooth relations between Max and the staff and headmaster, and one incident makes it pretty plain how headmaster Major felt about him.

Control of the school was shared by twelve prefects, who were selected as follows. The headmaster would on his own authority eliminate no-hopers, and then put up a list of about thirty names, these being the only possible contenders in his view. Nearly all would be members of the Upper Sixth Form, with perhaps half a dozen from the Lower Sixth as well. The school then elected the twelve prefects from the names on the list, by secret ballot, and the successful candidates then elected the Head Boy from among their number, by a further ballot, also secret.

To no one's surprise, Max was elected a prefect in his Lower Sixth year, and the following year, when he was in the Upper and Guest in the Lower Sixth, he was a long odds-on favourite to be chosen as Head Boy. When the result of the ballot among the twelve prefects was disclosed, however, some nonentity had come top of the poll, and Max had to be content with being Deputy Head Boy for his final year. The twelve, however (including the lucky winner, who was the most surprised of all), were so taken aback by the unexpected result that they held a post-mortem, and it became quite clear that Major had falsified the result to avoid having to co-operate with Max as his Head Boy.

This did not worry Max much, but the incident does leave something of a puzzle behind. One can readily understand Major's feeling that it would be placing altogether too much of a strain on the system – and, perhaps, on himself also – to expect him to work with someone he regarded as a known subversive. But in that case one is left wondering why he included Max's name on the list of possibles in the first place. Perhaps he feared too great an outcry if he left Max out entirely; perhaps Max was simply too prominent and popular to be omissible; perhaps

Major felt that if he could not subdue Max's spirit it was better to try to tame it with responsibility, rather than risk provoking him into outright rebellion; or maybe beneath Major's pique at Max's refusal to go the way he wished him to go, to Cambridge and the sciences, there lurked some residual respect, some lingering sense of justice, that whispered in the headmaster's ear that a youth of such qualities simply ought not to be left out in the cold. We shall never know, but it is an interesting matter for speculation.

From his early teens onwards Max has suffered from occasional fits of profound black depression. There is nothing uncommon about this, and like many sufferers, he has had much cause to be grateful to a close friend like Eric Guest. Long walks have always been a passion of Max's, usually solitary but sometimes accompanied by special friends, and in his schooldays this was the usual remedy he sought when such attacks were on him. He would call at Guest's home – to which he had to walk several miles to begin with – at all kinds of strange hours of day or night, and they would walk for untold miles through the local countryside, or along the Bridgwater Canal, while Max talked and Eric listened.

As often in such deep pair-bonds, one partner – in this case Guest – was an exceptionally good listener. In return Max provided his friend with what Eric Guest regards as the best part of his education – far more than university brought to him. Max fed him an endless diet of books and, most of all, of ideas. They talked, as such inseparable boyhood friends do, of almost everything under the sun, and it was a deeply rewarding and formative process for them both.

Among the books, Guest remembers Max acquiring Joyce's *Ulysses* when he was about sixteen. It instantly established itself as his personal *vade mecum*, and it has remained so ever since. Max's reading is exceptionally wide and deep – there has always been a conspicuous lack of trivia and frivolity on his bookshelves. His younger cousin, Roger Walden, remarked with a chuckle that when he and his family used to travel north to Swinton to visit Max and his parents, 'I never saw many Biggles books around', although as a teenager Max had a weakness for the 'William' books of Richmal Crompton (he still has); Thomas Mann, especially *Der Zauberberg* (The Magic Mountain), has been amongst his favourite reading since his teens, but Joyce and *Ulysses* have always been supreme. When Max received what is perhaps the ultimate accolade of acceptance by the British establishment, an invitation to be the castaway on *Desert Island Discs*, *Ulysses* was the book he chose to take with his eight records.

One other aspect of this friendship deserves special mention, on which Guest remarks with an air of considerable surprise. In all the years of their intimacy, the two of them have rarely talked about religion, and they have never talked about sex. Guest's role has been that of Max's confessor, a sympathetic ear in times of trouble, his contact with the world outside music. He is a down-to-earth North countryman, without being remotely assertive or opinionated. Rather, he is softly spoken, steady, sensible, fathomlessly loyal to his friend without for a moment being bereft of his own opinions – he is critical of Max, and quite severely so, when he thinks there is reason to be. He is a very calming, soothing person to be with – Max could hardly have chosen his best friend better.

Although Guest was special, he was not Max's only very close childhood friend, however. There were others. One was vitally important to him over a period of about five years, although they then lost contact. Another, like Eric Guest, has always remained close.

Max met both these friends through Trevor Hill, who was in charge of a nightly radio programme of the BBC in Manchester. The programme was called *Children's Hour*, and was a mixture of readings, educational features and entertainment for children up to the mid-teens. It included a regular spot, 'Your Own Ideas', in which talented children could perform – a kind of amateur talent contest in the serious, even then rather old-fashioned style of the BBC in those days, entirely lacking in glitter or razzmatazz.

Max had begun sending in pieces of music he had composed for consideration by this programme shortly before he began at Leigh Grammar School, and by the time he was thirteen he had become a regular participant, both as composer and performer, playing his own and established composers' music on the piano. One day another guest, a girl called Joyce Palin, who was there to play the piano, overheard Max playing in another room. She asked Trevor Hill to introduce her. He did, they took an immediate liking to one another, and quickly formed a firm friendship which lasted until they left their respective schools and went on to different colleges of music, after which they drifted apart.

Joyce lived in Withington, a southern suburb about the same distance from central Manchester as Max's home suburb of Swinton to the north-west; thus they lived about nine miles apart. Over the next four or five years they spent an enormous amount of time together, virtually exclusively playing and talking about music. Their meetings were almost all at Max's instigation, for the simple reason that Joyce's home had a telephone and Max's did not, so it was impossible for her to ring him to suggest a meeting. He had to go to a phone box and ring her, and would then take the bus to her home, where they would spend hours happily absorbed in music. The time they spent together was almost always at her house, again for a sound reason: there were two pianos there, while Max had only one.

They often played together on *Children's Hour*, sometimes playing music for two pianos or for four hands, sometimes with Max playing piano and Joyce the violin. Otherwise they would go for Max's favourite long walks; or he would accompany Joyce to her ballet classes. She had gained a teaching qualification in ballet by the age of twelve, and although the law prohibited her from actually giving lessons for gain she thought this was nonsense, and took on occasional children as pupils. Max loved to watch her classes and used to help her by working the curtain. Joyce was also a precociously gifted actress and regularly took part in plays on *Children's Hour*; Max often used to go along to watch rehearsals. But mostly it was music, music, music.

It has to be understood that for these two, extremely young though they were – they met when Joyce was about twelve and Max a couple of years older – their music was not play or a hobby, in any sense whatsoever. To both of them music was already the most important thing in their lives; both knew with total certainty that they were going to make music their lives, and both took the music to which they devoted such vast amounts of time, effort, concentration and passion completely seriously. Joyce states matter-of-factly that if by some chance either of them was faced with conflicting demands of music and school homework, it was the homework which went by the board. This was at a time when homework was not merely obligatory, but strictly enforced, and to disregard it was a serious matter. Furthermore, both Max and Joyce were pupils at schools where such things were almost certainly taken a good deal more seriously than in the general run of schools. In other words, their commitment to their music was a wholly mature, deadly earnest and, in a real sense, adult matter.

Since they were both performing regularly on *Children's Hour*, a great deal of their time was taken up with rehearsals. All radio was live in those not-so-distant days, so there was no second chance if a piece went awry, and no hiding place for the lazy, the incompetent or the ill-prepared; the effect of this was that both Max and Joyce were being treated as professionals at the age of thirteen – and Max had been so treated since the age of ten or possibly even nine. He wrote pieces for the two of them to play together, and he contributed a lot to Joyce's general musicality with his criticism of her playing, invariably constructive and offered in a genuine desire to help.

Within a short while of his debut on 'Your Own Ideas', Trevor Hill was anxious to find a more regular vehicle for his talents. It soon materialized with the start of *Out of School*, a monthly magazine programme for teenagers. Max immediately became its very youthful resident composer – anticipating certain later developments by about forty years; and he would often enliven the programme with compositions depicting his contemporaries at school (for example, in a piece called *The Green Imps* – from the school's green uniform blazers).

They had other things in common. Both were only children, and both were easy and comfortable as loners, though neither was in any sense anti-social. Neither of them was spoiled, either. Both had parents who were firm and sensible, even strict in certain matters. And they both had the special need for one, or a very few, exceptionally close and secure friendships. Joyce believes that this is characteristic of only children – a need for friends of a very special kind, whom they can trust utterly, without reservation. This is what Max straightaway became for her, and she for him.

Their families got to know each other, and also became friendly. Joyce still remembers the great kindness of Max's mother towards her own mother when her father was suffering a long and terrible last illness. Outside their families, however, the two of them kept their friendship to themselves: Joyce knew none of Max's other friends, and Max knew none of hers.

It should not be thought that their relationship was in any way a dour or priggish affair: they had enormous fun. The fact that it was mostly the fairly rarefied kind of fun that would please two extraordinarily intelligent young people, both intellectuals and both with strong inclinations to solitariness, does not make it any the less fun.

There was one memorable outing that took place when Max was about eighteen and Joyce about sixteen. Max had saved his pocket money all term for it but Joyce's mother warned her in advance not to go mad at lunch, because, she said, Max hadn't got much money. If this resulted in Joyce having a rather scanty lunch, she said, there would be a steak waiting for her when she got home.

When the day came the weather was dirty – high, swirling wind and heavy rain. Max arrived for Joyce, however, and off they went. It chanced that Max was into health food at that time, and the first thing they had to do, he announced, was to visit a certain healthfood shop he knew to buy some millet seed. So they walked several miles through suburban Manchester in a steady downpour to the shop, where they were told regretfully but firmly that there wasn't a stalk of millet to be had, but that they might try the pet shop a little distance away.

They went back into the rain, and when they got to the pet shop all was well: there was millet seed in abundance. But 'What sort of bird is it for?' asked the woman there. 'It's not for a bird. It's for *him*,' Joyce cried at the top of her voice, finally erupting.

They now had to travel into Manchester city centre. At a half-drowned Joyce's insistence they took the bus. Then came the matter of lunch, and Joyce, mindful of her mother's injunctions, dutifully took things easy. Their visit to the cinema went off well enough, disturbed only by the lingering dampness of Joyce's clothes and the persistent rumbling of her under-provided-for stomach. Max paid for the cinema tickets, and Joyce paid their bus fares to her home. When they got there her mother, who adored Max, promptly made a great fuss of him, clucking over his bedraggled state, while Joyce stood dripping and forgotten in the background. Then, 'Would you like a steak?' she asked. 'There's one in the fridge.' He accepted with alacrity; and Joyce had the pleasure of sitting watching as he wolfed it, courteously offering her a portion as he went. It is a tale she still enjoys telling; and her mother still adores Max to this day.

Joyce thought then, and still thinks, that Max was very fortunate in his parents, in particular his mother, who, she believes, regarded the world as revolving around her son. She never had the impression that his mother ever had to *make* him do anything. She was plainly devoted to him, but for all the doting she expected him to do well at whatever he decided to do, and to work hard to ensure that he did. His father, Joyce thinks, was always a little nonplussed by the yawning distance between his son and himself. Tom, she believes, had rather hoped that a son of his would be the sort of boy who could look under the bonnet of a car and understand the mysteries of what lay beneath it. Max has never even learned to drive a car. Tom would have liked a son who would accompany him to a football match. In fact there has never been a point in Max's life when he would have been seen dead at a football match. However, they both accepted the enormous difference between them with equanimity.

Max was a very special friend to Joyce. They needed each other and were always there for each other. Although Max was never niggardly in supporting musical activities at his school – returning good for evil – any such activities were far beneath his own level of ability, and Joyce too was considerably above almost all her contemporaries at her school. So they needed each other for musical stimulus at their own advanced level, to speak the same language.

Joyce is quite certain that Max was a child prodigy. One could not compare him to anyone else in those days, she says, because there was no one within view with whom he might be compared, in terms of his ability or the power of his personality. For his parents 'it must have been like having Everest in the background'. Musically, he left everyone else far behind. Much of the music he wrote at the time Joyce knew him was extremely avant-garde. But, importantly, even then he had the gift that he still has, of tailoring his music to the performers or the audience. Thus the pieces he wrote for the youthful performers and listeners of *Children's Hour* were entirely appropriate – with the result that the children enjoyed them, often writing in with requests to hear them again. They were also full of Max's highly distinctive sense of humour and fun.

One day around the same time as Max met Joyce Palin, Ian Kellam, a boy of Max's own age and a similar working-class background from Sheffield, was at the BBC *Children's Hour* studios to sing on the 'Your Own Ideas' spot, and heard another boy playing the piano. Ian, who also played, immediately realized that the other boy, who was of course Max, was possessed of a talent far beyond his own. They were introduced, and from that point the story is remarkably similar to that of Joyce Palin. They got to know each other very quickly, and became fast friends equally quickly. Kellam makes no bones about it: 'Max's music made a tremendous impression, but it was Max himself who made the greatest impression. I very quickly came to love him as much, I suppose, as one man can love another.'

Kellam understood a great deal about Max in their first few meetings. 'There was vast intelligence written all over his face,' he says, 'and, more than that, there was great fixity of purpose. Even at the age of thirteen I could see that here was someone who was going to go places and get to the top of his calling.'

They saw a lot of each other from the beginning, travelling across the Pennines on the train to visit each other, and Max immediately became the most important person in Kellam's life. As well as sharing Max's working-class background, Kellam, like Max, was deeply, intensely musical from a very early age. Unlike Max, however, Kellam disliked his father, and they spoke to each other as rarely as possible. By contrast, although Max's musical genius was a surprise, in that nobody could have either predicted it or said where he got it from, he grew up in general a secure, balanced child, certain of his parents' love and support. This made it easy for him to avoid destructive self-doubts about his music, among other things; whereas Kellam did not have this bedrock of security. It was accordingly a great relief to him to find someone from a similar background who not only shared his musicality, but knew so much more, and could teach him. In a sense, Kellam felt that if music was good and respectable enough for someone like Max, it was a proper thing for someone like him too.

Kellam's impressions of Max are remarkably similar to those of Joyce Palin, and those of both are very much like Eric Guest's. Kellam found Max exceptionally self-reliant and self-possessed for his age; and he also observed, like everyone else, his unusual ability to be content with his own company. At the same time he found him very easy to get on with: if Kellam loved Max, Max showed the same kind of affectionate feelings in return. They went for long walks together (anyone who got close to Max became used to long walks, if they were not already), and Kellam has precisely the same tale as Eric Guest to tell of Max's contribution to his general education, showering him with an endless torrent of new books, music, composers and ideas. But as with Joyce, the overwhelming emphasis of their friendship was on music. They talked endlessly about it, pouring out ideas and examining them from every conceivable angle with the tireless energy and inexhaustible interest of the young. They talked about music for, literally, years.

When Max and Joyce Palin left their schools she went on to the Northern School of Music and Max went to read music jointly at the Royal Manchester College of Music and Manchester University, dividing his time between the two institutions. The two of them drifted apart and did not meet again until very much later. Ian Kellam, however, like Eric Guest, has remained a close and affectionate friend of Max's throughout his life, and remains so to this day. He has made his own way as a composer, mainly of church music; and his respect for Max the composer is as undimmed as his love for the man. Max has written several pieces for him, including a piano sonata on the grand scale. It has never been performed in public, but the inscribed score is among Ian Kellam's most prized possessions.

Music was the governing passion of Max's early years, as of his later life, on all levels, spiritual, emotional and intellectual. With the important exception of Eric Guest, his most intimate friendships had music as their foundation. He had other interests: he had his walking, alone or with a special friend. He was very interested in, and knowledgeable about, natural history: his cousin Roger Walden remembers spending hours with Max looking at the teeming life in some ponds near Max's home, and being astonished to find that at the age of about eleven, he knew all the minute creatures' scientific Latin names.

Max's reading was already prolific, and fairly precocious, as shown by his early taste for Joyce and Mann. He himself says that by the time he was fourteen he was 'living, not so much in school, which I found very boring, mostly, but in the Swinton and Pendlebury libraries, and the Henry Watson Music Library in Manchester'. He was keenly interested in the other arts as well, which he says was generally regarded as very odd at school. He was fond of railways – he has been a railway buff, in a non-fanatical way, all his life.

There were concerts to listen to at the Albert Hall and other such places, with the Hallé and the BBC Northern Orchestra, as it was then known. (It was subsequently rechristened, first as the BBC Northern Symphony Orchestra – in that phase of its existence its members used to refer to the BBC's flagship orchestra, the BBC Symphony Orchestra, as 'the BBC Southern' – and then as the BBC Philharmonic Orchestra.) Max regarded the BBC as 'his' orchestra; on one occasion, when he was about twelve, he was introduced to the principal conductor, Charles Groves (not yet Sir Charles at that point), and showed him a small piece he had composed. He cannot remember Groves's reaction – probably a benevolent pat on the head and a rumbled congratulation – but the little episode was to have a surprising twist forty-six years later.

There was one other important discovery that Max had to make about himself during this generally very happy period of his adolescence. It might be thought from the account of their friendship that Max and Joyce Palin were youthful sweethearts but this was not so. When he was fourteen or perhaps fifteen Max realized that he was homosexual. This discovery, so often the cause of untold anguish, confusion, self-doubt and self-loathing until it has been assimilated and come to terms with (which in innumerable sad cases never happens) seems to have caused Max remarkably little trouble. He believes his parents knew, although it was never once discussed, or even mentioned: they were aware, he says, of his paying certain people a great deal of attention, but he suspects that they would have been incapable of articulating what they knew or thought, or thought they knew.

This is one of a number of close parallels between Max and Benjamin Britten. Britten too was homosexual, though he realized the fact later than Max, and came to terms with it only partially and only after a good deal of agonizing. Britten also had a fairly unhappy time at school and a headmaster who was less than sympathetic to his musical ambitions, who was not above trying to frustrate them or grabbing the credit for them.

His friends saw in the young Max a fearless integrity, and that is still one of his most highly visible qualities today. So are his intense resolution and fixity of purpose, and the self-reliance and self-possession that characterized him even as a child. However neither then nor now have those qualities ever overlapped into self-absorption. Max's unusual degree of contentment with his own company, and the relative freedom from the great twentieth-century phobia of loneliness that it implies, have also undoubtedly always been part of his conscious life. Whether this has anything to do with his homosexuality, neither he nor anyone else can say with any kind of certainty. Possibly it does represent a practical acceptance and coming-to-terms with certain aspects of it. It may equally well be simply that Max prefers his own company.

What matters more than anything else, however, is his total, unwavering commitment to music. Max is and always has been a passionate and forceful man. He holds views about most things: for example, he is strongly and outspokenly political. Most of the views he holds he holds strongly – there is nothing wishy-washy about him. As might be expected of such a man, he also has a lot of interests, which he takes seriously enough to devote time and energy to them – in other words, anything he does at all, he does properly. He has been full-blooded about his personal relationships with other people, but in the end, anything that comes into conflict with his music will fail. It is to his music that Max is committed, and to his music that he is ultimately true. Anyone and anything else has to be viewed in the light of that fact. This was as true when Max was thirteen years old as it is today. Ian Kellam knew it, Joyce Palin knew it and Eric Guest knew it. In other ways also, but in this respect most of all, the child was father of the man.

2 ~ The Gang of Five

Perhaps the most famous anecdote in circulation about Max is his headmaster's scoffing response to his request to take music as a School Certificate subject. John Timpson told it, for example, in introducing Max as a member of the *Any Questions* panel in 1985. As a result of Major's laughing philistinism Max simply did not get an O-level in music. That did not matter too much, but when it came to A-level he needed the qualification. Accordingly, when the time for A-levels came round, he said nothing to Major or anyone at the school about music, taking languages and sailing through them without difficulty. Meanwhile, he wrote off in advance to the examining board and arranged with them to take the music examination on his own initiative – a quality he quite clearly was not short of.

The examination itself was scarcely a test at all for someone as musically precocious as Max. He took the written papers at a strolling pace, and then, with all the candidates who did sufficiently well in those papers, had to go to Manchester Girls' High School to sit the oral part of the examination. Among other things, the candidates had to be ready to answer questions from the examiner on Beethoven's Violin Concerto. Thanks to his assiduous practice on the piano at home, and his regular work-outs with Joyce Palin, Max could play the entire work in piano reduction – 'of course', as he will say when telling the story. As far as the examiner was concerned, however, there was no 'of course' about it: she seemed to be thunderstruck by this revelation. When she had recovered her poise, she asked Max to play an excerpt, which, of course, he did. She then asked him what other works of Beethoven he could play without a score. 'You name it,' said Max. 'Symphony No. 1,' she suggested. Max played some of it. Then she tried 'Symphony No. 2', and he played some of that. The 'Eroica' followed, and so on, until he had played bits of all the symphonies one after another – and that was more or less the end of the examination.

On the strength of his performance in this examination he was awarded a Lancashire County scholarship to read music in a joint course at Manchester University and the Royal Manchester College of Music. He had chosen Manchester in order to be close to his home, and so to have access to his piano, which was by now an indispensable part of his daily life.

It is worth considering this episode in Max's life. By any standards, it is no mean achievement for a boy of seventeen, finding himself frustrated at school by the deliberate design of his headmaster, to circumvent the obstacle by so clear an act of self-will as Max deployed. The examination itself may not have been very demanding musically for someone of his gifts, but when he arrived at the hall for the first papers he found himself among hundreds of other young people, all clutching written recommendations of varying degrees of radiance from their headmasters and headmistresses. Max by contrast was all on his own, with no comrades from his own school to offer company and moral support, and certainly with no recommendation whatsoever. However he may make light of it now, it must have been very daunting indeed at the time. To have carried it off with the equanimity, indeed, the panache he seems to have shown indicates a degree of detachment and self-possession quite extraordinary in someone scarcely more than a boy. It is a quality he accepts he had in more than ordinary measure as a boy and as a youth, and it has never deserted him.

We have already seen how this determined effort by Max on his own behalf resulted in his headmaster making a proud mention of his triumphant success in music A-level on the school speech day – 'which taught me something about human nature', as Max comments when he thinks about the incident today. In fact, his final, considered verdict on his school when asked what, if anything, he derived from his time there, is the observation that 'mostly it taught me that I had a fight on my hands; and in that way it was very constructive.' The fight he refers to relates to his determination to become a composer, which had by now taken permanent root, and it was with this intention strong within him that he embarked on the next stage of his education.

On his last day at school Max celebrated by playing right through the piano version of Brahms's Variations on the St Antony Chorale with another boy and then, as he had so often done over the years, walked through the countryside along the seven or eight miles of the Bridgwater Canal from where it ran through the school grounds to his home, with Eric Guest for company.

Between leaving school and beginning his course at university, Max visited Hamburg, writing enthusiastically to Guest about the music at a Russian Orthodox service he attended out of interest. He also talked cheerfully, but with evident wonder, about the fact that he was 'running around Hamburg and Schleswig-Holstein in my short pants, showing off hairy legs to advantage – but nobody thinks anything of it!' – an illuminating comment on English attitudes of the time.

Soon, though, it was time to make a start on his studies. At Manchester he had to read composition and musical theory at the Faculty of Music of the University, and take a piano course 'across the road' at the Royal Manchester College of Music, as it was then called. (It later amalgamated with the Northern School of Music to become the Royal Northern College of Music.)

Max's piano course was given by Hedwig Stein, and he enjoyed it very much. It was the only element of his degree course, or, indeed, of the whole of the higher level of his education that he did enjoy. For the rest of it, he was pretty miserable. The education, he found, was very obvious and made no demands. The theoretical part broke down into several separate courses. There was counterpoint and harmony. This suffered from the drawback, where Max was concerned, anyway, of being simply too easy. The musical history course 'consisted not of finding anything out but of learning facts by rote and regurgitating them in the approved manner'; and then there were such things as score-reading. These were routine, which was fine; the only problem was that Max had already mastered them. This left the composition classes, which, clearly, ought to have been the centrepiece and highlight of the entire course. But, alas, it was not to be.

The Professor of Composition at the University was Humphrey Proctor-Gregg, later the manager of the Carl Rosa Opera Company. Initially Max was excited and eager to meet him, because he was known as a composer of some talent himself, and Max had never met a real composer. Unhappily, the relationship was doomed before it started. Proctor-Gregg's musical roots were firmly embedded – if not, indeed, anchored in concrete – in the nineteenth and very early twentieth centuries. His favourites were Donizetti and Delius – an unlikely couple – and he appeared to like few if any other composers at all. He had absolutely no time for contemporary music, even for modern composers who even then were recognized as relatively approachable: he refused to listen to Bartók, for example, or even Hindemith.

Proctor-Gregg was a great admirer of Sir Thomas Beecham, and very much under his spell. No doubt this had a lot to do with his admiration for Delius. Certainly his own compositions were very reminiscent of Delius's music, according to Max's fellow student Elgar Howarth, one of few people to have heard any of the younger man's work. Probably also borrowed from Beecham was Proctor-Gregg's customary disparaging dismissal of Bach as 'awful stuff'. No respecter of persons, he also habitually referred to Beethoven, rather oddly, as 'that dreadful German bow-wow'. Beecham was a dangerous and volatile mixture of entrepreneur, showman, talented musician, mountebank and egomaniac – not, therefore, any kind of model for younger and lesser men. It seems quite likely that Proctor-Gregg was sufficiently under Beecham's influence to pick up some of his mannerisms, flamboyant affectation of iconoclasm among them.

At all events, he and Max were not destined to get along, and within a very short period of Max's arrival in Proctor-Gregg's composition classes, he had, in effect, been thrown out of them. He liked the wrong kind of music, listened to the wrong kind of music, composed the wrong kind of music, and made it clear that it was his intention to go on composing that kind of music. This was taken by Proctor-Gregg as indicating that he was incorrigible, and he lost no time in pointing out to Max that he had nothing to teach him. Max took the hint, and made himself scarce from Proctor-Gregg's classes for the remainder of his time at Manchester.

The professor's legacy to Max consisted of two pieces of advice: 'Don't listen to any music written before 1550: it's dangerous'; and 'No music written after Delius is worth bothering with.' Why early music is dangerous was never made clear. Max supposes the injunction was intended to mean (if it meant anything) that such music might give one dangerously independent or alarmingly unorthodox ideas – but this can be no more than guesswork. However, he never forgot the two stern pieces of advice from his professor, and he has spent the whole of his distinguished career as a composer conscientiously disregarding them.

In having found his period at university generally dreary and of little use, Max is far from unique. As with many who ultimately derived little real gain from it, however, the time was not altogether wasted. Enlightenment, development and real education came instead from the friends he made and the associations he formed with his fellow students; in this respect, Manchester was a source of true riches – at least for a time. For by a coincidence of almost staggering dimensions, Manchester in the early and mid-1950s brought together five young men who, each in their own individual way, have proved the most striking and original talents in the musical life of the nation over the four decades since.

The first to come to Max's attention was Alexander Goehr. Born two years earlier than Max, in 1932, he was already something of a celebrity among the music students of both the University and the College by the time Max arrived. He was then a second-year student of the College, studying composition with Richard Hall. Very soon Max began to hear frequent reports of him and early in his own second year wrote to him suggesting that they should meet. They immediately became close friends.

Goehr was a very conspicuous figure. To begin with, he was the son of one of the most illustrious musicians in the country: his father, Walter Goehr, in addition to being one of the leading conductors of the day, was also, even more significantly, a former pupil of Schoenberg, then only very recently dead and still a figure of almost mythical potency to anyone with a real interest in modern music. Schoenberg's music was virtually never performed in Britain, and was usually regarded with incomprehension and hostility. But to would-be avant-gardistes it was a totem and a symbol, of modernity, of rebellion, and of rejection of the tired, conventional world of British musical life. Walter Goehr's connection with this shadowy but titanic, almost mystical being lent him, and by association his son also, a nimbus of glamour that may be difficult for contemporary readers to conceive.

On top of this, Goehr also came from London, and this, too, carried a significance that the present reader may not immediately grasp. As a result of international travel, television, instant communications and myriad other developments, the world of today is almost infinitely smaller than it was in the 1950s. For a boy or a very young man from the provinces at that time, London was a kind of Shangri-La of mystique and allure. An awareness of this is necessary to any under-standing of how a young man like Alexander Goehr – always known to his intimates as 'Sandy' – would have appeared to his less sophisticated contemporaries from outside London.

Max himself, of course, had a highly personal kind of sophistication of his own: there was nothing of the wide-eyed provincial hick about him. But he was ignorant of London and its spurious glamour. Perhaps the best way of putting it is that he was a provincial boy, saved from any appearance of conventional provincialism by his exceptional intelligence and by a total absence of the gaucheness that the notion of provincialism suggests. He was, in fact, a natural sophisticate waiting to emerge from a chrysalis. Goehr was in many ways the catalyst which facilitated that emergence.

And so they met; and they talked, and talked. Actually, it was Goehr who did most of the talking, while Max and the others who gravitated towards him listened. Goehr was already very much the professional: he had been signed up by a major publisher, Schotts, and his far greater worldliness lent him a natural pre-eminence in this small, intense musical circle.

The other members of the inner circle were a clarinettist named Harrison Birtwistle, a young trumpeter, Elgar Howarth, a year younger than the others and three years younger than Goehr, who arrived a year later to study composition at the College with Richard

Hall, and a huge, shambling bear of a man, John Ogdon, two years younger still and fresh from Manchester Grammar School, who already played the piano like no one else who had ever been heard.

Much has been made of this group, sometimes referred to as 'The Manchester School'. The mid-1950s was a time for the formation of groups and coteries. John Osborne, Arnold Wesker and a few others had started off a new wave of playwrights who quickly became known as the Angry Young Men, writing what even more quickly became termed as Kitchen Sink Drama. A new generation of writers, a remarkable number of them young, working-class North countrymen, and most of them certainly angry, began introducing the same note of gritty realism into the novel and the short story. Anthony Hartley, Thom Gunn and a gaggle of lesser talents had formed a loose confederation of poets known simply as The Movement. It was natural, therefore, to think of these young musicians, all outstanding and original talents, as a movement. The truth, as usual, was rather different.

Goehr, as we have seen, was without doubt the leader of the group, and did most of the talking. Ogdon was a quiet man, but his abilities at the piano already set him apart. One story about him aptly illustrates his vast talents. The Parsee composer Sorabji had written a huge work for piano called *Opus Clavicembalisticum*. It lasts for about three hours, and is a piece of the most fiendish virtuosity. At this time it was widely regarded – even, apparently, by the composer himself – as unplayable. The others gave the score to Ogdon, who promptly sat down and played it through at sight.

Ogdon often visited Max's home, where he was made a fuss of by Max's parents, and occasionally stayed the night, sleeping on the sofa. He met Eric Guest, who noticed that he quite frequently made references to his father in terms such as 'My father's gone in again.' Guest took it that this must be a way of intimating that his father was in Strangeways Prison, and naturally kept a tactful silence. It was only later that he realized that Ogdon was referring to his father's periods in mental hospitals: his father suffered from a condition that Ogdon himself inherited, and which was later to cause him great misery and suffering, culminating in his tragically premature death.

Elgar Howarth was a fine trumpeter, and also had a strong interest in composition and a liking for contemporary music whenever he got a chance to hear any. Among the things which drew him to Max was the fact that Max was often to be found with scores of works by Berg, Bartók, Schoenberg and even sometimes Boulez and Nono. He found Max a highly charismatic figure, slender and nimble, with an elfin quality about him, and, of course, the striking blue eyes.

It was with Harrison Birtwistle (always known as Harry, as Howarth was always called Gary) that Max became particularly friendly. He was a shy, private young man from Accrington, where he was born a few weeks before Max, in July 1934. He had been unhappy at school, which probably explains a lot of his retiring, withdrawn nature, but he became very close to Max who, though like Birtwistle an only child, was a far more outgoing and demonstrative character. Birtwistle's studies were entirely at the College, where he studied clarinet with Frederick Thurston and (like Goehr and Howarth) composition with Richard Hall, an unusually progressive teacher, who actively encouraged his pupils to compose in what was still, nearly fifty years after Schoenberg had pioneered it, the dangerously avant-garde and modern idiom of twelve-tone music.

Max, meanwhile, had already become *persona non grata* in his composition classes by the time he was in his second year, and was writing a thesis on Indian music instead. During his time at Manchester he also made several visits to Darmstadt, where the twin gurus of the European avant-garde, Pierre Boulez and Stockhausen, held their court. Max has never been influenced by the music of Stockhausen, whom later in life he has dismissed as lacking in humour. Still, at that time they got on reasonably well. Certainly they talked animatedly about music. On one occasion they were sitting immersed in conversation when a wine glass on the table between them spontaneously shattered into fragments. Max attributes it to the dynamic vibrations set up between the two of them.

In addition to getting to know the most modern composers as well as was possible in those days, Max was also taking a deep interest in the subject of his thesis, Indian music, and in very early music – the latter in defiance of the injunction of his intended mentor in composition, Humphrey Proctor-Gregg. He still saw a lot of Eric Guest, who recalls that among other early composers, the looming figure of John Taverner was already beginning to capture Max's especial interest. Taverner, a composer of considerable talents but also a somewhat shady character, lived from about 1495 to 1545; but he also lived in Max's imagination, as something of an obsession, from when he was about eighteen to the production of the opera named after him, in 1972, when Max was thirty-eight.

In sum, Max's time at university was marked by a signal lack of stimulation from the formal education that he was there to receive, and greatly compensated for by the presence of a circle of exceptionally talented and inspirational friends among his fellow-students, with the continuing presence of Eric Guest as a steadying, comforting influence.

Max was an unconventional student in a number of ways. Some, as we have seen, were to do with the subject of his studies and his attitudes to them – the trips to Darmstadt, getting himself thrown out of classes, the interest in Indian and medieval music, the impatience with convention and conformism. It should be remembered in this connection that Britain in the mid-1950s was still a highly conservative, conformist society, in almost every way. This extended to the world of music: Vaughan Williams was at that time still regarded as a modern composer – his late works were the British conception of 'new' music. Benjamin Britten was still thought of as the very latest thing, with Michael Tippett uneasily associated with him but figuring as a sort of wild card, about whom nobody was quite sure. Malcolm Arnold was composing, and going his own way as always, considerably despised in serious musical circles for having dared to venture into the field of popular music by writing film scores and so on, and even being presumptuous enough to make quite a lot of money from doing so. (Richard Rodney Bennett and, to a lesser extent, Max himself have since been rebuked by their more serious-minded well-wishers for the same reason.) There were other composers about, but there was nothing approximating to a genuine avant-garde. Max and the others filled this breach.

Max found time to serve as best man at John Ogdon's wedding, and one day he received a message that puzzled him greatly. 'What do you think?' he asked Eric Guest. 'Harry's been on the phone. I've got to meet him in Liverpool, and he won't tell me what it is. I've got to get myself dressed up as well. What the hell can it be about?' Guest couldn't hazard a guess, so Max dutifully dropped everything and went off to Liverpool in great haste. On his return he called at Guest's home to explain. 'I've had to be best man at Harry's wedding,' he said. 'He's married a chorus girl at the Windmill!' Max has no recollection of this at all, but Eric Guest remembers it clearly.

He also found the time to do odd holiday jobs: one winter vacation he worked for the Post Office on that traditional and trusty source of urgently needed cash for whole generations of sixth-form and university students, 'Christmas parcels'. The difference was that whereas most students needed the money for essentials the following term, Max spent his entire earnings on an unexpurgated edition of the *Arabian Nights* that had taken his fancy.

Max's second year saw the event which, judged in the context of his career as a whole, must almost certainly be regarded as the most notable of his time at the University, or at any rate as having the greatest significance in the long term. At the Christmas concert the College choir and orchestra put on a performance of the *Christmas Oratorio*. The work includes a very high part for trumpet. The instrument required is a trumpet in D, which was very difficult to find. From somewhere, however, a battered, pre-war instrument was unearthed, and the young Gary Howarth, still in his first term, was deputed to play the part. Max was enormously impressed, and immediately announced his intention of writing a piece for Howarth. He did so, and the result was the Sonata for Trumpet and Piano, opus 1.

This short three-movement piece (it lasts about seven minutes) shows some evidence of the composers who were influencing Max at the time: Stravinsky, Bartók and, to a lesser extent, Messiaen. The trumpet part is sinewy and difficult, and the piano part is itself a fearsome test; but with Ogdon at hand to play it, Max felt safe enough in letting himself go. It is a bright, cheerful piece, with some flamboyant and highly exhibitionist work for the trumpeter. And it is clearly identified by Max himself with his apprentice works. Equally, however, one can hear in it his own distinctive voice, and confirmation of this comes from no less an authority than Håkan Hardenberger, the great Swedish virtuoso trumpeter. Speaking in 1993, he observed that the style of Max's Concerto for Trumpet and Orchestra, of 1988, was quite clearly identifiable with the same man's writing for the instrument in the Sonata. Another way in which this earliest of his works that he still acknowledges contains the seed of something that was to blossom much later is in the opening three-note fanfare, which later surfaced as the opening motif of the opera *Taverner*.

Howarth and Ogdon performed the Sonata at the College, and it caused a sensation. Much more significant, however, was the undertaking by the Arts Council to put the work on in London. They agreed to include it in a programme, but added a rider that the piece would almost certainly have to be dropped in the end, because in their opinion it was unplayable. This warning caused some hilarity in Manchester, where a large audience had sat and listened attentively to Howarth and Ogdon playing it.

The piece was duly shown to be playable, even in London, on 9 January 1956. It took place in the Great Drawing Room of the Arts Council's headquarters in St James's Square. The programme was perhaps the most uncompromisingly modern ever to have been heard in Britain at that time. It began with Webern's Piano Variations, opus 27, which was a pretty emphatic declaration in itself: Webern was still regarded then as just about the last word in mere noise – plinketty-plonk music or, as it was later to be christened, 'squeaky gate music'. This was performed by John Ogdon, who also played a work by the German composer Elmer Seidel; in addition, as well as Max's Sonata, once again played by Howarth and Ogdon, there was a piece for cello and piano by

Skalkottas, and works for clarinet and piano by Elizabeth Lutyens and Goehr, in which the clarinet parts were played by Birtwistle. The programme notes were headed 'New Music Group Manchester'. This is of some interest, because it is the only documentary testimony that such a group ever existed.

Shortly afterwards Max wrote excitedly to Eric Guest:

> Our London concert at the Arts Council was a fantastic success – particularly my Trumpet Sonata. As a result we've got another concert at the Wigmore Hall. I've got people interested in playing my stuff (odd people in the world, aren't there?) and two prospective publishers – Schott and Universal – I've had letters from both asking for my scores so I suppose I can choose. (I'll go to Schott's.)
>
> Fantastic, isn't it?!
>
> The papers liked us – except the *Daily Mail* which said the whole thing stank. The *Guardian*, *The Times* and the *Telegraph* liked us a lot – the last two particularly my piece. The hall was packed out with people standing at the side. The standard of performance was phenomenal and the reception (acc to those who should know) the most enthusiastic that audience has given anyone for years.
>
> For most of the programme I turned over for John Ogdon at the piano, but for my piece I crept in at the back, among those standing. When my piece started everyone nearly jumped out of their seats – they didn't know what had hit them – then they took great interest, and I felt the tension rising. When the last gargantuan discord stopped, and the applause started, the man next to me (a dapper fellow smartly dressed in a navy blue suit) said, 'Who the hell wrote that?' 'I did,' said I and his face dropped a mile . . .

Max was called on to the stage to experience the heady feeling of taking his composer's bow for the first time, and afterwards met numerous people, including eminent musicians, but, as he goes on to say in the letter, 'after the nervous tension and the excitement I was in no state to take it in, and just said, "Hello, very pleased to meet you" to everybody (just like my schoolboy dreams!!)'. One congratulation he did take in sufficiently to remember it afterwards was from Walter Goehr, Sandy's father, who told him the trumpet piece was excellent. The other significant meeting was when Howard Hartog, the head of the music publishing firm of Schott & Co., bought him a drink and asked him to go to see him some time soon.

After all this excitement, after his considerable and well-earned sense of triumph, his letter to Guest ended on a sad little diminuendo:

Next week I'm going to Paris to see Sandy Goehr. I'll pretend I'm ill at the university. That place is so dull, but the Indian music thesis is interesting to do. I hope your university isn't as boring as ours!

Around this time he composed the work that bears the opus 2, *Five Pieces for Piano*. It is a difficult piece of spiky and complex polyphony, and shows the clear influence of Schoenberg and Boulez. It was written for Ogdon, who gave the first performance in Liverpool.

There is little more to say about Max's time at university. He finished his thesis, and in due course received his degree. How much he valued it, except as the bald statement of his having received a higher education, requires little comment. However, a comment he made to Eric Guest during his time at university contains a revealing parallel with his curt summary of what he had learned from his grammar school. Just as the most potent lesson of his schooldays had been his insight into human nature from the behaviour of his headmaster, the only significant lesson he took away with him from his time at Manchester, he thought, was that 'Composing is only 10 per cent. You've got to give 90 per cent to the struggle to get heard.' Thus it may just possibly be claimed on behalf of his university that if nothing else, it helped him in one significant way: it showed him that a musician cannot live in an ivory tower, divorced from the rest of the world, and that art is as nothing if it fails to communicate. That certainty has coloured the whole of Max's subsequent career; and although it is true that it has earned him more kicks than ha'pence at times in that career, in general it has contributed much to his popular success. As such it can only be seen as having been a potent force for good.

As for the 'Manchester School', they very rapidly found their own directions. Some of their friendships have lasted until this day, some ended sadly a few years later in ill-feeling and even bitterness. But really, as suggested earlier, the idea of a school or movement of young composers is a misconception. If they ever did constitute such a school it really only lasted for the one concert in London and the earlier ones in Manchester. It is much more sensible to think of them as a group of five exceptionally talented individual musicians who happened by accident of birth and circumstances to come together at the same college at the same time, and who formed, for their brief time there, a deep but not in all cases permanent bond of friendship and a common front against the conservative, lack-lustre musical ambiance of their time. Once they had made their own very large contribution to changing that, the raison d'être of their confederation ceased to exist, and it dissolved.

We have seen how the musical landscape looked in the Britain into which Max had now sallied forth, and he had made his intention clear: he was going to inject a little colour into it if he could. As a parting shot he sent an article to the musical magazine *The Score*, edited at the time by William (later Sir William) Glock, who published it in the issue of March 1956. It was a spirited, sometimes fiercely polemical onslaught on the dreariness and the dead hand of conservatism in British music of the time. It is an interesting demonstration of Max's consistency of thought: the attitude towards the composer's craft set out in the article are, by and large, the attitudes he still has today.

Among the qualities that this article demonstrates most clearly is Max's enormous energy – it comes crackling right off the page as one reads – and another is his self-confidence. Both have been of vital importance to him throughout his life – someone once defined genius as being as much energy as anything else. Max's has rarely failed him. Certainly throughout the course of his education he only let his guard down once. Talking, as always in times of crisis or anxiety, to Eric Guest, he confessed that he was possessed by one all-consuming terror, of ending up like Sibelius, that is, burned out, with thirty years to live and nothing left to say. 'I really think I'd have to kill myself,' he said, 'if I ran out of inspiration.' Fortunately, such moments of lowered vitality have been rare; but the remark is a chilling, and perhaps a little awesome, reminder that extreme creativity is a driving force of colossal power, and not, perhaps, an altogether unmixed blessing.

The next decisive step in Max's career was now at hand, but there is one small and mildly amusing postscript to this period of his life. A clue to it is found in a footnote in the programme of the milestone concert at the Arts Council. Among the performers, Ogdon and Howarth, it noted, appeared by permission of the Principal of the Royal Manchester College of Music. But, it went on, 'Harrison Birtwistle appears by kind permission of the Musical Director, the R. A. Plymouth Band, Park Hall Camp, Oswestry'.

The 'R. A.' stands for 'Royal Artillery'; in those days, of course, all young men were required to do a period of National Service in one of the armed forces. These being no respecters of persons, young composers and other artists, however gifted, had to do their stint like everyone else; and there was no reason why Max should have been an exception. Not that he himself in any way expected to escape the common fate: when his call-up duly came he accepted the inevitable with resignation, realizing the futility of complaining about it, and went off cheerfully enough to face the preliminary medical and intelligence examinations, fully expecting to pass the next couple of years enduring the privations and boredom of life as a temporary private soldier.

He was home within a few weeks. The army had carried out IQ and aptitude tests and a series of personal interviews, at the end of which they said, in effect, that if Max was not a genius he was at any rate the nearest to one they had ever seen, and that the best service he could perform for his country was to go home and carry on composing music for it.

There is no way of telling, especially after this length of time, what, if anything, lay behind this extraordinary and – apparently, at least – generous attitude on the part of the army authorities.

One or two reasons do suggest themselves fairly readily; but it is idle to speculate. What is certain is that Max accepted his reprieve from National Service with even less complaint than he had accepted his call-up to it, and he was never bothered by the army again.

So it came about that instead of peeling potatoes in an army camp, the next step in Max's life took him to Italy, and to Signor Goffredo Petrassi, a leading Italian composer of his day. Max had heard and liked some of his music, and knew that he also had an excellent reputation as a teacher, so when he found out about scholarships awarded by the Italian government to study with Petrassi for a year he immediately decided to try for one. He asked Howard Hartog, the head of his publishing firm – he had by now signed up with Schott's – and William Glock, who was at the Dartington Summer Music School and had also published his polemical article, to act as his referees, and succeeded in securing one of the scholarships. He had also considered a course with Messiaen, but he had already visited Italy, and formed the deep love for that country that has remained with him ever since. A powerful additional incentive to go to Italy was that with Messiaen he would be only one among many pupils in a large class; Petrassi, by contrast, had told him straightaway that he would take him on as an individual pupil, rather than simply as a member of his regular classes. It was no contest.

Max was due to go to Rome late in 1957. In the meantime he began laying the groundwork for what was to be among the most seminally important aspects of his life and career, by taking on teaching practice. Teaching, inculcating compositional technique and the vital importance of that technique into young people, has been one of the dominant preoccupations of Max's entire life as a musician. He has inspired generations of children and young adults, teaching always by example, by the force of his iridescent personality, by his whirlwind-like energy, his enormous and, in the best sense, childlike enthusiasm, and by the unfeigned youthfulness of his own outlook and approach. He has also always been a highly unconventional teacher; his experiences at his own school and the unrelenting tedium of his university course left him with a horror of conventional teaching methods associated with lecture-rooms and the dry-as-dust monotony of 'learning facts by rote and regurgitating them in the approved manner'. All these early-formed attitudes are shown in another letter to Eric Guest:

> I'm doing TP [teaching practice] too! The lectures are mostly complete nonsense and I cut as many as I dare, but I find the school practice itself very pleasant. I'm at Salford Grammar . . . four days a week doing music – it's done properly here with General Cert. at ordinary and advanced level. I have lots of VI form work: I've only been there a week but the VI Lower had a diet of Berg, Schoenberg, Webern and Bartók and the lower school from form I up have had Bartók. It's surprising how much theory they do – the first two years have one period theory, one period history and one period singing each week, after which theory and history are optional. I find it very interesting to work with a handful of V and VI form – it gives much more opportunity for getting to know individuals and their ways of working, though some of them are clots. The younger boys are great fun . . .

This very early experience strengthened his conviction that there was no obstacle to the successful introduction of 'difficult' modern music to young school pupils, and that provided only that the teaching was not conservative and stuffy, young people were far better able than most of their elders to assimilate all aspects of modern music, including the vital ingredient of enjoying it for its own sake.

In his leisure at this time Max wrote incidental music for a university play, and for a lecture by a leading gynaecologist of the north-west of England, Dr Rickards. The lecture, with its music, including some for surgical instruments, was entitled 'A Womb With a View'.

Soon, however, he was off to Rome, and Petrassi.

The relationship between Petrassi and his pupil, the way in which the one taught the other, was fundamentally very simple: Max would compose music, Petrassi would ask him questions about it, and this went on for the whole of Max's eighteen-month stay in Rome. Put that way, it sounds absurd; but a senior composer who attempts to teach a beginner is really setting out to teach the unteachable. Max himself, after half a lifetime of teaching young apprentice composers, not to mention vast numbers of ordinary children who never thought of themselves as composers at all, says of teaching: 'All you can do is help and encourage the pupil to do his own thing. And of course the experienced man can help and advise on matters of technique.'

So what happens between an experienced teacher and his pupil is that the pupil is encouraged to compose, it doesn't matter what. Max, for example, spent almost his entire period with Petrassi composing two works: his *St Michael*, a sonata for seventeen wind and brass instruments, and *Prolation*, his first piece for full orchestra. When he had composed a section of the work in progress, he would take it to the next session with Petrassi, who would ask him questions about it. This is far harder, and far more likely to result in the eventual production of a good piece of music, than it sounds. Petrassi's questions were particularly difficult and pertinacious, and they kept Max on his composing toes much better than any more formalized system of examination and exegesis would have done, even supposing that a method of 'teaching' something as dependent on the individual creative personality as composition could be devised.

Max had to justify everything he did; if he could not, or if his explanations were lame, he was subjected to an intensive examination, which ultimately stripped the work he had done to the bare bone. Flaws in technique and in conception were mercilessly exposed, and he was enabled to take several paces back and assess his work objectively. Towards the end of his time in Italy Max felt that he had learned a lot, 'just from being interrogated'. His technique was more accomplished and assured, and he had gained considerably in confidence, simply by knowing with a lot more certainty why he was doing what he was doing.

He was also happy to be in Rome, a city he had fallen in love with on a visit two or three years before, while he was still at Manchester University. He had written then to Eric Guest, 'Rome is the most beautiful city I have ever seen. Every street, every square is full of interest . . . ' He had rapidly made close friends with a young Roman named Eugenio, who knew the city like the back of his hand and was delighted to have a chance of showing off its hidden beauties and its secret nooks and corners to a foreign friend who was very willing to fall under its enchantment.

Now, writing again to Guest, soon after his arrival to begin his work with Petrassi, Max still felt the same magic at work on him:

Rome is a marvellous place to live in – I live between the Vatican and the river, and near enough to the Borghese gardens. It is still hot enough [he was writing at the end of November] in the afternoon to lounge about in squares or parks in the sun, but at night it's v. cold. I'm living for the first time in my life with a telephone. This is great fun, although at first it was a real agony answering in Italian. I'm producing comparatively vast amounts of music, going to concerts and seeing lots of people and sights . . .

And a couple of months later in January 1958 he was enthusing: 'Rome is marvellous, hot and full of Christmas, which goes on till Jan 6th, with bagpipers dressed in sheep in the streets, riotous crowds fireworking, fairs and wild massed masses in the churches. Also the SUN . . . '

Among the many causes Max had for pleasure during his time in Italy was his meeting with the Italian serial composer Luigi Nono. Their initial acquaintance quickly became a firm friendship. Another source of satisfaction to Max was the assurance that none of his old flair for languages had deserted him. In the course of his eighteen-month stay in Rome he went from scarcely being able to speak more than a few halting sentences and elementary inquiries to a fluent, colloquial Italian which has never left him, thanks to his regular holidays in various Italian cities (Italy is still his favourite place to spend a holiday). It so happened that his recently acquired Italian turned out to be very useful soon after his return to England. He went to Dartington Summer School in 1959, and found that among the guests was none other than Nono. He delivered his lectures in Italian while Max provided a running translation.

The two works, *St Michael* and *Prolation*, that remain as a testimony to Max's Italian adventure are both still acknowledged. He had also, just before his departure for Rome, had the satisfaction of a first perform-ance by the New Music Ensemble, conducted by John Carewe, at the Dartington Summer School of a sextet for wind instruments, *Alma Redemptoris Mater*. The title is taken from a medieval plainsong, with which Max plays intricate games in the short piece. He also makes use of a motet based on the same plainsong and bearing the same title, by John Dunstable, one of his first great loves among the early composers against whom he was warned by Proctor-Gregg at Manchester.

Two other pieces from this time survive in the catalogue of Max's published and acknowledged works. *Stedman Doubles* is a notoriously difficult piece for clarinet and percussion. Its title is taken from change-ringing, but it was in fact one of several works that were directly influenced by the Indian music that Max had studied for his thesis. (He submitted the others to the Society for the Promotion of New Music, but destroyed them when the Society rejected them.) It was originally written for clarinet and three percussion players, but was never played in that form. It finally received its first performance in 1968, when Max revised it, rewriting the clarinet part and compressing the three percussion parts into one. The other surviving piece is the Clarinet Sonata, a long (25-minute), flamboyant and demanding piece, first performed at the 1957 Darmstadt Festival, with Max playing the piano part.

Of the two pieces written in Rome, the *St Michael*, a grand sonata for seventeen wind and brass instruments, was not given its first performance until after Max returned home to England, where it was performed to a good deal of blank incomprehension at the Cheltenham Festival in July 1959.

As for *Prolation*, this is a highly complex piece for full orchestra, including a large percussion section requiring three players. The work takes its title from a term used in medieval music to denote the relationship between the semibreve and the minim: in 'major prolation' there were three semibreves to a minim, in 'minor prolation' there were two. From this Max extrapolated a series of numerical ratios, reflecting durations of related parts of the music. However, this is extremely involved and makes no difference whatever to whether one likes the music or not, and it is by no means the last piece by Max in which the composer employs enormously complicated mathematical building materials for his music which can be cheerfully disregarded by the listener (with, incidentally, Max's full approval). Max's own brief verdict on *Prolation* is that 'It's such a vigorous piece, it almost suggests electronic music.' Eric Guest says that it is in some way based on the east window of a church the two of them visited, at the village of Bashall Eaves, just across the Yorkshire border; but it is not clear how the two are related to each other. What is certain is that there was a riot in the concert hall at the first performance of *Prolation*, in July 1959. It was not the last time a new work of Max's would provoke this reaction, but it was the first, and, according to Guest, 'Max was rather proud of this.'

It made, at any rate, for a suitably rousing finale to Max's happy spell in Italy. All good things come to an end, and soon after this performance of his piece, he returned to England. He was nowhere even close to making any sort of a living from composing, and realized that he would have to find some other source of income straightaway. Shortly after his return a vacancy was advertised in the *Manchester Guardian*: a Head of Music was required by Cirencester Grammar School. Max applied for the post, and got it. It was a fateful turn of events. The great part of Max's life has been governed by two preoccupations. The composition of music is one, and he had committed himself to that from a very early age. His acceptance of the position at Cirencester unlocked the door to the other.

3 ~ No Frontier

Many famous men have been schoolmasters at some time in their lives, but there have been few famous schoolmasters: one thinks of Dr Arnold, and then starts struggling. Fiction helps with Mr Quelch and Wackford Squeers, and that's about it. To this distinguished list one can, however, add a fourth: during his three-year spell as music master at Cirencester Grammar School, Max Davies was possibly the best-known schoolmaster in the country.

This was partly on account of his growing reputation as an up-and-coming young composer of the post-Vaughan Williams and even post-Britten generation. But it was mostly as a result of the methods he employed as a teacher at the school.

The very fact that one schoolmaster's teaching methods should become the subject of articles in national newspapers and numerous programmes on radio and television says a great deal about the British education system at the time. In a system less starched, in a less rigidly conservative country, Max's methods might have been thought perhaps a trifle unconventional. In a 500-year-old grammar school in a sleepy English market town, they were regarded as quite extraordinarily iconoclastic. Yet these supposedly revolutionary methods really amounted to nothing more than the concept of getting the pupils themselves, the children and young people for whose benefit the education system existed, involved in the subject of the course – getting them right to the heart of the matter, writing and performing music of their own.

When Max arrived at the school at the beginning of the Christmas term of 1959 everyone immediately knew that they had someone different in their midst. He dressed differently, for a start: pullovers and slacks instead of the more formal garb customary among grammar schoolmasters of those days; and he never wore the black stuff gown that was still sported by many masters, certainly amongst the older generation. His teaching methods were radically different from those used in the past, or anywhere else in Britain at the time, and so were the results he obtained – spectacularly so. He also departed from convention in establishing an easy-going, informal atmosphere with his pupils, even down to the use of Christian names, although they generally addressed him as 'Sir' or 'Mr Maxwell-Davies', an early instance of the misapprehension that he has a double-barrelled surname. Another radical departure from the traditional atmosphere of distance and formality between schoolmasters and pupils was clearly shown by the fact that several of the pupils formed an inner circle of close personal friends, who spent a great deal of time with him, both in and out of school hours. In the late 1950s this was highly unconventional. Max was lucky in his school, and in his headmaster.

Cirencester Grammar School, under the headmastership of John Barnett when Max applied for his post and for two of the three years he spent there, was on the progressive side, without being outrageously avant-garde. This meant in effect that Max and his unconventional ways were accepted, but were still noticeably out of the ordinary – few if any other members of the staff there chose to adopt similar methods. A few of the older, stuffier members of the staff did indeed regard his attitudes and methods as subversive, mostly on the grounds that his informality with his classes was liable to endanger discipline. Max dispatched this argument in the most telling way possible, however: although he never once felt it necessary to punish any pupil, by corporal chastisement, by detention or by any other method, in all his three years at the school he never had any disciplinary problems in his own classes.

As far as the pupils were concerned, the response was quite clear; not surprisingly, they were all for Max. It was a refreshing change for them to have a master who was close enough to them in age to be able to remember what it felt like to be a schoolboy himself, and who thus found it easy to understand and sympathize with them and their problems; who was unambiguously human, lively, and youthful in outlook – not, in other words, any kind of a fuddy-duddy schoolmaster. Most refreshingly unusually of all Max treated his pupils as equals, never talking down to them, never even *composing* down to them – he was and still is emphatic that music composed for children must never involve writing down to them.

Among his first innovations as music master was to form a school orchestra. He also acted swiftly to revolutionize the repertoire of the school choir. Until then it had been a very conventional affair, rarely if ever performing anything more adventurous than folk songs and hymns. Within a short time of his arrival, Max had the choir performing not only his own works, but also large volumes of the music of his own favourite early composers. It was the first time most of the pupils had ever heard the music of Byrd, Dunstable, Tomkins, Victoria, the Gabrielis and countless others, and for many of the musical ones among them it was an unforgettable experience. In particular Max introduced a lot of Monteverdi's music into the repertoire, anticipating by a good ten years the Monteverdi renaissance of the late 1960s. Another ambitious project was a performance of Handel's serenata, *Acis and Galatea*, in which he directed the Cirencester town chorus and the Stroud orchestra.

Under his firm, exacting guidance the fledgling school orchestra quickly ascended to a good standard of playing. It improved steadily throughout Max's time at Cirencester until, in his last year there – 1962 – it was fit to perform a complete concert at the Bath Festival, no less. From very early on in Max's tenure the orchestra and the choir, sometimes together, sometimes separately, sometimes broken down into smaller ensembles, gave frequent concerts for the rest of the school, and this enabled Max to introduce the flood of unknown music to anyone who was receptive to it, not just to his own music pupils.

He was also able to make contact with the wider body of pupils when he took occasional General Study periods. These were widely appreciated as treats, because they could always be relied on to be fascinating in one way or another. Sometimes Max would treat the class to a piano recital. Sometimes he would simply sit and reminisce about his travels in Italy, Darmstadt, Hamburg and elsewhere. If the sun was shining he would suddenly leap up and summon the class to follow him out, and take them for a walk round the City Bank, the grassed-over remains of the ancient town's Roman wall. He also greatly impressed his pupils by his fluent German.

Of the various ways in which Max was a highly conspicuous figure, the fact that he was quite frequently heard on the radio was probably the most powerful. He gave a number of talks on aspects of contemporary music, and was quite often asked to introduce new works of his own on the odd occasions when they were broadcast. This was long before either local radio or the radio and television phone-in programme had been born or thought of, so it was a great thrill to the pupils to hear the voice of someone they knew on the radio, or to read an article in the paper about him.

His contacts further helped him to enliven the life of the school: John Ogdon, newly famous as the first British winner of the Tchaikovsky Piano Competition in Moscow, came and played for them. Still greater thrills were in store as well.

By the time of Ogdon's visit Max had moved out of the digs he had occupied at first, and moved into his first home of his own – he had always lived with his parents prior to his departure for Rome. This was the first floor of a sort of small barn set in the enormous gardens of a fine

Georgian house. Although it was right in the centre of Cirencester it was very secluded and, most important of all, quiet; Max has had a horror of noise from early childhood to the present day, and, especially when he is composing, extraneous noise, such as jet aircraft thundering overhead, very easily drives him into a frenzy. The barn had been used for storing apples from the estate orchards, and the first floor was called the Apple Loft. It was whitewashed and plain, and Max, who has always preferred such decor, kept it that way as he turned it into a bed-sitter. He had a small cooking stove, though in general he ate out to save time. There were also his first grand piano, lent to him on more or less permanent loan by a wealthy woman friend, and his precious clavichord.

This was where he slept, and where he entertained the inner circle of particular friends among the pupils when they went to see him outside school hours. Often they would go straight from school at the end of the day, buying cakes in the town and assembling at the Apple Loft to drink endless cups of instant coffee as they talked or listened to Max playing the clavichord.

On the occasion of John Ogdon's visit Eric Guest was also staying for a few days. Before Ogdon's arrival Max had locked the clavichord with a flourish, remarking to Guest that 'I don't want Ogdon getting his big hands on that.' On the first night of Ogdon's stay they all got drunk (on Grand Marnier, Guest recalls with a reminiscent shudder). When they got back to the Apple Loft Max did some hilarious impressions of Peter Pears singing Britten folk songs, with the aid of a book of John Clare's poems, and then ceremoniously opened up the clavichord, played one great chord, *fortissimo*, and broke three strings – precisely the catastrophe he had feared it would suffer under Ogdon's huge paws. They then fell asleep, Guest in Max's bed, Max on a camp bed, and Ogdon on the floor under the piano for some reason.

For the pupils who visited the Loft it was a magical place of friendship, conversation and fun. They didn't stop learning and gathering new experiences when they were off duty. Roger Holmes was a sixth-former when Max arrived at the school, and was not one of his music pupils, but he was a budding recording engineer, and a member of the inner circle. He would help Max to put his hi-fi record-player right if it malfunctioned. He remembers vividly how when he visited the Loft on one occasion Max put on a record and the room was suffused with rich, glowing romantic sound, the complete opposite of the austere, astringent Elizabethan music to which Max had already introduced them with such success. Max assured him that the composer would become popular one day. It was the first time Holmes had heard

Mahler, who did indeed become popular – in fact, he achieved cult status – a few years later.

Another member of the inner circle, Neil Martin, who was one of Max's music pupils, says that he had never encountered anyone, before or since, who worked so hard – a comment that has been made by all who have encountered Max at any stage of his life: it is impossible to miss his astonishing energy and vitality. In his years as a schoolmaster, this enabled him to continue to find time to compose his own music. In the course of his first year at Cirencester he produced four works which have survived in his catalogue of published and acknowledged works. Two of them were composed specifically for the school orchestra, which was already, in this first year of its existence, of a standard high enough to merit being stretched by these pieces.

Five Klee Pictures is just what it says: vivid translations into orchestral terms of five of Paul Klee's pictures. In *A Crusader* an obsessive march theme is gradually taken over by an equally obsessive motif on the side-drum; *Oriental Garden* is a delicate filigree of oboe and clarinet themes; *The Twittering Machine*, one of Klee's funniest and most celebrated pictures, also translated into music by Günther Schuller in his *Seven Studies on Themes of Paul Klee*, is based on a relentless, bouncy, nine-note figure in the brass which surrounds itself with a wild assortment of sounds from the large percussion section (five players); *Stained Glass Saint* begins as a sad, majestic, slow movement and gradually turns into a noisy piece of parody; and *Ad Parnassum* is a virtuoso showpiece for the flutes, oboes and trumpets.

The other piece Max produced for his young orchestra was *William Byrd: Three Dances*. This is, as the name suggests, an arrangement rather than an original work, although it appears in Max's list of published works. The three dances are a volta, a quick-moving Italian dance in triple time, a slow alman, and a coranto, which, as its name suggests (it is a variant of *courante*), is a very fast movement.

Max was constantly arranging other composers' music for the orchestra and the choir, and rewriting large amounts of it for smaller ensembles of voices or instruments, and then, more often than not, himself preparing the individual players' or singers' parts in his own time. He spent a lot of time coaching all these groups personally, and also had to get his music pupils through their GCE examinations. There were the frequent concerts by the choir and the orchestra, separately and together, in the Bingham Hall (the school's concert hall) and Cirencester parish church, but he still managed to find time to arrange visits to concerts outside the school: he took parties to orchestral concerts at the Cheltenham Festival, for example.

Even this punishing workload did not stop him from somehow finding time to compose two other works in the course of 1959, *Ricercar and Doubles on 'To Many a Well'* and, perhaps his first masterpiece, *Five Motets*.

Ricercar and Doubles is based on a medieval carol of the name in the work's title. The melody is worked first into a ricercar, then two doubles, or variations, the first a scherzo and trio, the second a slow movement.

Five Motets is Max's first published choral work, and was originally written for vocal forces alone. He later added parts for sixteen instruments, which mostly double the voices. The forces are divided into three separate choirs or groups, with a direction that they be placed as far apart as the logistics of the venue permit, including setting groups to the side or rear of the audience, each with its own conductor if necessary. The intention of all this is to heighten the antiphonal effect. The two SATB choirs are set widely apart in the left- and right-hand groups, with the four solo voices (again SATB) in the middle group. The left- and right-hand groups have choirs of brass and woodwind instruments respectively, each augmented by a chamber organ, and the central group of soloists is accompanied by a string quintet.

The three odd-numbered movements are large-scale celebrations of Christ, the two even-numbered ones providing quieter, more serene relief. The second is the well-known hymn 'Alma Redemptoris Mater', which Max had arranged from Dunstable's motet while still at university. In this setting it is scored for male voices and low instruments, and the fourth movement is a duet for unaccompanied soprano and contralto soloists.

The following year, 1960, saw Max adding only two new works to his list, both written for the school musicians, which indicates how busy his work at Cirencester kept him. The results of his teaching methods with his music pupils were to be still more spectacular this year.

Those methods were described in elementary terms by Neil Martin, who went on to be a teacher himself. According to Martin, Max's method consisted 'basically of saying to a pupil, "Sit down, here's some manuscript paper, here's a pen, now watch this, listen to this, and write some music on it." That kind of immediate, powerful direction, which got music out of people who . . . well, for example, I'm sure *I* wouldn't have written music. And it wasn't only the writing of it; it was immediately getting it performed, listened to, criticized, changed. Wonderful.'

Martin, who feels certain that he would never have written a note of music without Max's unique methods, was in fact one of his most able pupils, and composed several substantial pieces while a pupil at the school. He has no doubt of Max's qualities as a teacher and as a musician. 'Oh, yes, he was a genius, there's no question. Looking back, I'm not surprised I was so overwhelmed.' For Martin, the most striking thing about Max during his time at Cirencester was the intensity of his entire life – everything he did was at full voltage; nothing was done by halves – a characteristic noticed by everyone who has known Max at all well at any other point in his life.

The other quality all the pupils noticed, and liked and admired Max for, was his candour, his utter lack of hypocrisy. He had an endearing custom – endearing to the pupils, at any rate – of talking quite openly about other members of the staff and their idiosyncrasies. Generally speaking, this is not done at all in scholastic circles. What made this blithe candour – or perhaps it was youthful ingenuousness – into a bond between Max and his pupils was that he unerringly laughed at the same masters at whom the children were laughing already. It told them plainly that he was one of them, rather than one of the enemy.

Most of all, though, to quote Neil Martin once again, 'it was his incredible talent for getting music out of us – getting us to compose, getting decent performances out of us'. The same comment is repeated again and again by anyone who learned under Max: sheer force of personality enabled him to get things out of people that no one else would have been able to extract, and that they themselves would never have believed was in them in the first place.

All this he managed in a general atmosphere of amiability, getting on easily with the children – there is no recollection of slave-driving in any of his former pupils. On the other hand they all testify that if anyone ever showed an indolent or couldn't-care-less attitude, failed to turn up or, worst of all, was not dealing fairly with Max, he could fly into towering rages, which could be a most terrifying experience for those on the receiving end. He had, as he still has, a very effective shout, surprisingly loud and ferocious coming out of such a small, slim frame, which, if worked up to the necessary temperature, he would use on anyone; but they accepted this because they could see the essential justice underlying it – there was no fear or favour about it. The children's judgement in this has since been proved correct: he will use the same resource as readily against adults and professionals as he did with his teenagers thirty years before. It was only another facet of his invariable, and quite unforced, custom of treating the pupils as equals, and they, with the unfailing eyes that children have for such rare courtesy and consideration, recognized it as such and responded to it.

In so far as there was opposition, as distinct from the odd bout of harrumphing from stuffier masters registering disapproval of Max and his modern methods, it usually arose when members of other people's classes had been hijacked by Max for some musical duty or other. He certainly was ruthless in commandeering people in the middle of their French or geography classes when he needed them for a final run-through of some piece they were about to play or sing. This was all very well, but the feelings of the other masters may well be imagined; they had exams to get their pupils through too. The occasional irascibility that this brought out in other members of staff could not have been greatly assuaged by the realization that the pupils were invariably on Max's side: if there was ever a clash of anything else with musical activities, at least if the pupil concerned was one of Max's musicians, there was never any doubt which was more important.

Generally, though, the respect he received from the pupils was matched by the support he got from the headmaster and the other staff. The headmaster, Barnett, gave him as free a hand as possible, recognizing that the publicity Max was attracting could only be good for the school. Obviously, major events, such as the taking over of the parish church on occasion, or the visit of the Argo record company to make a record of the school choir and orchestra, which necessitated stopping the traffic outside to avoid external noise, could not have been achieved without a great deal of support. In time Max repaid this confidence by dedicating a piece to Barnett.

There were frequent highlights to excite the school over Max's years there. The first of these came early in December 1960, with the first full performance, in the parish church, of a big new work for Christmas by Max, composed for the school forces. This was *O Magnum Mysterium*, a hefty forty-minute piece comprising four carols, two instrumental sonatas and a fantasia for organ to finish it with a flourish. The original carol of the same title is based on a Wakefield Shepherd play. Eric Guest had lent Max a copy of it while they were still at school, so the piece had evidently been incubating in his mind for a fair while before its composition at this time. This new work was accompanied by works by Soriano, Arcadelt and Giovanni Gabrieli, arranged as always by Max for the forces to hand. There were various other pieces on the programme as well, including several composed by pupils and a carol by Max's assistant music mistress, Rosemary Hammond, but the climax of the concert was undoubtedly *O Magnum Mysterium*, which the school choir and fourteen instrumentalists from the orchestra performed beautifully. The concluding organ fantasia was given a spectacular premiere by Allan Wicks, the organist of Manchester Cathedral.

A couple of months later, in February 1961, there was great excitement in the school when the BBC TV arts programme, *Monitor*, featured Max and Dudley Moore in a programme entitled *Two Composers, Two Worlds*. As so often with television, the programme misrepresented and trivialized its subjects, partly for the perennial reason that there was insufficient time to treat its subject seriously. Presumably the controllers of television take a profoundly pessimistic view of their viewers' attention span. The main flaw in the programme, however, was that having grown out of the initial idea of two young composers (both were twenty-six at the time of the broadcast) following utterly different courses, it went on to force everything that followed into the strait-jacket of this parallel-development-but-look-aren't-they-different theme. The result was that Max was portrayed as the earnest, unsmiling composer of 'serious' music, oozing gravitas and deadly serious high purpose, while Moore was made out to be an almost clownish figure, unreeling volumes of trifling ephemera. There is a grain of truth in both these ludicrously coarsened pictures of the two men, but of course they miss the point in both cases, since, annoyingly, real people do not fit into such neat, symmetrical cut-out shapes. The programme design demanded a perfect antithesis with no overlaps or grey areas. When Max and Moore failed to provide one, the programme-makers manufactured it.

The main effect of this, in Max's case anyway, was that the programme failed completely to reveal his skittish sense of humour and fun, never far below the surface, in his music as well as in his social life. Still, it did show him in well-known places in the town of Cirencester and the school, together with lots of shots of pupils, several of whose own compositions were played, so the school was generally very well pleased with it. In addition, for all its faults the programme did attempt to show how Max succeeded in getting music from pupils in whom no one would have thought music lay hidden.

Having described him as a revolutionary, the narrator asked Max to talk about his own music and about his teaching methods. On the subject of his own work he replied that he was often accused of writing music that was meaningless. He went on: 'I take it for granted that what I write has got a meaning. I think a composer should be able to take that for granted – otherwise he shouldn't be in the business at all. What does keep me awake at nights is the method of expression, the technique of composition. That is the composer's first concern.'

He added that he was very encouraged and pleased by the reception his music had received at Cirencester, 'particularly with the children at the school, who enjoy it'. This is a favourite theme of his, that young people, without a gradually accumulated stock of prejudices, find far less difficulty than their elders in assimilating his music. Max is at pains to emphasize that young people *enjoy* his music, and his former pupils enthusiastically endorse his view. The programme concluded with the observation that he 'must avoid the ivory tower, and judging by his impact on children, and on critics, he's being pretty successful'.

The school buzzed with a variety of musical activities. The dramatic society needed incidental music for its production of Barrie's *Peter Pan*. It was composed by members of Max's music class because, as he guilelessly remarked in his brief introduction to the play, he had not had time to do it himself. Instead, he rounded up half a dozen or so of his musicians, parked them in the Apple Loft, gave each of them a section of the play for which he needed music, and told them to get on with it. In half an hour there was a fearsome din going on, with everybody composing at once, trying out bits on the glockenspiels and other oddities in the room and directing a barrage of questions at Max about whether you could do glissandos on a cello, how this or that would sound on a flute, and so forth. The music was a great success, including a fantasia on the National Anthem written by Max himself. It performed a series of merry pranks on the anthem, and raised a few elderly eyebrows on the night of the play's performance, but the school loved it.

Neil Martin formed a group, Pro Musica Optima, from sixth-form members of the choir, and composed a substantial *Communion Service* (made up of the *Sanctus*, *Benedictus* and *Agnus Dei* from the Mass) for it. They performed it in local church services and in a number of concerts.

The week after the performance of *Peter Pan* the school put on a concert which brought the music correspondents of several national papers down from London. The main reason for the special interest was that the second half of the concert was taken up by a performance of the great *Vespers* of Monteverdi. As we saw earlier, Max's 'discovery' of Monteverdi preceded his sudden exhumation and temporary attainment of cult status by several years. However, all the visiting VIPs were also given the chance, in the first half of the programme, to hear the usual mixture of early music and pupils' compositions, plus a Prelude for harpsichord by Max himself (now withdrawn). The entire concert was a triumphant success, the *Vespers* in particular, though it had to survive a certain amount of premature applause resulting from the fact that scarcely anyone in the hall had ever heard the work, so that no one knew when the end was due.

On Ascension Day 1961, Max decided to revive an ancient Cirencester custom. At 6.30 that morning he took a small wind band to play from the top of the parish church's 160-foot tower. A large number of the school got up early and gathered in the churchyard to listen. By this time the local newspaper had realized that anything involving Max was very likely to be newsworthy, and appeared promptly to interview the children down below. When some wag reported plaintively that the music had been spoiled by the persistent song of a cuckoo in the churchyard it was all dutifully reported.

The year 1961 was as busy as any other for Max with the ordinary work of the school, but he still found time to compose three new works, two of them for Cirencester. *Te Lucis Ante Terminum* is a setting for SATB choir and a twelve-piece instrumental ensemble of the compline, or evening hymn. It has three verses of rich harmony for unaccompanied voices, separated by instrumental movements, the first a short andante, the second requiring improvization on given note groups. It was premiered by the school chorus and orchestra in the parish church in November of that year.

The same month saw the first performance, by the Amici Quartet, of Max's String Quartet, in a BBC invitation concert. Though fairly short – it lasts less than fifteen minutes – it is one of his most concentrated pieces, based on material from one of his own carols.

The other new piece had some amusing repercussions. It was a brief carol, a pretty little piece called 'Ave Maria – Hail, Blessed Flower', and it was first performed at a concert given by the school forces at the Royal College of Music in London, under the auspices of the Society for the Promotion of New Music – another tremendous thrill for the children. The Society billed the performance as 'a concert of original music composed at the school'. It included the *Peter Pan* music and numerous compositions by pupils, Rosemary Hammond's carol and the two choral pieces composed that year by Max. The concert was another triumph for Max and his young performers, and made a hit not only with the audience on the night but also with the critics. The *Daily Telegraph*'s reviewer reported it under a headline 'A Colony of Boy and Girl Composers', and spoke enthusiastically of the 'astonishing works' on display.

The fleeting notoriety of the little carol 'Ave Maria – Hail, Blessed Flower' came not from this concert, however, but from a curious departure from its normal practice on the part of the magazine, *The Musical Times*. Under its new and radical editor, Andrew Porter, this august monthly published the carol in its supplement, where normally there would be found some traditional piece of choral music, sometimes worthy but always utterly safe. This piece of Max's provoked something of an uproar, extracting fierce howls of outrage. Writing in *The Times* on 6 October, on the other hand, 'Our Music Critic' (William Mann) felt able to describe the carol as 'nothing but a gentle little piece of polyphony in A minor with a flattened fifth to its scale, and a lilting six-eight metre, each part singing nicely (there are one or two awkward intervals) . . . ' So he clearly did not see anything in the little piece to get anxious about. Nor did most of the other professional critics: Jeremy Noble, also in *The Times*, Colin Mason in *The Guardian*, Noël Goodwin in the *Daily Express* and others all said very favourable things about it.

Not so the public, if the sample whose comments were printed in the next issue of *The Musical Times* are anything to go by. 'I consider myself one of the younger generation, appreciative of sensible modern trends,' declared one Donald Cashmore of Surrey, before continuing, 'it is high time someone made a firm stand against this unnecessarily unpleasant music which has little interest in its melodic lines and altogether creates a hideous dirge.' The same reader also asked, 'Is this a hoax by *The Musical Times*?' Alfred Corum of London N1 declared knowledgeably that 'a choir, above all a church choir, which would persevere with it after a first reading must be a very rare thing indeed', and another expert on choirs and what was within their grasp, E. A. H. Martin of Kent, agreed: 'a choir singing extempore would not sing such grinding discords unless they were all deaf. I doubt whether a hearing choir *could* sing so many minor seconds.' Colin Crabe of Kent was more than merely musically outraged, and demanded to know 'what possible connection has the praise of Mary with those melancholy, purposeless progressions?'; but of all these 'Disgusteds' the prize for hyperbolic damnation of Max's inoffensive little carol had to go to the Rev. K. S. S. Jamal of Suffolk, who went so far as to declare that 'Personally I think it is an affront to God, and I am speaking both as a priest and as a competent organist and experienced choirmaster.'

As a mild riposte to this overflow of spleen the magazine playfully reminded its readers of another publication's verdict on another new piece of music a while earlier: 'Altogether it seems to have been intended as a sort of enigma – we almost said a hoax' – thus a paper called *Harmonicon*, in 1825, à propos of Beethoven's 'Pastoral' Symphony. And in case that failed to chasten the ranks of the disgusted, it gave the last word to Max himself, who remarked drily that 'It must be easy to do, because our kids got it on one rehearsal.'

This absurd episode can only have reinforced the conviction that underpinned Max's entire philosophy of music teaching, that mid-twentieth-century children need mid-twentieth-century music, and that children need not necessarily share their parents' prejudices about what does and does not constitute music. He elaborated on this in another BBC radio programme, broadcast a short while later, early in 1962. He saw nothing unusual about his achievements at Cirencester, he said, and felt that similar results ought to be possible in many schools. He went on to give some description of his methods. 'We have got in the school', he said, 'several young composers – young composers who have not been taught about consecutive perfect fifths, who have not done Palestrina counterpoint or anything approaching that sort of thing. They have written music within their own concepts. I have not tried to impose anything from outside, just realized what the person was trying to get at, within his own limitations, and deliver that as well as I could.'

This goes straight to the heart of Max's innermost principles as a musician, both as composer and as teacher. It was the method of helping him adopted by Petrassi in Rome before he went to Cirencester, which was also used by Roger Sessions, his mentor in his subsequent studies in the United States. But far more than that, it has been at the heart of Max's own method as a teacher from his beginnings as a schoolmaster right up to his Summer School for young composers held every year in the Orkneys and the numerous other ambitious projects in which he makes his contribution to the musical future of the country today.

The most pronounced (and encouraging) difference between Max's period at Cirencester between 1959 and 1962 and the present is that nowadays his methods, if not exactly commonplace, at least are not regarded as revolutionary or downright seditious. The schoolmaster Neil Martin confirms that the musical world, and in particular the musical teaching world, is still intensely interested in what Max did at that time, and many music teachers are profoundly influenced by the methods he pioneered. This process began while he was still at Cirencester. Dr Eric Roseberry was a county music organizer in Huntingdonshire from 1959 to 1964. He says: 'I was very much inspired by his work at Cirencester, and we performed a number of his things – chiefly *O Magnum Mysterium* – and invited him to direct a composition class at our annual Summer School of Music at Orton Hall, Peterborough, where he also introduced (with great eloquence) a performance of his (then) new String Quartet. Max was great fun and very friendly.'

If it is difficult now to grasp precisely why he was seen as such a rebel, or revolutionary – both terms were applied to him almost as a matter of routine in the radio programmes and newspaper articles devoted to him – it was in truth a simple matter. Max treated all his pupils, from eleven to eighteen years of age, as equals – which is to say, as adults. He never patronized them, never composed down to them either, but always conscientiously made sure that what he produced for them was within their reach. Even if it was only just within their potential, it was within it, so that although they might well be stretched, they were never over-stretched.

The results of these beliefs and practices, he told one BBC inter-
viewer, were that

> The sort of music [that the children produce] is naturally quite
> unconventional. A young mind gets hold of a musical image
> which is fresh, rather raw sometimes, but completely free. I have
> been surprised at some of the results. The extreme sophistication
> of some of this still knocks me over, and the imagery of some of it
> surprises me perhaps more.

He added a comment that might have been scripted as a retort to the
self-styled arbiters of what choirs would and would not find acceptable
in *The Musical Times*:

> I should like to see more music written for and by amateurs. I'm
> rather tired of the situation where composers are writing only for
> professionals and ignoring the amateur completely, and where so
> many people say, 'No, I can't possibly write music, it's far too
> difficult.' That's rubbish, you can make music of a sort, anyway,
> and get a great deal of enjoyment out of it.

In 1962 Max's time at Cirencester was nearing its close: he had
decided that he wanted to return to the other end of the teaching and
learning process, and do some more studying for a while. However,
there were still musical excitements to come, beginning in February
with a contribution to one of the Robert Meyer concerts at the Royal
Festival Hall. These concerts were specifically for children – the Meyer
motto was that adults were not permitted entry to the auditorium unless
accompanied by a child – and their programmes were always a mixture
of large numbers of highly varied complete short pieces and excerpts
from larger works, all the items being introduced with a certain amount
of unpatronizing description and background. In this concert Max
introduced the choir, making a point of mentioning that they had had to
be up at half past four to get there in time (Robert Meyer concerts
always took place in the winter). They then sang *O Magnum Mysterium*,
which they thoroughly enjoyed, and the young audience loved every
minute of it. The concert was also later broadcast on the radio.

The following month saw the visit of Argo already mentioned, to
make the record of *O Magnum Mysterium*. This went without a hitch.
The school choir and orchestra were at their impressive best, and the
resulting LP record went on to receive excellent reviews.

For their finest hour, though, the young musicians of the school had
to wait until the penultimate month of Max's time as their master. In
June 1962 they travelled to Bath, where they were scheduled to put on a

complete concert in that year's Festival. The programme was the usual mix of early and contemporary music: there were pieces by Victoria and Praetorius, early instrumental pieces, some in arrangements by Max; there was thirteen-year-old Robert Kneale, playing his own Prelude for Harpsichord. The greatest interest, though, was in a long and substantial work by Max's star pupil, Stephen Arnold. It was a Theme and Variations for Violin and Harpsichord, and it was played at this, its first performance, by none other than Yehudi Menuhin, the founder of the Bath Festival, and at that time still very much in personal charge. He spoke warmly of the piece, saying that he had much enjoyed exchanging ideas with its sixteen-year-old composer, then played it with great panache, with Max playing the harpsichord part. The concert ended with the choral and orchestral pieces from *O Magnum Mysterium*. Both local and national newspapers reviewed the concert enthusiastically, and most of the performance was repeated later in a recorded broadcast on the radio. But nothing sent a greater frisson of excitement round the young musicians and their supporters than when Sir Adrian Boult and Michael Tippett (not yet Sir Michael) were seen taking their places in the audience.

After this there was one last concert in the parish church back in Cirencester, which, as one newspaper put it, 'marked the end of a musical epoch'. A good half of this concert took the form of a harpsichord recital by Max, in the course of which his virtuoso account of Bach's *Chromatic Fantasia and Fugue* brought the packed audience to its feet, to stand for a full minute in silent admiration (it was not done to applaud in church at that time).

Just before the end of the summer term – Max's last – the choir, orchestra and a great many friends, most of them former pupils who had left the school, held a farewell buffet for him in one of Cirencester's hotels. It was a high-spirited affair, which ended in Max's tie being ceremonially cut into pieces, one for each person present to take away as a memento of the occasion.

Busy though the year had been, with more than the usual number of high points interspersed with periods of everyday routine, Max still managed to compose a number of new pieces of his own, including three very substantial ones. The *Leopardi Fragments* is a setting in the form of a cantata of short texts by the Italian poet Leopardi. The texts are sung in solos and duets by soprano and contralto soloists, separated by decorative passages for the eight-piece instrumental ensemble.

The *Sinfonia* is a symphony in four movements for chamber orchestra. It was written for the English Chamber Orchestra, and was the first major orchestral commission Max had secured. It grew out of structural elements in the Monteverdi *Vespers*, to which he had devoted so much time for the school, preparing a performing version and coaching the pupils in the piece. Two other big works of this time, his String Quartet and the *Leopardi Fragments*, share this structural debt to the *Vespers*. Max himself has described the relationship between his own works and the Monteverdi as being similar to that between Picasso's paintings based on a Velasquez original and the original from which they were taken. Asked if there had been any special reason why he had titled the work *Sinfonia* instead of *Symphony*, he grinned and said simply, 'Yeah, it wasn't big enough.'

The following sketch of the work is based on a description of it by Max himself. The first movement, lento recitando, is based on the 'Domine ad adjuvandum' of Monteverdi, and is a dialogue of recitatives for woodwinds, with fast propulsive tuttis, each based on a single chord. The second, allegro molto moderato, opens out into expressive melody based on the same chords, with the duet 'Pulchra es' from the *Vespers* now the bass of the music. The third is a sonata allegro with much ornamentation in its development; and the fourth and final movement, lento, is a meditation mainly for the strings, with interludes for the wind, based on the hymn 'Ave Maris Stella', which was to be a source of inspiration for Max on more than one occasion in the future. The piece received its premiere at the Royal Festival Hall, played by the ECO conducted by Colin Davis, in May 1962.

The last of the three big works was another milestone in Max's career: his first commission from the BBC for the Promenade Concerts. For it he chose to write the first of his three major works based on the figure from early music who more than anyone else obsessed him for a very long time during the first half of his life: John Taverner. The work was the *First Taverner Fantasia* or, to give it its full title, the *First Fantasia on an 'In Nomine' of John Taverner*.

The *in nomine* was a style of instrumental music popular in England in the sixteenth and seventeenth centuries, and was so called because such pieces were based on the *in nomine* section of the *Gloria Tibi Trinitas* mass by Taverner himself. Max's piece begins with the oboes giving out the original plainsong, then oboes and bassoons with Taverner's theme. Then the main body of the piece starts, allegro, working up to a big climax with brass, wind and handbells, followed by a long coda. The work was premiered at the Prom of 15 September, with a number of Max's former students from Cirencester in the audience, many of them having travelled long distances to be there to see him off, for he was shortly to leave for the United States. In the other works in the concert the BBC Symphony Orchestra were conducted by Sir Malcolm

Sargent, but Max had to take over the conducting of his own piece because Sargent found it too difficult. Not that he was the only one. '*I* found it difficult,' Max admits cheerfully. 'I couldn't conduct it. Just stood up there and beat the bar patterns!' However, the orchestra was a match for the occasion and Max's conducting, and the audience, according to the former pupils who were part of it, loved the piece.

This was more or less the last act of an eventful year before he left for the USA to resume, for a while and for the last time, in any formal sense at least, the role of student himself. It was also the end of a crucial phase of his life. His three years at Cirencester had been arduous, taxing even to someone with twice the normal allocation of effervescent nervous energy. They had also, however, been highly rewarding. Perhaps the most important effect of his spell as a schoolmaster was to confirm in him several key attitudes to the teaching of music, which would determine how he handled very different but perhaps more important teaching tasks in the future.

The lynch-pin of his whole philosophy of teaching was summed up by the narrator of the BBC *Monitor* programme back in 1959, who at one point said: 'For Maxwell Davies composing and teaching are two aspects of the same single-mindedness . . . for him there is no frontier between composing and teaching.' It was to prove a singularly perceptive, even prophetic remark in a rather flawed and unsatisfying programme. We shall be reminded of it more than once in tracing the subsequent course of Max's life.

4 ~ Princeton

Max left Cirencester not only because after three years as a teacher he had decided he wanted to do some more studying himself, but to have more time for writing music. The ground had been prepared for this move years earlier, in 1957, when he attended the Summer School at Dartington, in Devon. Among the illustrious visiting tutors that year was Aaron Copland, in whose composition classes Max played some of his work. Copland was deeply impressed, and asked if he had considered going to America to further his studies. Max had never thought about it, and said so. Copland said it was time he did think about it, and suggested in particular that Max would benefit from lessons from his old friend Roger Sessions, who taught composition at Princeton University. There were scholarships available through the Harkness Foundation, and Copland offered to act as one of the necessary referees in Max's cause.

Two further referees would be required. Copland was on his way to Aldeburgh to see Benjamin Britten, and offered to raise the matter with him. Max, however, felt that he was not yet ready for such an upheaval. They parted on cordial terms, with an understanding that Max would contact Copland whenever he felt ready for the venture. Towards the end of his spell at Cirencester he did so. Copland was as good, and as kind, as his word, and wrote to Britten who readily agreed to act as one of Max's referees, along with Copland; Max asked Howard Hartog to be the third.

It was all fixed up by March 1962, when Max wrote to Britten thanking him for his kindness in acting as referee, and confessing that the prospect of his trip to the USA was 'quite terrifying', but adding that he felt it was necessary. He had already said, in his letter the previous December formally asking Britten to be his referee, that although the trip scared him stagnation frightened him more. Anyway, in late 1962, frightened or not, he sailed in the *Queen Elizabeth* to begin a two-year composition course with Roger Sessions, Earl Kim (who had been a pupil of Schoenberg) and the rest of the music faculty at Princeton.

As usual, Max made an immediate and vivid impression. Stephen Pruslin, later to play a crucial part in Max's musical life, as well as becoming one of his closest friends, was a graduate student at Princeton at the time. (He is generally known as Steve, which is how he is referred to henceforward in this book.) He uses the same word as numerous others have done to describe his first impression of Max: 'a mercurial man', he says, with a quicksilver mind and responses, which worked at incredible speed. According to Pruslin, the Americans in general quickly found Max charming, articulate and quintessentially English. English people might disagree about the last epithet, but he did very quickly amuse his hosts, at the same time establishing his own small claim to the eccentricity widely supposed by Americans to be a national trait of the English, by having his telephone disconnected, on the grounds that 'It might go off.' On another occasion, at a dinner party very soon after his arrival, he again startled his new American friends. The conversation turned to the Beatles, who had just begun to make their impact on the world. As the only Englishman present Max was naturally expected to know more about them than anyone else, so it was the cause of some amusement, mingled with astonishment, when he confessed that he had never heard them.

In the main, however, the first impressions, which were to be confirmed as time went on, were of vast talent coupled with a highly unusual degree of self-possession. It was noticeable that during composition classes, when the other students put their works up on the piano rack for dissection, analysis and discussion by the class, this all went on with abandon; when Max put something of his up there would be a few very polite questions and then an equally respectful silence.

People were aware that in Britain he was already, at twenty-eight, a quite well-known composer, who had had works performed by professional musicians on many occasions, including at the Proms; that he had a music publisher of international repute who regularly published his compositions; and that he had received commissions from highly reputable sources, including once again the BBC and the Proms, both institutions greatly respected in the USA. His fellow students could not help noticing, also, that he was treated by the faculty, including Sessions, very much as an equal – even down to the fact that he was invited to dinner noticeably more frequently than anyone else! The eminent American composer John Harbison and his future wife Rosemary, both students with Max, were struck by his highly un-student-like self-possession. As Rosemary Harbison puts it, 'He was fully aware of who and what he was as an artist; he was quite sure of where he was going.' All this made it so much the more remarkable to them, and pleasing, that he was never superior or stand-offish in any way, but was 'utterly lacking in any kind of airs and graces' – Steve Pruslin's words, which are echoed in one form or another by the Harbisons and everyone else who was at Princeton with Max.

It is striking how often throughout his life, people have commented on this quality of his, of remaining quite unassuming while having a good deal to be assuming about; and it especially endeared him to the Harbisons and others because visiting students from Europe, in particular those who had already begun to make reputations for themselves as artists, were not usually slow to remind their American contemporaries of how primitive they were, and how young, brash and unsophisticated the culture of their country. It is a dismal reflection on Europeans, but one heard only too often from Americans, who, in general, seem quite unnecessarily forgiving about it.

The students therefore tended more or less unconsciously to treat Max from early on as a fully mature composer, and as much farther advanced than the rest of them. This made them all the more appreciative of his unfeigned interest in all their musical activities. They were also very pleased when he remarked one day that there were more composers at Princeton than there were in the whole of England.

In general, however, Max did not say much in class. Indeed, the others all wondered if he was actually studying with Sessions, until one occasion (Max was not present) when the class was discussing whether it was possible to eliminate the sense of pulse and still have musical discourse. Sessions remarked that he would have said that the answer was that it was impossible until he had heard Max's *Sinfonia*, which he had found, to his surprise, pulseless but convincing. It was from this that the others realized that Max was indeed a full member of Sessions's class, and that the two of them were in fact looking closely at some of Max's work. Needless to say, the tribute from Sessions further enhanced Max's standing among the students.

He was in fact having private lessons with Sessions as well as taking part in the open classes. The methods used by the tutors at Princeton, especially Sessions, were essentially the same as those of Petrassi, especially in the inexorable demands that Max justify every mark he made on the manuscript paper. The significant difference was that Sessions was quite happy to talk about his own works as well as scrutinizing Max's. Max was working hard on his opera, and long-standing preoccupation, *Taverner*: he had determined that his time at Princeton should be largely devoted to getting the back of this major work broken while he had the chance. By a happy coincidence it so happened that Sessions was writing his own opera, *Montezuma*, at the same time, and this enabled them to bounce ideas off each other, compare progress and methods, and generally try things out on each other, which helped to cement a firm friendship and also a usefully close working relationship between two composers, as well as teacher and pupil. Meanwhile Max was also getting on very well with the other teaching staff, notably Earl Kim and Edward Cone. The notable exception was the senior professor, Milton Babbitt, whose manner Max found irritatingly high-falutin and affected. Among the students he very quickly made an especially close friend of Steve Pruslin.

Mostly, though, it was work. In Max's case this amounted to something of a luxury. He was not in any way priggish about being work-addicted, but he took the writing of music very seriously; he loved it, and now, at Princeton, for the first time in his life he was in a position to work uninterruptedly. It was also the first time he had been able to relax and write music without having to worry about money.

So for most of his time he sat in his apartment, now satisfactorily telephone-free, and concentrated on John Taverner. We have seen already that he had been thinking about this shadowy, turn-of-the-sixteenth-century figure since his teens, and the *First Fantasia on an 'In Nomine' of John Taverner* was his response to his first Promenade Concerts commission, during his last year at Cirencester. Now he settled down to serious work on the opera that he had wanted, and planned, for years to write about his brother composer.

His fascination with Taverner had begun when he first became interested in early music while still at school. Over the years of his boyhood and youth he was the best customer of the Henry Watson Music Library in Manchester, to such an extent that by the time he left school he had borrowed pretty well every score the library possessed. Among all the other things he discovered there, took away and played or pored over, he borrowed huge volumes of Tudor sacred music, including a great quantity by Taverner. He was initially attracted by the music, which he thought was magnificent; from there he quickly became fascinated by the figure of Taverner himself. His story embraces many of Max's most enduring interests and speculations. This is not surprising, for they are among the most all-pervasive themes in the whole of Western culture and philosophy: why artists create and feel the urge to create; religious belief and its perversion into fanaticism; cruelty and repentance; and betrayal, including the betrayal of self.

How well he got on is shown in a letter he wrote to Eric Guest in March 1963, in which he says he has finished the first three scenes of Act 1. Otherwise the letter is entertaining and revealing about some of

Max's musical attitudes of that time, including a confirmation of his feelings about Milton Babbitt:

> Things aren't going too badly here. I said TOO MUCH about and to the New York 'IN' 'new music' people – a lot of crappy phoneys, either dazzling each other (and no one else) with maths, which is supposed to excuse boring music – this faction led by Milton Babbitt – or fooling around burning musical instruments on stage or putting *drills* in pieces or making all SILENT – this faction led by Cage. But the string quartet was broadcast twice, and the Princeton High School Choir do the *Magnum Mysterium* and the Princeton Symphony Orch is to do the *Taverner Fantasia* next year . . .

The contrast between the unaffected manner, friendliness and lack of airs and graces that made such an impression on his fellow-students, and his impatience and contempt for members of musical high society, whom he regarded as mere poseurs, could hardly be more striking. The Harbisons spent some weeks with him in 1991, when he was once again in the United States for the Ojai Festival in California, and after almost thirty years their impression of him was precisely the same: a man who did not suffer fools readily, but who was still the same direct, straightforward, honest person, who would have no truck whatsoever with postures.

Yet again in the same letter to Eric Guest, Max reveals some of his feelings towards the United States in general. Guest is about to join him in the States for a touring holiday by Greyhound bus. In answer to a question about the possibility of hiring a car, Max wrote: 'I wouldn't advise it unless you enjoy driving because it's my idea of hell, on the wrong side of the road, at never under 60, with incredible multi-lane flyovers as complicated as Clapham Junction to be manoeuvred and decided in split seconds, and every car as long as a train and the police NASTY, with revolvers . . . ' In the next paragraph he goes on: 'I warn you, you'll hate many things – it's only because I've the peace of this attic to retire to that it's tolerable.' And forgetting that he has reserved his definition of hell for the spaghetti road junctions, he continues, 'New York is all hell.'

Clearly his feelings about America were mixed – or perhaps it was merely homesickness having its say when he saw the negative side of things. On one occasion, certainly, he suffered from one of the profound black depressions to which Eric Guest has referred. Guest's father worked in the Mines Rescue Station, and there was a telephone in the family home that was reserved strictly for mining disasters and other emergencies. One Christmas, probably that of 1963, this phone rang. The only emergency it disclosed, however, was Max, suffering from severe depression and announcing, 'I'm not supposed to be here. I'm breaking the terms of my fellowship. But I just had to get away. See you tomorrow.'

Having said all that, he did go on what Steve Pruslin describes as the 'obligatory' grand tour of the States with Guest, impressing the Harbisons once again with his readiness to meet America and Americans without condescension. They went westwards, visiting, among other things, ghost towns left uninhabited and eerie overnight as claims petered out during the Gold Rush. In Oregon they halted for long enough for Max to do some lecturing and take a class of music teachers, and to suffer a minor crisis of conscience as a result. As he always did when it was possible, he confided in Guest. The problem was that in the classes he had marked the music teachers' efforts rather severely, not knowing that their rates of pay were going to be determined by the marks they gained on the course. The discovery of this, plus the teachers' dismay and, here and there, tears, had greatly disconcerted Max.

It was easily enough put right: he simply recalled the exercises and marked everybody up to a suitable level. As an exercise in cooking the books it could not have been simpler, and gave universal satisfaction. As an indication of Max's unwillingness to inflict hurt, it is very reminiscent of the incident at school when he came top in languages, to the mortification of the other boy who had worked far harder to achieve the same result. And it also gives a clear indication of Max's cheerful indifference to officialdom: the fact that he was falsifying the marks and almost certainly cheating their employers out of a certain amount of cash that the teachers were not strictly entitled to, was less than nothing to him. As a matter of fact he did not even recall the incident: it was Eric Guest who remembered it.

A rather fuller review of Max's feelings about America, about Princeton and what he was doing there, and about his state of mind in general, is given in a long letter he wrote very early in his stay to Dr Donald Mitchell, the musicologist and critic, close friend and associate of Benjamin Britten, who knew of Max from his work at Cirencester, and had got to know him in person when Max took part in Eric Roseberry's Summer School at Orton Hall in Peterborough. (Mitchell claims that his immortality was assured when he was press-ganged into playing the bass drum in the world premiere of one of Max's works there.) Max's letter to him is worth quoting not only for the picture it gives of his life at Princeton but also because it reveals that he was not quite as supremely self-possessed and confident as the other students thought.

The University music dept. is overawing in certain respects – the other graduate students *know* far more than I do, and have encyclopaedic knowledge of scores. The staff are horribly knowledgeable – Milton Babbitt is the one electronic composer I met who makes sense, Sessions is slow but thorough, Kim . . . is fabulous as a composition teacher, Strunck is a diehard forbidding musicologist, and the others are well up to this standard. Schenker and higher maths are ex-cathedra dogma here, everyone is expected to know 'notation' (= ligatures and all that old rot! not half so interesting as the *music* itself) – in fact I'm very, very glad I'm not expected to get a degree here – I never could make it – now, at least, that I'm so old & *set*!

New York is a 90–minute bus ride away, with half-hourly buses and the last one home at 1.00 a.m., so it is very convenient and tempting to go to NY for innumerable concerts. One given by Gunther Schuller and crack instrumentalists of Cage, Ives, Cowell, Wolpe and Varèse was so well played it was unbelievable, and was so sold out neither Varese Babbitt nor I could get in, and had to be *smuggled* in. The *music* was cold and hardly competent – no tradition, obvious! I came out into the snow and felt wretched and utterly miserable.

Your fellow-critics here are an unbelievable bunch of utter cretins – people just don't believe me when I say not only am I on *speaking terms* with London newspaper music writers, but that 2 of them are very good friends! The filthy rubbish Schonberg, for instance, writes in the NY Times is so incompetent and *wrong* it is tragic, as he ruins good people and makes clots, such is his power . . . Stravinsky is right in attacking these fools. No serious musician here would be seen speaking to one of them – it really goes so far. But what can one do?

I finished the text of the opera *Taverner* . . . I already set most of the 1st scene (in full score!) – this is the most intense and exciting thing I ever did, and has cost so much energy . . . it burns my fingers! . . .

I don't know yet if America is *really* bearable – I worked so hard I hardly noticed. I sent off to Schott's already a drastic rescoring of the five enormous motets I wrote in '59 – this a huge job in itself. Already there are 49 pages of very closely written full score of *Taverner* . . .

There is another long section of this letter which cannot be quoted because it concerns someone who does not wish to be named; but the substance of it is worth relating. One of Max's inner circle of personal friends, and also one of his most talented music students during his time at Cirencester, was still a pupil at the school at this time, and was desperately unhappy. He was intensely musical, but his parents were unsympathetic and would not contemplate allowing him to have a piano or other keyboard instrument, which was essential for his studies. The boy had had the use of a clavichord, which he had been lent, but the owner had taken it back for his own use, and he had no means of getting hold of another instrument. Max asked Mitchell to find and buy a clavichord as a matter of urgency, enclosing a cheque for £100 and promising to send any reasonable amount over and above if the instrument found was more expensive. At the same time he swore Mitchell to absolute secrecy, particularly where the boy's parents were concerned. A little later he reiterates this: 'Again, please tell nobody I paid for this, because it isn't "generosity" – the thing [i.e. the clavichord] is absolutely necessary and I have the money lying idle, so it might as well be spent very wisely thus – which may be misunderstood . . .'

The final few words suggest the reason for his insistence on doing good by stealth; part of it was on account, no doubt, of the boy's parents' total lack of sympathy for his devotion to music; but such a munificent gesture on the part of someone who had until very recently been one of the boy's masters, especially when there had been and still was a powerful bond of friendship between the two, could clearly be misconstrued – and not only by exceptionally suspicious minds – as Max evidently realized.

It is, indeed, perhaps even more likely to be so misconstrued today, especially in the light of Max's open declaration of his sexual orientation. Since that is so, the matter should be cleared up here. There was definitely no sexual link between Max and the boy in question, while Max was a master at the school or at any other time; furthermore, on the authority of more than one of the innermost circle of pupils who were Max's personal friends as well as his students at Cirencester, there was never any homosexual link between Max and any of the boys at the school. Max's purchase of the clavichord for the boy was precisely the act of great kindness that he himself denies it was: a selfless act of rescue on behalf of a friend whose musical deprivation was causing him great spiritual anguish. Max saw the anguish, remembered the friendship, and did something generous and practical to remedy it. The lurking fear that such an action might be misconstrued says more about contemporary conditioning and stereotyping than it does about Max.

At about this time, early in 1963, Max became embroiled in a protracted, at times bitter and always absurd squabble, caught between two giants in the world of music publishing, both of them internationally famous names, and both anxious to have Max on their books. He had been signed up with Schott for several years, and they wanted him to stay with them. Donald Mitchell, however, at Britten's instigation, had joined Boosey & Hawkes as a music consultant. Britten was not happy at Boosey's at the time, and was anxious to improve his relationship with the firm by having Mitchell handle his affairs. At the same time he wanted Mitchell to try to revitalize Boosey's list by recruiting some younger talents. Mitchell's brief, quite simply, was to see who, with Britten's encouragement, he could entice to join Boosey & Hawkes, with offers not only of better money but also of a relationship in which musical rather than commercial considerations were paramount. Max was an obvious candidate: Britten had known of his work at Cirencester, and regarded him as the ideal representative of the younger generation, to whom he could safely hand on the torch of pioneering work with the young.

In the end Mitchell took Max from Schott's and Nicholas Maw from Chester's. In Max's case, however, it was a somewhat messy business. A letter from Max to Mitchell in February of 1963 explains the position:

> About B & H – Schott's . . . are falling over themselves just now to publish my pieces quickly, and I've no complaints . . . I receive an annual 'retainer' of £100 (this could be bigger, I admit!) and £20 for each new piece . . . in 'advance of royalties' – however, real royalties only start when they've covered the 'cost of production' which means in fact I pay for my own publication!!! However I was reconciled to that ages ago, being convinced that if a publisher doesn't do something of that nature on the swings he'll diddle you on the roundabouts. Royalties, after all these deductions, come to about 3/4d per annum. I have no standing contract with the firm – only the £100/annum 'retainer' (I suppose euphemism for 'bribe') and a new contract for each new piece. I couldn't live off *that lot* clear, but the P. R. S. now adds a very tidy sum each year. I frankly dread the thought of 'earning a living' when I get back to England, having had the liberty to compose all day here! I shouldn't like to leave Ian Kemp [then in charge at Schott's] now after all he did, disapproving 'disloyalty' etc . . . '

Only two days later Max was acknowledging a letter from Mitchell that had crossed with his own, and now he was talking enthusiastically about the terms Boosey's had offered him. They were enormously better than the deal he was on at Schott's, and it is quite clear from his letter that the possibility of escaping his dreaded 'earning a living', which he thinks would have had to be by teaching part-time and doing the odd broadcast for schools, had more than overcome his qualms about seeming (or being) disloyal to Schott's.

He adds a word to the effect that he does not want any repeat of his early experiences at Schott's, of having new works lying gathering dust on shelves for long periods before publication, then goes on to express anxiety about his opera, *Taverner*, which was growing fast now that he was able to compose full-time, and incidentally provides a progress report on the work:

> what about the opera? I'm already well into the music for scene 3, and it's by far the most ambitious and by a very long chalk the *best* music I've made . . . I'll be quite honest here – composing *Taverner* is the most shattering musical experience I had, and despite possible difficulties with the authorities (the established church) I would like it to be available.

Finally, he appends a brief postscript in which he returns to the main cause for his joyous move to Boosey & Hawkes: 'P. S. Does this mean Boosey & Hawkes think my work will *pay*!!!? It wd be marvellous were it performed enough for that! . . . '

Further letters keep up the enthusiastic tone, but about a month later, on 22 February, Max sent a cable to Mitchell stating baldly that Schott's were going to make a serious bid to keep him on their books; and shortly thereafter the Chairman of Boosey's was writing to Mitchell stating that it would be unethical for the company to increase their own offer in order to outbid Schott's. He has, he says, already written to Max telling him that he must honour any moral or contractual obligations he may have towards Schott's, and not feel that he has been put in any dilemma by Boosey's offer.

Max now replied, pointing out a little snappishly that Boosey's had done nothing wrong, that Schott's offer of serious terms would not have happened without Boosey's offer in the first place, and that there had been not the slightest hint of it prior to Boosey's intervention. Clearly there had been murmurs from Schott's about 'loyalty'. He also wrote in the same terms to the boss at Schott's – 'only fair to you', he commented to Mitchell.

Letters continued to flow copiously back and forth across the Atlantic in the three-cornered discussions of Max's publishing contract, but eventually, on 21 March, Max sent a cable to Donald Mitchell in London ending with the words 'Prepare contract'. Mitchell then wrote telling Max in the most emphatic terms that he must write to Schott's stating that their counter-offer was unsatisfactory and categorically terminating his relationship with Schott's, before Boosey's could send him their contract. And there was further correspondence between Max and Dr Ernst Roth, the chairman of Boosey's, about some silly stories that mischief-makers had whispered in Max's ear about Boosey's. Finally, another cable reached Mitchell: 'Roth's letter absolutely straight full of confidence go ahead letter sent to Schott's as required.'

The affair was still not over, however. Schott's now resorted to threats – and Boosey's hesitated. The draft contract, which had been promised the moment Max wrote formally to Schott's severing his connection with them, was not sent. A fortnight later it had still not been sent. An anxious letter from Mitchell to Roth sets out the latest state of play:

> I am convinced that PMD is a man of genius and the leading composer of his generation, and as such I should like to see him published by Boosey & Hawkes . . . The very fact that Schott's don't think he's worth the retainer you offer him . . . only reinforces my feeling that Schott's don't deserve to keep him. What would PMD's reaction be, I wonder, if we told him what his present publishers think of him?
>
> Moreover, and more importantly, PMD now *wants* to be published by Boosey & Hawkes, which leaves us in the absurd predicament that though (1) PMD wants to come to B&H and (2) we want him to come, (3) we are deterred by Schott's blustering.

Mitchell, who felt acutely the awkwardness of his position, having actively encouraged Max to ditch Schott's in favour of Boosey's, urged Dr Roth that the contract *must* be sent to Max without delay – otherwise, he argued, what would Max think? What would other composers think (they were bound to hear of the affair)? He himself, Mitchell went on, was a lot more concerned about what Max thought of him than what the boss of Schott's did. In short, he urged that if the rest of the musical world wanted to think that Max was disloyal and Boosey's were predators, let them think it, but let the contract be dispatched. The letter has a special interest, apart from the new episode in the continuing soap opera of Max's contract, in that Mitchell went on to reiterate that he thought Max was the leading composer of his generation – probably the first time on record that this had been said in so many words.

In late April, Dr Roth wrote a fairly anguished letter to Max, repeating that Schott's had raised a fearful commotion, accusing Boosey's of breaching unwritten codes of business honour, and Max of being disloyal. Roth suggested that both Max and Boosey's ought to clarify matters, and get their names clear, before going any further; and he reluctantly accepted Schott's demand that they should have another chance to persuade Max that he would be better off with them than with Boosey's. He ended, therefore, by urging Max to arrange to meet Schott's representative, a Mr Makings, as soon as he could, and get the matter finished with.

One wonders, at this point, how Schott's could have imagined that they still had a chance of hanging on to Max. Apart from being responsible for all the agonizing and delay, they had quite plainly offered him proper financial terms only when forced to do so by the appearance on the scene of serious competition; and after the composer had exercised his freedom of choice they had then done everything they could to make life awkward for him. No doubt they were relying on the notion of 'loyalty' which pervades British business – though it is very noticeable that when the chips are down this only ever cuts one way.

Max wrote sympathetically to Donald Mitchell, declaring in outspoken terms that if Schott's made it morally impossible for Boosey's to honour their original offer he was none the less not going to continue as before, but would, if necessary, publish *nothing*, and go back to schoolteaching instead. His amply expressed horror at the idea of having to do any such thing gives a good indication of how angry at Schott's behaviour he had become by this time. One suspects also that there was a strong element here of retrospective anger at how Schott's had been treating him financially – he would not have felt this so much until someone else came along with an offer that made him realize there were people who thought him worth a lot more than his present publishers did. As Mitchell had remarked in his letter to Roth, 'What would PMD's reaction be, I wonder, if we told him what his present publishers think of him?'

A pleasing element of reality is brought into this by one of Max's former pupils, the same boy for whom Max had bought the clavichord. Aided by the clear-sightedness of youth, unencumbered by such fictitious notions as unwritten codes of honour in business, 'loyalty' and the unmentionableness of money, this boy, now about eighteen, says in a letter to Mitchell: 'Schott's retainer is approximately 1/12 of your offer, I believe, so that all this flap about Max being "unfaithful" or something is rather irrelevant, isn't it?' Having thus uttered the most wholly sensible comment on the affair, the boy goes on to talk about the difficulties Max would face should he be unable to take up Boosey's lucrative offer. 'The point is', he says,

> that Max *needs* the money. His scholarship to USA has enabled him to start on *Taverner*. But he can hardly stomach USA for various reasons. When he heard of the B&H offer, he realized that he could come back *early* and still finish 'Tav'. He intended to come back in Sept this year [i.e., September 1963] . . . If he does so now he will have to get a job to breadwin, and, as 'Tav' is a *full-time* job, he won't be able to finish it easily. If he stays in USA, he still won't be able to finish it easily, because of environment, etc. Is there nothing to be done to help Max out?

At this point, in June 1963, Max took a break and flew home to England, where the matter of the contract was finally cleared up, and the way was clear for him to sign up with Boosey & Hawkes. When he got back to America he was feeling much better about life in general – the argy-bargy over the move to Boosey's must have been a terrible strain on his nerves, with fears of having to take a humdrum job lurking in the background. He had put right a mess he had made of one section of *Taverner*, and the London Philharmonic Orchestra was making encouraging noises about a big orchestral piece. A fee of £300 was being talked about quite seriously – big money at the time. First of all, though, Max made time for his holiday tour around the States with Eric Guest.

On both sides of this holiday he was working furiously on the opera. He had no time to produce a piano reduction – 'the ideas are too hot', he commented in a letter to Mitchell, so Steve Pruslin offered to do this for him: a noble offer, for it was a colossal task. Meanwhile, though, Max was also writing a piece for the Princeton High School Choir, which was booked to perform it at the Cheltenham Festival the following year (1964). The school was scratching round desperately to raise the air fares for the choir (about $200 each) and could not afford to pay for the reproduction of the scores of their piece. Max paid for the work, *Veni, Sancte Spiritus* himself. It was a substantial piece of twenty minutes' duration for soloists, chorus and orchestra.

He was also just embarking on two other projects, both of which were to have repercussions of considerable importance many years later. He describes them both in a letter to Mitchell written in September 1963:

> I am making an architectural film with Jonathan Mansfield – architect, also on a Harkness Fellowship – and as the musical and

visual shapes are related absolutely, we are working out (he with the aid of the computer) a notation which involves *all* the experience. I don't know quite how this will work out, but it should be quite an interesting venture . . .

He then moves on to the other project:

I am working on the text of a new one-act chamber opera. This is all set in an operating theatre, and involves film, dance, electronics, etc. I am arranging to see brain surgery and heart-lung ops, particularly inside the heart. This work, which will make *Taverner* seem like a children's bedtime morality, will be ready in two years – if you could get somebody to commission it . . .

And so, here, as early as 1963, when Max was stuck not too happily in a foreign land, we can see the first few preliminary chalk-marks and pieces of string marking the sites of two towering masterpieces of the future. The interest in architecture, and a parallel interest in the musical representation of architectural structures, was to find its ultimate expression in the sublime third symphony, which was to be first performed twenty-two years later, in early 1985. And the idea of an opera set in an operating theatre was to come to *its* final fruition in the shape of *Resurrection*, commissioned by the city of Darmstadt and first performed at the Stadtstheater there in late 1988. It is a noticeable feature of Max's career as a composer that his preoccupations tend to be remarkably long-lived, often incubating quietly underground for very long periods before suddenly bursting into brilliant life when everyone – except, presumably, Max himself – has forgotten their existence.

Shortly afterwards he completed the piece he was writing for the Princeton High School Choir, and was working hard on the piece for the London Philharmonic Orchestra, which had indeed been commissioned. There was a minor hitch with this piece, which was perhaps a blessing, for without it we should have been denied one of Max's first real masterpieces. The conductor who was to direct the orchestra in the piece, John Pritchard, at that time Principal Conductor of the LPO, had planned to perform Webern's Symphony in the same programme. So he wrote to Max via Boosey's (with whom Max was by now happily settled), asking him to write his piece for a smallish ensemble, to balance the Webern. The note, however, somehow went astray somewhere en route, with the result that when it finally surfaced six months later, Max, under the impression that there were no restrictions of any kind, had already written a very heavily scored piece for full orchestra –

indeed, it is for a slightly larger orchestra than normal, being augmented by a second tuba, a harp and an arsenal of percussion requiring four players. The piece was the *Second Fantasia on an 'In Nomine' of John Taverner*.

At about this time Max received a very pleasant surprise in the form of a telegram from the Gesellschaft der Musikfreunde in Vienna to inform him that his *First Taverner Fantasia* had won third prize in a competition sponsored by UNESCO in honour of the 150th anniversary of the Gesellschaft. He was invited to the commemorative concert in the Great Hall of the Musikverein, at which his work would be performed by the Vienna Symphony Orchestra under the direction of Hans Schmidt-Isserstedt, and there was also a cash prize of $500 to go with the honour. And honour it truly was: the first and second prizes went to Lutoslawski and Walton, and the unplaced composers included Berio and Roy Harris.

It turned out that it was the BBC Symphony Orchestra, which had played the work at the Promenade Concert in 1962, that had submitted the score and a tape of Max's piece. The orchestra got a very notable accolade in return for its gesture – the list of unplaced orchestras reads like a roll of honour: the Berlin Philharmonic, New York Philharmonic, San Francisco Symphony, Chicago Symphony, Boston Symphony, Suisse Romande, Japan Philharmonic, Austrian and Warsaw Radio Orchestras, among many others.

One award was rapidly followed by another. In a postscript to a letter to Donald Mitchell Max says casually, 'Mrs Koussevitsky's presenting me with the American International Music Fund award in N. Y. at a little ceremony on Tuesday.'

Far less agreeable was a row with the man at Cheltenham who had been responsible for the booking of the Princeton High School Choir for the Cheltenham Festival. He was now, according to Max, trying to back out of putting on a performance of Webern's First Cantata, which the High School children had learned off by heart. This was in order to avoid offending or embarrassing the conductor, John Pritchard: it was felt that Pritchard would cut a less than heroic figure if he was given only works by Haydn and Purcell to conduct while the chorus-master of the High School, Thomas Hilbish, conducted the Webern and Max his own *Veni, Sancte Spiritus*. It would, or at any rate might, it was argued, look as if Pritchard could not be trusted to conduct any work that was modern and difficult. Max suggested a tactful compromise, whereby Pritchard would conduct the Webern and Hilbish take over Max's piece, but when he rang to put the suggestion, Pritchard was not keen on the idea. This put Max in a very difficult position with Hilbish, and he ended up by getting irate with the cause of the trouble, threatening to cancel the High School's appearance altogether and to prohibit performances of his own works at Cheltenham Festivals in the future. Reporting all this to Donald Mitchell, he ends by saying:

> They [i.e. the Cheltenham organizers] must realise that people shouldn't be treated like this – also, *particularly* children, when they learn a work like Webern 1 *by heart* specially. Perhaps [the organizer in question] will say 'Go to Hell', but I'm not going to have people walked over.

In the same letter he announces, with frank relief, his imminent return to Britain: the letter was written on 19 February, and he was to arrive home on 15 April, 'only to go on to Berlin on the 16th – this I frankly look forward to', he writes, 'I was away from England and Europe long enough.'

Max had thus spent about eighteen months in America, taking the last formal lessons he was to receive, but, for the most part, enjoying the luxury of being able to compose at will without having to worry about money, the only limitation being how many hours he had sufficient stamina for. This he had undoubtedly enjoyed: indeed, it was his idea of paradise. The rest, as we have seen, he had viewed with mixed feelings at best. Still, he had made a favourable impression on the people he met there, and he had had fun at times, such as the holiday with Eric Guest.

In terms of achievement, the American experience was fairly productive. Max had, as we have seen, gone a considerable way with the opera *Taverner*, which was by far the biggest work he had yet conceived. He had written the *Second Taverner Fantasia* a very hefty piece for big orchestra of about forty minutes' duration, and *Veni, Sancte Spiritus*, another chunky piece, about twenty minutes long, for the High School. He had also gone some way towards the writing of another major work of this period, the *Seven 'In Nomine'*. These were in a way a kind of dry run for the Taverner fantasia, and began life in Earl Kim's composition classes. The first of the seven *In Nomine* pieces was by Taverner himself.

The *Second Fantasia* is intimately bound up with the opera, and could be thought of as a 'Taverner Symphony'. The musical material grew from that of the first Act of the opera, which, as we saw, Max had completed before he left Princeton. Indeed, some passages are virtually identical. The piece is in thirteen sections, all thematically united by three related melodic ideas which metamorphose one into the other throughout the piece. The first six sections make up a movement in sonata form, with introduction and coda. This part opens with an exposition of all three melodic themes in quick succession, the first on solo cello, the second (very brief) on solo viola, and the third on solo violin and then solo cello. The introduction concludes with a fanfare for brass and side-drum. Section 7 is a bridging passage to the scherzo and trio in sections 8 to 10, section 11 (heralded by dramatic trumpets) another to the long slow movement of section 12 (shades here of the Adagio of Mahler's Tenth Symphony), and section 13 is a coda, harking back to the material of the introduction.

The *Veni, Sancte Spiritus* is a setting of the Pentecost hymn and the biblical story of the mighty wind and the sound from heaven, scored for soprano, alto and bass soloists, who may be drawn from the choir if the voices are adequate, normal SATB chorus, and chamber orchestra without percussion, or even timpani. The orchestra spends most of its time doubling the vocal lines. It is considerably more difficult than, say, *O Magnum Mysterium*, written earlier for school choir, or *The Shepherd's Calendar*, written later for a mixture of school and university musicians.

Apart from the pieces of music written, what benefits, if any, did Max derive from his stay at Princeton? He held most of the staff of the faculty in high respect, and freely concedes that he learned from Sessions, Kim and Edward Cone in particular. John Harbison remembers him saying one evening, 'I'm building a technique that will last me for forty years.' The Princeton period and people helped appreciably in that, and some would say that that in itself was sufficient justification for the experiment. It is, however, open to question how much of it Max would have provided for himself in any case, had he not gone to the States. We have seen how assured he seemed to the others, and how clearly he appeared to them to see his way forward. Pruslin, the Harbisons and several other students, and Edward Cone of the faculty, all remember specific instances of this. Someone looked at the score of his Sonata for Trumpet and Piano, written seven years before, and commented that the harmony was very similar to the harmony Max was using at this time. Max replied: 'You can change everything else, but not harmony. Your harmony is in your genes.' Steve Pruslin says: 'In discussions of his pieces in class, there would always come a moment when he would say something to the effect of "this is how it was composed", and that always signalled the end of that particular discussion. He was saying, "This is my way of composing, and it's for you to find yours".'

On another occasion John Harbison asked Max if he spent much time in revising his works. He replied that he did so rarely, because it was like trying to conceal ugliness by putting on make-up: never very convincing. This is a remark that could perfectly easily have been made by Max at any moment from that day to the present: his attitude has not altered at all. One other snippet of conversation has stuck in Harbison's memory. He had shown Max a composition of his own with the comment that 'I'm really worried whether it's any good or not.' Max laughed and said, 'My God, if you worry about things like that you'll never write anything at all.' The laugh robbed the remark of any personal sting, but the attitude was there, already formed, which was to see him through much criticism, often savage, vituperative, personalized and unfair, in later years. It also offers early evidence of a streak of toughness in Max, which Harbison also perceived quite clearly: 'He wasn't in the least ivory-towerish,' he says. 'He combined subtlety and flexibility as a musician, and generosity and toughness as a person.'

Somewhere in Max, not necessarily far beneath the surface, is a very hard man – spiritually hard: capable of taking difficult decisions, and on occasion of being decisive to the point of ruthlessness if necessary. None of this invalidates his claim to be a kind, indeed generous, friend. But there are always people ready to equate kindness, decency, and especially generosity with weakness. Those who have tried it on with Max have had a tendency to find themselves lying on their backs, wondering where the blood is coming from.

This toughness has undoubtedly been valuable to Max over the years, but it has not been to everyone's liking, and a fair proportion of his friends deplore it, seeing in it an aspect of the man they glimpse only rarely, and do not like.

On balance it seems more likely that the real benefits of the American venture were of a less tangible kind. To begin with, all travel, all meetings with new people are intrinsically beneficial: they broaden the mind, expose prejudices to healthy challenge, comfortable orthodoxies to other cultures and other ways. Max made valuable new friendships, some of which were to last a lifetime, notably that with Steve Pruslin.

He is remembered by those who knew him at Princeton with affection and great respect. Edward Cone recalls that when a string quartet of his was being given its first performance in New York, he looked round to see who from Princeton was in the audience. Max was the only one. Cone was greatly touched by this loyalty. He also says:

> In our discussions about music, what I admired about Max was his completely natural attitude, free of cant and false intellectualism. That is not to say that he was anti-intellectual, but he was opposed to a tendency that he saw in the young Americans around him to substitute words and ideas about music (often half-baked ideas) for music itself. Once, addressing a class of such young Americans, I said, 'I find myself completely on the side of the young composer – a rather well-known one – who, when asked why he wrote as he did,

replied, "I like the tunes". The young composer was, of course, Max.

Probably the greatest benefit of all, though, was that Princeton provided him with a taste of what writing music professionally was like – that is, all the time he needed, without having to worry about making a living in other ways. If Max had never gone to Princeton and experienced this it might have taken him years longer to decide once and for all that he was simply not willing to earn his living any other way. He might never have made the decision, though that is unlikely – someone of his strength of will, who had decided early in childhood that he was going to write music for his living, would almost certainly have contrived to do so somehow – but even if he had been delayed by only a few years, his resolve might have foundered amidst the eddies and shoals of everyday, humdrum commonplace; and in any case his development as a composer to the full power of his maturity would have been greatly delayed, with incalculable repercussions.

So, early in 1964, Max returned to England, and was very glad to be home. Having finally sorted out the squabbling over who was to publish him, he had signed up with Boosey & Hawkes, who had been as good as their word and paid him an annual retainer of £1200 a year. Max's comment, made with great glee, is: 'I could live on that. And so I never did a stroke of work again!'

Incidentally, one comment on Max's standing as a composer at this time was unwittingly made by Schott's in the course of the unseemly wrangle: the boss there, Ian Kemp, was always absolved by Max from any personal responsibility for the affair, and from any suspicion of having done anything improper; on the contrary, Mr Kemp's personal part in the business seems to have been above criticism throughout, except, perhaps, that he ought to have kept a sharper eye on other people to make sure they behaved as sensibly as he did. In fact, as is often the case with such things, the whole affair was more a cock-up than anything more sinister. But at one point Mr Kemp conceded that he would have been more than ready to pay Max more or less anything he asked within reason; his problem, he went on, was that if he paid one of his contemporary composers a realistic amount, the others on his books would all start expecting the same terms; and that would be both impractical, in that the company could not afford it, and bad business anyway, because most of them were not worth it. The implication is unmistakable: they might not be worth it, but Max was. Coming from that particular source, at that particular time, the compliment paid cannot but have been sincere.

With Boosey's annual retainer providing him with a very respectable income, there followed a period of two years in which Max, though busy as always, was able to settle down and compose. When he first got back to London he quickly met up with his friend and former pupil from Cirencester, Neil Martin, by now an undergraduate at the University of London. They had continued to correspond throughout Max's time at Princeton, and met on Max's couple of brief visits home. Martin had a flat in Bolsover Street, in the looming shadow of the Post Office Tower. The building was owned by Derek Saul, a friendly man and a lover of music, much older than his ever-changing student tenants but young in spirit and outlook. Martin introduced Max to him and to the place, and thereafter Max was a frequent visitor, using Martin's flat as a pied-à-terre and sleeping on the sofa when he was in London. Quite soon he had become a tenant himself, and for a short period his small flat there (which was, in fact, Derek Saul's own sitting-room) was where he composed his music.

It was often a meeting place for groups of former Cirencester pupils and friends of Max's, gathering to go to a Promenade Concert together, or to hear a new work of Max's premiered. Other visitors included a Persian prince whom Max had visited while at Cirencester, and a ghost, christened Gregory, who was seen (and heard) regularly by Max and by Steve Pruslin when he came to live in London. Bolsover Street continued to be a regular meeting place and haven for musical wanderers long after Neil Martin had moved on and Max had ceased to be an official tenant there; and Derek Saul, who still owns it, remains a friend of Max, with this to say of his former tenant: 'There is in fact on my sitting-room windowsill a tiny piece of music in Max's own hand called *A Fiftieth Birthday Card for Derek* . . . The fact that Max lived here for a short time and welcomed the opportunity to do so – as I did to have such a marvellous person in my home – gave the place a stamp which it has never lost.'

Steve Pruslin had gained his Master's degree from Princeton and stayed on to teach there, but then won a scholarship that permitted him to spend two years living in Europe. He arrived in London two months after Max's own return home. He soon met numerous friends of Max's, including Harry Birtwistle, and they knocked about London together, talking endlessly about music, setting the world to rights, as Pruslin puts it, and generally enjoying being young, finished with formal education and its demands, and in London. They also made plans, including one that was to shape the immediate future for all of them, but for Max more than either of the others. First, however, came a period in which Max's life alternated between widely varying activity and rural tranquillity and calm.

5 ~ Interlude

The phase of Max's life that ended with his return from Princeton had been one of rapid change and continuous development. A few years later, in 1967, a new phase began, which was to be one of the most frenetically creative of his career. Between these two periods of high activity came one of relative calm, marked by the lowest level of musical output of his adult life. A period like this, even if of only brief duration, was probably necessary – a rest after the physical and emotional upheaval of temporary exile in the States, and a time of preparation, of lying fallow and gathering strength, for the volcanic outburst to come.

Such terms are relative, however. Max was young, in addition to having more than most people's quota of nervous energy. So it was not long after his return to England that he was up and doing, planning, organizing and hurling himself into new ventures. The first of these to bear fruit was a collaboration with his two comrades of Manchester days, Sandy Goehr and Harry Birtwistle. Together they organized the first of two Summer Schools of Music at Wardour Castle, in Wiltshire.

It was Birtwistle's idea. At that time he was eking out his minute earnings from composition by teaching woodwind instruments at Cranborne Chase, a fashionable private school for girls, near Shaftesbury, in Dorset. The estate consisted of a great house, dating from the eighteenth century, and extensive grounds which contained the ruins of Wardour Castle. The house accommodated the school, and, now, the Summer School of Music.

Birtwistle asked Goehr and Max to help out with the Summer School. Also involved were the Melos Ensemble, at that time probably Britain's premier chamber ensemble, the composer Hugh Wood and his wife, and the pianist Margaret Kitchin, who was the wife of the head of Schott's, Max's former publishers. The three composers all gave composition classes, there were various courses for instrumentalists, and a choir of students. It was, Max recalls, much like Dartington, but considerably more intense, because everyone there was planning in earnest to become a professional musician.

While they were still setting up this event, Max received two

welcome commissions. One was from the BBC, as part of the commemorations of the 400th anniversary of the birth of William Shakespeare. The other had far-reaching consequences: they reached about
12,500 miles, to be more precise. This commission was from
UNESCO, for performance at a conference it had arranged for the
summer of the following year, in Sydney, Australia. Before any of these
varied projects had begun in earnest, however, an earlier commisson
came to fruition in July, when the Princeton High School Choir gave
the first performance of *Veni, Sancte Spiritus* at the Cheltenham Festival.

Shortly after this the first Wardour Castle Summer School was held
under the presidency of Michael Tippett, and proved a great success. It
saw the first performance of a work that Max had been putting together
on and off over the past four years, the *Five Little Pieces for Piano*.
Lasting only about five minutes all told, these five miniatures were
played at the Summer School by Max himself.

After the Summer School Max applied himself to writing his
commission for the Shakespeare quatercentenary celebrations. The
piece was called simply *Shakespeare Music*, and consisted of a suite of
dances from Shakespeare's own day, set in Max's highly distinctive
style, for eleven instruments: woodwind and brass, an interesting
combination of strings – guitar, viola and double bass – and one
hyperactive percussionist.

By this time Max was beginning to crave the clean air and the peace
and quiet of the countryside. He therefore rented a cottage in the hamlet
of Tollard Royal, in Wiltshire, very close to the Dorset border. It was
the first time he had tucked himself away in a remote rural corner, but it
would not be the last; and it was a natural and obvious move to make.
Since his childhood he had had a ferocious hatred of superfluous noise;
worse than merely hating it, he found that extraneous noise interfered to
a maddening extent with his composing. He had returned from
Princeton a pretty well-known composer, by now clearly identified as
the leading light of the youngest generation of composers. This meant,
naturally enough, that he was going to receive more commissions, and
that had indeed begun already, with the two from the BBC and
UNESCO. His choice of this particular corner of rural England was
also in part at least in order to be closer to Harry Birtwistle and his wife,
Sheila, who were living in the nearby market town of Shaftesbury.

Max retired to Wiltshire reasonably comfortable on his generous
retainer from Boosey & Hawkes, and carried on with work on *Taverner*
until December, when the first performance of his *Shakespeare Music*
drew him to London. It was performed in a BBC Invitation Concert by
the Portia Ensemble under the direction of John Carewe.

After this he had only a very short time to relax in the new cottage and get on with his composing before he was off on another arduous journey, this time round Germany, Austria and Switzerland on a lecture tour. This took him throughout February and March to a number of ancient cities, among them Vienna, Linz, Graz, Salzburg and Innsbruck. But, as he wrote a little plaintively to Eric Guest in the middle of the tour, his main feeling was not so much of exaltation at finding himself amid centuries of musical tradition as of exhaustion at having to trail round in apparently perpetual snowstorms.

Eventually the tour ended, and Max was back in England for the first performance on 30 April of his largest, and possibly his most important, work so far, the *Second Taverner Fantasia*, given in the Royal Festival Hall by the London Philharmonic Orchestra, which had commissioned it, conducted by its principal conductor, John Pritchard (later Sir John).

Almost immediately Max was off again, this time to Australia, to attend the UNESCO conference on music education, for which he had been commissioned to write a work. The result was a large-scale piece for choral forces and soloists plus orchestra, *The Shepherd's Calendar*, and this, like his last choral piece, the *Veni, Sancte Spiritus*, was written for young, and specifically student, voices. At twenty-one minutes, it is about the same length as *Veni, Sancte Spiritus*, but it is significantly easier to sing, being more on a par with the children's elements of *O Magnum Mysterium*. It is a sequence of alternating choral and instrumental episodes – another parallel with *O Magnum Mysterium* – and, yet again like the earlier work, it allows comparatively unskilled performers to take part alongside more skilled ones – the less skilled ones taking the two percussion parts. The text is taken from the thirteenth-century Latin of the Goliard poets, and the whole piece makes up a song of the changing seasons.

The first chorus is introduced by a tenor solo, and ushers in spring. It is followed by a rustic interlude for woodwind and percussion, with recorders making bird calls. Then there is a calm summer chorus, followed by gentle music for string quartet and solo flute. There is a sad little autumn chorus, followed by another passage for woodwind and percussion. Winter starts with improvization, gradually drawing in all the instruments until the final chorus with treble solo brings the work to a conclusion. The piece received its premiere, performed by students of Sydney University and the Sydney Church Grammar School, with Max himself conducting. (His own verdict on his conducting ability at this time is that he was not significantly better than when he had conducted at the Royal Albert Hall because Sargent found his work too difficult.)

After the Sydney concert Max spent almost three months travelling round Australasia, often on the most extraordinarily hectic schedules, doing what he described in a letter to Eric Guest as 'visiting' (his inverted commas) numerous music colleges and universities. He goes on to translate 'visiting' as 'looking at what they did and giving lectures'. He also fitted in some conducting and gave numerous radio and television interviews and talks.

It was, he admits, utterly exhausting. He describes one day of the tour, admittedly one of the worst: 'I lectured at a training college in the morning, whizzed in a government car from Melbourne to Ballarat [a distance of about 50 or 60 miles] to a snatched lunch and another lecture and TV interview, was whizzed back to Melbourne just in time to catch a plane to Adelaide, where I was received at the airport by press with cameras and questions.'

By the time he got to New Zealand the strain of it all was beginning to tell on his nerves, and on his manners – or, at any rate, his finer sense of diplomacy:

> I was more than fed up with all this, and gave a radio interview that fairly made a sizzle (if anything can do there). The result was a melting of telephone wires to NZBC and Christchurch University Music Dept (saying 'how dare!'). I said that from what I had seen in NZ music education was 50 years behind the times, and that it was time the NZ authorities stopped giving so many scholarships to the Royal College of Music and the Academy in London, where as far as music theory, history, composition and musicology go they might as well go to the moon, tho' they certainly produce more than their quota of musically and generally illiterate performers – particularly singers and performers . . .

His wording and syntax leave uncertain quite what he means by the reference to their going to the moon, but the general tenor of his remarks and his own description of his frame of mind make it fairly clear that he was saying, in effect, that they might as well go to the moon if they thought they were going to derive any benefit from the classes he mentions at the Royal College and Royal Academy – the further implication being that the New Zealand students would be unworthy of these places.

There are indications that New Zealand was hell in other ways, too. Again writing to Guest, Max says:

> all-time low in NZ was where I was guest of honour at a soiree given by a university's Music Graduates' Society – an evening with tea and cucumber and potted meat sandwiches,

regaled with several specimens of NZ culture, including 'a New
Zealand setting of a New Zealand poem': two Victorian ladies in
pink stoles and perms came in and nodded at the pianist, who
rippled a dominant 7th, and they warbled in thirds and sixths
'Where art thou rising now, WOOKEY-BIRD?', etc etc, then
(verse 2) 'I shall take thee twixt my breasts, o wookey bird . . .'

'I was very moved, and needed my hanky,' he concludes, before going
on to say that several other places were nearly as bad. The dismal
catalogue of horrors ends with an especially plaintive lament: in
Dunedin 'I was disturbed all night by the traffic lights outside: every
two minutes all vehicles stopped on the red and the "cross now" sign
came on, accompanied by a vicious little buzzer, which buzzes as long as
the sign is lit. Christ, I hated it, for hours through the night!'

There were compensations from time to time, however: 'South Island
had little narrow-gauge steam trains – so had Brisbane and district, but a
different gauge'; 'there were a few beautiful wooden cowboy-style
towns in the S Island NZ interior, and wonderful winter landscapes';
'visited a friend of a friend who had a "station". I said, "How far does it
go?" They said, "That's all of it" (a range of snow-capped mountains
extending to infinity, full of sheep, they said, millions of them)'; and 'I
enjoyed the bush in Western Australia best – districts with extraordinary
tall trees and very odd bushes and flowers (altho it was "winter") – and
districts with nothing! Also, near Brisbane, the rain forest.'

In general, however, Max found both Australia and New Zealand
provincial and depressing. Oddly enough in someone who has spent
much of his adult life in remote hideaways, he liked the big Australian
cities best, describing them as 'fine; particularly Sydney, which is
magnificent, with lots of Victorian iron trelliswork and some very plain
early Victorian houses (built by convicts); some of the new buildings are
super, especially set off by that bridge – beautiful harbour with new
opera house . . . but', he was forced to add, 'there are about 50 miles of
suburbs around which are *hell* . . .'

His generally unfavourable response to Australia did not deter him
from accepting an opportunity that came his way while he was in
Sydney: an offer of a six-month position as composer in residence at the
University of Adelaide, in South Australia. With this post arranged for
early the following year (1966) he fled for home. He had hoped to return
in exotic and adventurous style, stopping off in every unlikely place he
could along the way. But in the end he was so utterly exhausted that he
came back to London in a single flight. 'Next time,' he declared in a
letter to Eric Guest, 'I'm coming back on a cargo boat, stopping off

everywhere I should.' It was a promise to himself that he would keep.

He arrived in London considerably relieved but tired out, and he did not have much time to recover his energies, because he had to go more or less directly to Wardour Castle for the second of the two Summer Schools that he, Birtwistle and Goehr conducted there. This year saw the first performance of a new work by Max, *Ecce Manus Tradentis*, and one by Harry Birtwistle, *Tragoedia*, which caused a tremendous stir of excitement.

Ecce Manus Tradentis consists of two musically related motets, the first short (four minutes) and instrumental, the second long (twenty minutes) and for SATB soloists, SATB chorus and the same ensemble of nine instruments. The short instrumental first part, *Eram Quasi Agnus*, was commissioned by the English Bach Festival and was not composed until later – it received its first performance in 1969. But the bigger vocal and choral second half was performed on this occasion at Wardour Castle by the Summer School Choir with the Melos Ensemble, and soloists Bethany Beardslee, Pauline Stevens, Ian Partridge and Geoffrey Shaw. It is a setting of passages from St Luke's and St Mark's Gospels in the Vulgate, and originally bore the name *Ecce Manus Tradentis*, which was eventually given to the two-part work as a whole. When the complete work was given that title, this second part was titled *In Illo Tempore*. As its name announces, it is a gloomy meditation on the betrayal of Christ, and Max himself has described it as the bleakest piece he had ever written. The words are chanted in sombre harmony, with a desolate instrumental accompaniment and interludes. The texture brightens, however, when the soprano soloist, in a kind of strange ecstasy, proclaims Judas's crime, and the piece slips into a nonchalant, gentle D minor to conclude.

With this second Wardour Castle school the venture came to a somewhat premature end. Premature because this 1965 school ended with a riotous party that went on all night, featured large numbers of people being sick in interesting places, and, most unfortunately, involved a fair amount of minor damage to the Cranborne Chase premises. It is interesting, though, of course, idle, to speculate on how different the course of recent British musical history might have been had the Wardour Castle experiment been able to continue for a few more years.

The Summer Schools had been important for a number of reasons. First, as concerned Max himself, it was almost certainly at the 1965 school that the expressionist period, which was shortly to bring him with an explosion of volcanic proportions to the very forefront of the British musical scene, first crystallized in his imagination. In his composition class that summer he had dissected three works in great detail and with considerable skill: Bach's *Two-Part Inventions*, the titanic first movement of Mahler's Third Symphony and Schoenberg's *Pierrot Lunaire*. The last was analysed in minute detail because at the end of the school there was to be a performance of the work by the American soprano Bethany Beardslee and the Melos Ensemble.

This performance was duly held in a concert hall bearing the homely name of The Old Kitchen, and took everyone, including Max, by storm. Beardslee's performance was theatrical and almost certainly set the scene in Max's mind for the similarly dramatic performances over which he was himself to preside not very long afterwards; but much more importantly than that, it also presaged Max's whole exploration of the world of musical theatre – and it was on that, as we shall be seeing, that the next, vital step of his career was to turn.

But if the Wardour Castle schools thus saw the first germination of a phase of Max's life and career, they also signalled the end of another: the 1965 school, with its nauseous and drunken conclusion, was the last time the so-called 'Manchester School' of composers did anything of any significance together. Max's friendship with Birtwistle lasted a few years longer, but in time first Goehr and then the other two were to go their separate ways.

Their final venture together had been a success, and a significant event for the musical public too. The younger generation of budding composers, performers and musicologists clearly identified the Manchester group as a new axis in British music, and they came to the schools in large numbers: there were around 150 students at each. After the second of the two events, Max, Goehr and Birtwistle had finally taken their places as the fully acknowledged new leaders of British music, and were at last taken seriously as such. Max's own last word on the school was typically generous: 'This will be remembered', he said, 'for the arrival of Harrison Birtwistle.' It is worth bearing this comment in mind, in the light of what was to happen only a short while later.

After the close of this second and final Wardour Castle school Max was at last able to retire to his Wiltshire cottage for a month or so to compose, and worked on *Taverner* and on another work that he had begun while he was at Princeton, the *Seven 'In Nomine'*. This work had its premiere on 3 December at the Commonwealth Institute, London, performed by the Melos Ensemble conducted by Lawrence Foster. This meant, incidentally, that 1964 and 1965 saw the first performances of no fewer than seven works by Max: *Veni, Sancte Spiritus*, *Five Little Pieces for Piano* and *Shakespeare Music* in 1964, and the *Second Taverner Fantasia*, the *Shepherd's Calendar*, *Ecce Manus Tradentis* – at least, the far more substantial of the two parts of it – and the *Seven 'In Nomine'* in 1965. So although, as mentioned earlier, these were somewhat lean years as far as the composition of new works was concerned, they were not at all bad for premieres.

As its name indicates, the *Seven 'In Nomine'* is a work in seven parts, each being an *in nomine*. The first of the seven sections of this work of Max's was based on an *in nomine* of Taverner himself. (The work is actually titled 'Seven "In-Nomines"', but that would be an unsightly miscegenation of Latin word with English plural form, so the faintly odd-looking form is preferred.)

The work was begun, as seen in the previous chapter, at Princeton, in Earl Kim's composition classes. Steve Pruslin, indeed, remembers that at least two of the seven pieces were presented for discussion and analysis in the classes. The first was based on an original *in nomine* by Taverner. The second was an entirely original work by Max, and was sent by him as a birthday gift for Benjamin Britten's fiftieth birthday. This fell in 1963, and there is a very brief and respectful accompanying letter from Max, marked Princeton, 4 October 1963, to Britten, wishing him warmest good wishes for his birthday and referring to the little piece enclosed; so we can feel sure that it was the first and second parts of the work which were seen by Kim's class at Princeton. The third *in nomine* was also a birthday present, this one for Michael Tippett's sixtieth, in 1965. The fourth was based on an original by the early English composer with the very English name of John Bull, and the sixth on one by Blitheman. This is the only one not formally titled '*in nomine*', being called instead *Gloria Tibi Trinitas* after Taverner's mass that was the foundation of all such pieces. The fifth and seventh are original tunes by Max. The whole work is part parody, part serious paying of respects, and is a piece of considerable wit.

Just after Christmas 1965 Max took a decisive step by buying his first home of his own. He left the rented cottage at Tollard Royal and moved into a larger and more comfortable one, bearing the odd name of Barter's Town, in the village of Charlton, near the larger village of Donhead Saint Mary, which in its turn is near the small market town of Shaftesbury.

The new home was a cottage 'up its own lane', as Max described it. 'No traffic goes past,' he wrote, and – one can almost hear the relief and satisfaction – 'it comes to a dead end 50 yards along.' It had electricity and mains-supplied water, neither of which was by any means to be taken for granted in the mid-1960s in very rural parts of Britain, and was 'very plain – stone and tile outside, plain white plaster, tiles and plain wood in (no beams or anything, but nice wooden seats)'. It had a good view out to the downs at the front, and a copse at the back, and about a third of an acre of land with some good old apple trees. 'No houses near,' he said happily, 'but a few in sight (1/3 mile away) in the village.'

One other reason why his move to this cottage was a source of happiness was that it brought him very close to Harry Birtwistle, teaching at Cranborne Chase. He too was living near Shaftesbury, and with Max now living in the same district they began to see a great deal of each other, to their mutual pleasure.

It is in the purchase and doing-up of this cottage that we should look for an explanation of Max's decision to go back to Australia for a six-month stint as visiting composer in residence at Adelaide. This decision was more than a little puzzling in view of his extremely jaundiced view of Australia on his earlier visit. However, enlightenment is at hand in the letter to Guest in which he talks about his new cottage. 'I know it sounds mercenary,' he says of his decision to go back, 'but the main reason for this is the money, which will replace that which I spent (advance from Boosey & Hawkes!) on the cottage.'

The other immediate consequence of the purchase of his cottage and his imminent absence in Australia for at least six months was that he felt compelled to give up his tiny pied-à-terre at 53 Bolsover Street: 'can't afford to have this hanging on while I'm away so long. Anyway I got to hate it in London – mainly due to the traffic (the noise and neurosis it causes).'

Towards the end of 1965, Max was trying to help Harry Birtwistle, who had applied to become a member of the Performing Rights Society, and had been told that he was ineligible for admission on the grounds that he had not yet had enough performances of his music. Max wrote to Benjamin Britten to ask if Britten would intercede on Birtwistle's behalf:

> I remember Alexander Goehr and myself met with the same treatment when we tried to join, and it was necessary to appeal – we are now both members.
>
> Mr Birtwistle has at least as many performances as myself in Europe and the USA, if not in England, and I think it is particularly unjust that he be excluded now, particularly as he has a BBC commission for schools broadcasts (already in print) which children all over Great Britain will be learning *by air*, so that he stands to lose an enormous sum of money which he and his family desperately need, and also particularly as there is now the question of an opera for the English Opera Group . . . I hope you will find

a moment to drop [the PRS] a line. If Goehr and myself are members, I think this situation is very unfair; I see Harry Birtwistle as at least as good a composer as myself, and, apart from England, he is probably more performed.

Britten evidently did intervene, along with his friend and librettist Eric Crozier, because a couple of weeks later Max was writing again to Britten, to tell him among other things that he and Birtwistle were both very pleased about the concern the two older men had shown in the matter and to thank Britten for taking so much trouble over it. This episode was to be important in the light of subsequent events.

Early in the New Year, Max departed for his stint in Adelaide. Before taking up his post there, however, he stopped off in Perth, Western Australia, to give a lecture. Coincidentally, this itinerary meant that in both places he bumped into the Australian poet and novelist Randolph Stow. They had met before, and taken a liking to each other. Also, Max knew some of Stow's work, and liked it. Their chance meetings in these two Australian cities were to have their consequences later on.

Stow had first heard of Max in the winter of 1964–5, when he was living on a ranch in New Mexico, writing a book. There he received a letter from Max, addressed to him care of the Professor of Music at the University of Western Australia, at Perth, saying that Max was interested in setting some of Stow's poems from his early collection, *Outrider*.

Stow replied that he liked the idea of having his poems set to music, but that he was not planning to return to Australia, so they would not be able to meet when Max was there for the UNESCO conference. As things turned out, however, they were to meet before too long all the same, thanks to the coincidence that Stow too was in America on a Harkness Fellowship. When he had finished writing his book on the ranch he drove 'all the way up and down the map', as he puts it, 'until I had been in almost all the states', and ended up in New York. There he went to Harkness House to see what mail had arrived for him, and found Max there on a flying return visit to Princeton. They had lunch together with the Harkness Foundation people, and then parted with expressions of mutual esteem.

They both felt, therefore, that their meetings in Australia were somehow providential, and started talking. Among the things they discussed was the possibility of Stow's providing the libretto for an opera for children by Max. Stow had been fascinated by the medieval Suffolk folk legend of the Green Children of Woolpit. In the end this scheme was aborted, because Stow found his way to England, and to

Aldeburgh, where he met Eric Crozier. He happened to mention his idea for the opera, and Crozier said, 'I've been trying to get Ben' [i.e. Britten] 'to do that for years.' Stow abandoned the idea on the spot, feeling that the competition in this case was too powerful to be worth taking on. Anyway, he confessed much later, 'I soon began to see that it wasn't Max's sort of thing. It was too sweet and harmless, compared with *Taverner*.' (As a happy postscript, he did not drop the idea entirely: it survived to become a theme in his novel *The Girl Green as Elderflower*, published much later, in 1980).

For the moment, then, they went their separate ways, and Max got down to his work as a teacher of composition. On the whole he enjoyed his six months at Adelaide. This was largely because his class of composition students was exceptionally talented. Apparently the word had gone round that he was to be the temporary Professor of Composition, and a number of highly talented young composers had found various ways of getting themselves into his classes. The group included Ross Edwards, Wesley Barker and Gillian Whitehead, now all among Australia's (and, in Whitehead's case, New Zealand's) most eminent composers, and Graham Dudley, a prominent figure in music education in Australia: as Max remarked with a laugh, thinking about it many years later, 'Every bloody person in that class – they all did very well for 'emselves.'

Max's methods were on the whole similar to those of his own masters, Petrassi, Sessions and the others, except that he tended to be less formal. Not that he was slack, or that he permitted slacking in his class. 'I was a bit stroppier' [than Petrassi or Sessions], he says. 'On one occasion I noticed that attention was beginning to wander – and some of the girls were knitting! So I jolted them by announcing, in a very loud voice, that I'd have an essay from every one of them the next day. And I did, too.'

In so far as he found any spare time to work on his own compositions, he was still busy on *Taverner*; but he had also begun work, even at this early date, on *Worldes Blis*, a colossal piece for full orchestra which was to cause something of a storm when it finally saw the light of day. That, however, was not to be until 1969, three years ahead.

In the meantime, after his six-month spell was at an end, he paid a quick visit to Sydney, to spend a short time as acting Professor at the University there, covering for the incumbent Professor who was lecturing in the United States. And there in Sydney, who should he meet but Randolph Stow, yet again, this time intending to head for Britain, where he planned to live. This time they decided to stick together, and came home together.

   As he had declared he would in a letter to Eric Guest, Max did what he had intended to do the previous time, and ambled home by way of every exotic port he could find. Together the two of them put in at Singapore, Bangkok, Calcutta, Delhi, Bombay, Teheran, Istanbul and Athens, to name only the places he could afterwards remember.

   All in all it had been a good trip this time: in one of his letters of the period to Eric Guest he said, 'I enjoyed my stay here – got some good work from my students and did some worthwhile concerts . . . ' And a little later: 'I'm back . . . I think this cottage is smashing (much better than Tollard). Was in lots of places on the way back: this was a wonderful trip. I arrived back here absolutely all-in.' A good trip; and, on the whole, a good year, too.

6 ~ *Metamorphosis*

When Harrison Birtwistle left the Royal Manchester College of Music he went on to the Royal Academy of Music in London. Among the people he became especially friendly with there was a young clarinettist, Alan Hacker. Later, in 1964, Steve Pruslin came to London, to begin with on a scholarship to write a thesis on Mahler's Ninth Symphony, but in the event to settle and live permanently: and, as we have seen, he, Max and Birtwistle knocked about together a great deal, and talked endlessly about music. In the summer of 1964, and the following year, the four were brought together at the Wardour Castle Summer Schools of Music. They were the four moving spirits behind the formation later on of a group of performers and creators who were to have an electrifying effect on the musical life of Britain in the late 1960s and beyond.

Actually, they founded several groups between them. Sandy Goehr, who was also at Wardour Castle, and Alan Hacker founded one group called the Brighton Festival Ensemble. Two other groups, one of them very quickly to become the most famous and influential of them all, were formed some years later. But the most important for the time being was founded by Birtwistle, Hacker and Pruslin. Max would undoubtedly have been a founder member proper, and was one in spirit, but at the precise time of the group's foundation he happened to be away on a brief trip to, he recalls, Australia. He was invited to join up immediately on his return, and did so. Max himself says that, as with the Wardour Castle Summer School, the first germ of the idea came from Birtwistle.

The new group was dedicated to the idea of securing properly rehearsed, committed and proficient performances of the works of the two composers, and, as a secondary objective, performances of a similar standard of Schoenberg's seminal masterpiece, which they regarded as the cornerstone of modern music, *Pierrot Lunaire*. Their aim was to put on what they considered 'authentic' – that is to say, theatrical – performances of this work: something which had not been done since Schoenberg's own performances of it in the early years of the century. (It must be remembered in this context that in the mid to late 1960s

Schoenberg's piece – his work in general, in fact – was not at all the commonplace part of the musical life of the country that it has since become. *Pierrot Lunaire* was at that time almost unheard, indeed almost unheard of, in Britain.)

To this end it was decided that the group should comprise exactly the same instrumentalists as the ensemble for which Schoenberg had written his work: flute, clarinet, violin, cello and piano, plus a female singer. The flautist would also play piccolo and other members of the flute family, the violinist would double viola, the pianist would play a variety of other keyboard instruments, and they decided to add one player who had not been in Schoenberg's line-up, a percussionist. The third very important objective of the planned ensemble was to perform works of music theatre, which interested all of them. Drawing on both the twin objectives, Pruslin came up with the name the Pierrot Players. The word players, he explained later, combined suggestions of both music and theatre, and was as such a more accurate description of the group as they planned it than a purely musical term such as ensemble.

Thus the formation of the Pierrot Players was already a living impulse as early as 1964. As the four principals talked further in the following summer at Wardour Castle and then later on when they were all back in London, it gradually took on form and shape, until it finally became a reality very early in 1967. The Pierrot Players gave their first performance on 30 May that year, at the then newly opened Queen Elizabeth Hall, in the South Bank arts complex.

The members of the new group pretty well chose themselves. About the singer there was never any doubt: Steve Pruslin had heard a young soprano called Mary Thomas several times, and had been, to use his own word, stunned by her performances of contemporary music. She had already won a high reputation as a member of the celebrated Deller Consort. She had made a highly acclaimed recording as Dido in Purcell's *Dido and Aeneas*, and had given numerous performances of the Monteverdi *Vespers* among other vogue works of the time. She had also conducted a secondary career, under another name, as a singer of light music, and was a fine jazz singer and pianist. Pruslin recruited her on the spot.

Alan Hacker took his place as the group's clarinettist *nem. con.* He had a powerful say in the election of the flautist, Judith Pearce, and he also recruited the cellist, Jennifer Ward Clarke. As a matter of marginal interest, the first flautist they considered was an unknown young Irishman, James Galway; but in the end they felt that he might not integrate into the group. He went on to become principal flute with the Berlin Philharmonic Orchestra instead, and the rest, as they say, is history. The violinist they chose was Duncan Druce, and the first percussionist was Tristan Fry, later to be the drummer in the guitarist John Williams's rock group, Sky. The line-up was completed by the pianist and general-purpose keyboard player, who was, of course, Steve Pruslin himself.

In the first year of their existence the Pierrot Players established themselves rapidly: in addition to the new hall on the South Bank they appeared at the Cheltenham Festival and at a Macnaghten concert at the Conway Hall; and they gave world premiere performances of five big works by Max and two by Birtwistle.

The first concert, on 30 May 1967, featured the work after which the group was named, a dramatic performance of *Pierrot Lunaire*, a large work by Birtwistle with a text by Pruslin based on Greek tragedy, and as overture, *Antechrist* by Max. This is a densely packed piece of about six minutes' duration for the interesting combination of piccolo, bass clarinet, violin, cello and three very fully occupied percussion players. It is based on a thirteenth-century motet followed by a set of variations.

In July the Pierrot Players took part in the Cheltenham Festival, giving the premiere of Max's piece *Hymnos*, a spirited thirteen-minute piece of extended virtuosity for clarinet and piano; and the following February they gave a Macnaghten concert at the Conway Hall, in which they premiered two major works.

The first of these was a piece that Max had written between two and three years before, in 1965, in response to a commission from the Serge Koussevitsky Music Foundation in the Library of Congress, Washington, DC; and although no one (perhaps not even Max himself) realized it at the time of its composition it marked the beginning of a new and distinctive phase in his career that was to be one of the most productive, lively and controversial. Without doubt it was this period that was to see his coming of age as a composer and the true making of his reputation; and yet the reputation thus made was to a large extent meretricious: even now, twenty-five years after that sudden explosion of creativity and resultant notoriety, he is still frequently judged by it, as if the intervening twenty-five years had never happened, and as if the music he has written during them is no different from that which he produced then – none of which is anywhere close to the truth. It is important to bear in mind, though, that this applies almost solely to those critics who were and still are hostile to Max and his music. The flood of works that Max produced in the period we are about to examine were found so outrageous by conservatives that they are still to this day trying to use them as a rod to beat his back with, irrespective of all subsequent changes.

The work immediately in question was *Revelation and Fall*, and if any work can be positively identified as the beginning of Max's expressionist period, it is this. It also marked his first venture into the genre of music theatre, with which his name was soon to be almost synonymous for some years.

Taking the term expressionism to mean, broadly, a style of art characterized by extreme subjectivity, violent expression of emotion, bold, even garish use of primary colours (whether in paint, music or words) and a deliberate stretching of the chosen medium to its furthest limits, this piece fits in all directions. It is a setting of an intense text of the same title by the tragic and neurotic Austrian poet Georg Trakl, described by the composer as a monodrama, for soprano soloist and an ensemble of sixteen instruments. This was one of the earliest concerts in which the Pierrot Players made use of guest performers. In time they were to invite many guests to join them for occasional concerts, including the cream of British orchestral players of the day.

The soprano part, sung by Mary Thomas, was a virtuoso piece of alarming range and vocal savagery, the despairing howl of Trakl's text always poised on a razor edge between barely maintained control and total abandon. The violent effect is heightened by the theatrical presentation: the soprano appears in a scarlet nun's habit, taking the part of Trakl's incestuous sister, and she delivers her most violent outburst by shrieking into a megaphone. Much of the writing for the instrumental ensemble is equally violent.

The other work of Max's at this same Macnaghten concert in February 1968, was his *Missa Super l'Homme Armé*, billed as a parody mass for singer or speaker and six instrumentalists. Hovering between parody and serious examination of his recurring themes (most thoroughly explored in *Taverner*) of weakness and betrayal, this represents a new 'farthest north' in Max's stretching and contortion of ancient music. It begins as an arrangement of an anonymous fifteenth-century mass, but soon collapses into parody, ultimately metamorphosing into a foxtrot, an early twentieth-century dance step that was to become something of an obsession with Max. The text deals with the betrayals of Christ by Judas Iscariot and St Peter, and the piece is once again, like *Revelation and Fall*, delivered by someone in religious garb, though the soloist delivers his or her part dressed in a habit belonging to the opposite sex, to emphasize the inversion of meaning of the piece.

It is interesting to note, however, that Max did not originally envisage this as a piece of crypto-religious music theatre: the words were originally intended to be delivered by a boy's voice on tape. In that guise it was much closer to *Ecce Manus Tradentis* – which uses substantially the same text (from the Vulgate) – than to *Revelation and Fall* and the music theatre works that followed it.

Works of this kind have from time to time offended the devout, who have seen them as merely anti-religious invective of a peculiarly violent tone. This is a mistake, though, as a more thoughtful examination of them will quickly reveal. Max is far too serious a musician, and a man, to indulge in such cheap gestures. He has, to be sure, always eschewed formal religion: in one interview he gave, to the *BBC Music Magazine* in 1992, he dismissed it contemptuously, observing that 'religion is a dirty word, and I don't want to be associated with that'. Yet the forms of religion, the trappings, the ambiance and particularly the musical forms associated with it, have held considerable fascination for him throughout his adult life. His one large-scale opera is on a fundamentally religious theme, and for a very long time he has nurtured plans for another, on St Francis of Assisi – although he has always said that it would not be a devotional work in the style of Messiaen's opera on the subject, but about the saint as a man.

The point is that irrespective of Max's own attitude to religious conviction, he is deeply and perennially interested in matters of truth, both as a musician and as a deeply thinking man. He is concerned about the communication of truth, and about communication in general – he is a communicator himself, and he worries greatly about the methods of communicating used by individuals, institutions and governments today. Since for many people religion is as profound a truth as it is a profound nonsense to others, he is *de facto* interested in its methods of communicating; and if he finds them corrupt, as in *Taverner*, he regards it as a very serious matter.

One suspects also that the dignity and gravity of religious ceremonial attract him, while he is too intellectually rigorous, too incapable of the necessary suspension of scepticism, to be able to accept the doctrinal core of religion itself. Alexander Goehr once speculated that one day Max might perhaps feel able to espouse the Anglican faith, and predicted that if it happened we would see 'White Max', as opposed to the 'Black Max' of the 1960s and later. This was a plain reference to works such as the two under discussion here, and *Taverner*, in which Max can see little in the heart of religion except self-deception and betrayal. In the event, of course, the readiness to embrace Christianity has never materialized, and it is a reasonably safe prediction that it will not now do so.

At all events, this Macnaghten concert must have been a powerful experience. Later in the same year, 1968, accompanied by Robin Yapp, a music-loving friend of his and Birtwistle's, and also their dentist in the small town of Gillingham in Dorset, near their homes, Max went to Aldeburgh to hear the first performance of Birtwistle's opera *Punch and Judy* (libretto by Steve Pruslin). After this, in the remaining part of the year, he had only one more work premiered: on 30 May, the anniversary of their first concert, the Pierrot Players again appeared on the South Bank, this time in the smaller Purcell Room. The programme included *Stedman Caters*, a chunky and difficult piece of fifteen minutes for sextet comprising flute, clarinet in B flat, harpsichord, viola, cello and percussionist. It is distinguished among other things by the fact that the viola player and the cellist are required to double on various percussion instruments. The title of the piece is a term from change-ringing: Stedman Caters is a pattern of changes rung on nine bells. This piece has nine movements, played continuously, 'like a succession of points in a seventeenth-century fantasia', as Max has said of it. Appropriately enough, it includes a rich range of bells and bell-like sounds.

From the outset the Pierrot Players' policy was consistent: they set out not only to improve the outlook for Birtwistle and Max, but also to help other young and struggling composers, and to further the public exposure and reputation of those they admired from earlier generations who they felt were neglected. To this end they performed a lot of Schoenberg's work; they also performed the work of, for example, Earl Kim, Max's former teacher at Princeton. Their most valuable service to music, though, was without doubt their regular commissioning of other young composers. By the end of the group's existence they had commissioned works from at least forty apart from their own pair. They included a few big names such as Boulez, Henze (first performances, not commissions) and Elliott Carter, but the great majority were young, struggling, and only too glad to receive a commission, a bit of exposure, a vote of confidence, a chance to watch real live musicians trying to make sense of their notes and, not least, some money (which came from the Arts Council). More often than not, indeed, other groups would have thought about commissioning a piece from some young composer, then got cold feet about him, and waited. The Pierrot Players would then commission him, everyone else would promptly take that as the seal of approval, and he would get commissions elsewhere.

Steve Pruslin is certain that this was the greatest single contribution the group made to the cultural life of the country. They never broadcast their public service as a major part of their image, he said, as most groups did, but did so in a quiet and sustained way, and this aspect of the group's activities was particularly close to Max's heart. Pruslin believes that this is largely accounted for by Max's terrible memories of how he had had to come to maturity in a virtual vacuum, with no support and no one to guide him through the difficult days, or even to take him seriously. These memories were so vivid that he was determined that the composers of the next generation should not have to struggle in the same way. So the group, at Max's own instigation, regularly took risks with *very* young composers, by giving them their first platform ever, in London or elsewhere. This is a matter of 'tremendous pride' (Steve Pruslin's words) with him and Max alike; it is also one reason why there are a great number of composers, now approaching middle age, who will not willingly hear a bad word said about either of them.

In their first year of existence the group ran its affairs, as is almost a tradition among fledgling arts companies, on a shoestring and with everyone mucking in and doing his bit to handle the administration. Friends were beguiled into helping in any way they could: the ten-fingered being commandeered for typing duties, anyone remotely suspected of financial acumen for the accounts, and so on. Money, needless to say, was a perennial problem. Max himself put in a fair amount out of his own pocket. Steve Pruslin contributed by doing huge amounts of essential and unpaid administration work.

Because the Pierrots were serious – very serious indeed – about their artistic and musical purpose, however, this chaotic state of affairs could not go on for long, and in 1968 Max put matters right. That, at any rate, was what he tried to do, thought he had done, and, in general, actually did do. The fact that his action contributed to certain unhappy consequences later on could not possibly have been known at the time, nor was what happened the fault of Max or the other person involved.

What he did was to call in the Pierrots' first professional manager, an Australian entrepreneur and impresario named James Murdoch. Max had met him in Sydney, during his six-month spell in Australia while he was teaching at Adelaide University, when Murdoch had put on several concerts of Max's music in his home town of Melbourne.

In many ways Murdoch was a great success as manager. Max says that he had 'a huge flair for publicity', and this is echoed by all the former members of the group. In a very short time after his arrival, he also had something to sell. Unfortunately, as we shall see, his arrival also introduced an element of strain into the group – or, more likely perhaps, his personality acted as an amplifier for certain cracks that already existed, making them more serious and ultimately precipitating a crisis in the group's affairs.

Without doubt, 1969 was Max's *annus mirabilis*. It was marred by a very unhappy ending, but before that came a grand procession of triumphs, with one *magnum opus* following another in an astonishing explosion of creativity.

It was not merely the suddenness of the torrent of works that made this period of his life so remarkable, but also the nature of the works themselves. Nothing that had gone before could have prepared followers of Max's career for the work he now turned out – although an acute observer at the Macnaghten concert a year before, hearing the twin expressionist works premiered then, *Revelation and Fall* and the *Missa Super l'Homme Armé*, might have wondered what they presaged. For this phase was expressionism writ large, the pieces bold, extravagant, on the surface flamboyant, colourful, even garish; and their effect on audiences tended to fall at one extreme or the other; people found them electrifyingly new and exciting or hideously, intolerably outrageous, not music at all.

There was, however, a quiet introduction: the first of no fewer than seven new pieces was first heard on 13 January, and was the first of Max's arrangements, or realizations as he prefers to call them, of a piece of early music – in this case, of a *Fantasia and Two Pavans* by Purcell, for the basic Pierrot Players ensemble of six instrumentalists. The piece is very funny, Max's stated intention being, as he put it, to restore 'Purcell's intensity of feeling, sense of fun and sheer outrageousness'; and the fun begins with the choice of instruments. Instead of being scored for a flute doubling piccolo, this piece is for the other way round, piccolo doubling flute; clarinet in B flat, viola and cello are ordinary enough, but the harpsi-chordist doubles on an out-of-tune upright piano (a favourite of Max's); and the percussionist has charge of a marimba, a band kit comprising a bass drum, side drum, tom-tom, hi-hat and suspended cymbal, and (only optionally, alas) a football rattle and a railway guard's whistle. The piece itself is riotous, with the fantasia full of comical effects and finishing with the two pavans heavily disguised as Max's favourite foxtrots.

This was a good start, and good fun. But in April there came something very different, which delighted a part of the musical public and scandalized rather more of it. It has become possibly Max's best known work, although one suspects that it has that status among those who loathe his music rather than among his admirers. The work is the famous, or notorious, *Eight Songs for a Mad King*. At the time many people found this work variously offensive, horrifying, incomprehens-ible or plain mad. Although since then it has become accepted as a work of genius, and (to Max's great satisfaction) no longer leaves people mystified or repelled (at least, not so many people), it is still a profoundly disturbing work. It is a ferocious portrayal of insanity, and on first hearing its main effect is genuinely shocking.

Eight Songs is a setting of eight texts by Randolph Stow, delivered by a baritone soloist and accompanied by flute (doubling piccolo), clarinet, violin, cello, piano (doubling harpsichord) and a single percussion player, who must be extremely physically fit, having an enormous array of instruments and other bizarre objects to play. As well as a wide range of conventional percussion, his equipment includes a didgeridoo, an anvil, a scrubbing board, a squeak, a football rattle, a railway whistle and a collection of mechanical birdcall toys.

We have already seen that Stow had wanted to collaborate on a work with Max ever since their series of meetings, and having come to Britain with Max via various exotic ports of call, had stayed on permanently. In August 1968 he visited the home of a new acquaintance, the historian Sir Steven Runciman. In the course of the visit he was shown, to his delight, Sir Steven's collection of mechanical musical toys. However, he lost interest in the remainder of the collection when Runciman told him that one instrument, a small mechanical hand-organ, 'perhaps the least impressive to look at', had once belonged to George III. His interest grew when he heard that the king, during his long confinement in a padded room on account of his progressive insanity, had kept a collection of pet bullfinches, and had used the device to try to teach the birds to sing to him.

Stow carries on the story:

This really touched me, because of something I'd lately read . . . I had been re-reading some . . . family history, including the memoirs of a great-great-grandfather who had seen the mad king with his own eyes. He was an army captain who was stationed at Windsor for a couple of years after the Napoleonic wars. In late life he wrote: 'His Majesty was at this time insane, and occupied a padded room in the castle, just over the terrace, in the care of an attendant. The terrace was closed against the public, but the officers on guard, when visiting their sentries, frequently saw His Majesty at the windows. His appearance was most venerable, with a white flowing beard down upon his breast. Previous to his insanity it was related of him that he accosted a sentry on the terrace one morning, asking his name and if he had a family; the man replied, "Yes". The King then said, "Come along with me to the garden, and I will give you some cabbages." "Please, Your Majesty, I must not leave my post." "Oh, well, well, come when you are relieved, and I will fill your sack with cabbages."' [This excerpt comes from *A Brief Sketch of the Long and Varied Career of Marshall MacDermott, Esq., J.P., of Adelaide, South Australia.*]

This was the germination of what eventually became *Eight Songs for a Mad King*; and the incident of the king and the cabbages became the first of the eight texts. Not long afterwards, Stow paid Runciman another visit, this time with Max. The two took an immediate liking to one another, and Max was duly shown over – and instantly fascinated by – the collection of mechanical instruments. He was captivated by the hand-organ in particular. Runciman remembers that 'Max was delighted with it, and played it so often and so strenuously that it has never quite recovered, some of the pins having been loosened!'

So Stow went away and wrote the eight texts, basing them on George III's own words, as set down by Fanny Burney. Max composed the final work over February and March of 1969, dedicating the piece to Runciman. It was first performed in April at the Queen Elizabeth Hall by Roy Hart and the Pierrot Players, Max conducting. Roy Hart was a South African baritone with an astonishing vocal range, necessary for this part. He had been introduced to Max by James Murdoch. One of the brightest theatrical inspirations of the piece was that the instrumental players performed in bamboo cages (not unlike the cages used by the Japanese for troublesome prisoners of war during the Second World War). At the party afterwards Max insisted that Runciman act as co-host, and presented him with the autograph score.

The work as a whole is ambivalent, on several levels. Beneath the apparent mockery in the demented soloist's crazed words and antics, there is a terrible sympathy, a tender and deeply penetrating depiction of madness: of how it must feel to *be* demented, in particular to be aware of the onset of the dementia with the other side of the same mind that it is already eating away. Then again, the cages occupied by most of the instrumentalists are partly a simple reference to the cage-birds that George III tried to teach to sing; but also a poignant reference to the caged condition of the king himself; thus they point out the dual roles of the ensemble, as at once the king's captives and the king's keepers. Meanwhile, the music itself works to highlight the ambivalent impression the piece is intended to evoke in the audience. As an example, in Max's words: 'In no. 5, *The Phantom Queen*, an eighteenth-century suite is intermittently suggested in the instrumental parts, and in the Courante, at the words "Starve you, strike you", the flute part hurries ahead in a 7:6 rhythmic proportion, the clarinet's rhythms become dotted and its part displaced by octaves, the effect being schizophrenic.'

The work begins with an ear-splitting discord from the ensemble, after which the soloist begins his incantation of the texts. The words are not sung, nor is the delivery exactly Schoenberg's *Sprechgesang*, or 'speech-song', in which the voice starts off by singing each note, then falls away from the pitch. Nor, on the other hand, is the soloist a straightforward reciter. What he does have to be, however, is a consummate actor; and he has to possess a voice of quite startling range and power. He delivers the words in a series of hoots and growls, the vocal line now swooping to a low, groaning howl, now soaring to a high, anguished screeching as the madman's emotions flicker between extremes of elation and benevolence and terrible flashes of awareness of his true condition. Meanwhile the chamber ensemble around him gives a kind of instrumental commentary on the monologue. There are numerous quotations and occasional parodies of diverse composers from, as Max says, Handel to Birtwistle. He himself wrote of the work, shortly after its composition: 'In some ways, I regard the work as a collection of musical objects borrowed from many sources, functioning as musical stage props, around which the reciter's part weaves, lighting them from extraordinary angles, and throwing grotesque and distorted shadows from them, giving the musical "objects" an unexpected and sometimes sinister significance.'

The soloist holds dialogues at various points with individual members of the instrumental ensemble: with the flute in no. 3, the cello in no. 4, the clarinet in no. 6 and the violin in no. 7. These refer to George III's conversations with his pet bullfinches in their cages; but the notion of talking to birds in cages has undertones of talking to oneself, often regarded (usually wrongly, since the context, the things said and the manner of their saying are not usually taken into account) as 'the first sign of madness'.

The crux of the piece is no. 7. At the end of this number the king reaches into the cage of the violinist, with whom he has been con-ducting one of his little dialogues, seizes the violin, and breaks it. This is in part a symbolic killing of one of the caged bullfinches; but that act in itself is much more than merely a frustrated assault on his little companion. It is the mad protagonist's final admission that everything he has been doing is false, because it has all been part of the nightmare, upside-down world inhabited by the mad: in other words, it is the king's own admission of his madness; and it is this acceptance that enables him to prepare for his own death in the final number of the piece.

The text of this final number is poignant: it gives the soloist lines to utter that have a measure of dignity, almost of serenity, which neatly counterpoises the mockery earlier in the work; similarly, the words are almost spoken, even murmured, and the tone is almost sane, with the merest hint of cracking beneath the surface. Only the last word of all, 'howling', picks up the maniacal quality of the rest of the declamation, echoing wildly as it fades into silence. There is a deep sadness, for the soloist himself but also for some abstract version of himself – perhaps for some concept of an immortal soul, which is whole and untainted. The number, and the piece, end with the soloist enduring a final moment of lucidity, in which he realizes that he – the real he, the inhabitant of this nightmare – is not yet dead, after all, but that 'Poor fellow, He will die howling. Howling.' Thus the end of the work throws out the final ambivalences of the piece as a whole: we are left, at the end, wondering first if the madman was really George III at all, or some poor madman who thinks he is the king, and second, if the protagonist was really mad after all, or whether, perhaps, the difference between him and the rest of us is simply that he ends up recognizing that he is mad, while we do not.

Of the critics, only William Mann bothered to point out that 'some of the huge audience protested vociferously' – or maybe he was the only one who was actually there. At all events, there was a certain amount of booing and jeering; but it was immediately howled down by the majority, which must have been extremely gratifying for Max. In general, the piece was received with tumultuous applause and a standing ovation, rare among reserved South Bank audiences; and it has since become one of Max's most popular pieces, with several hundred performances clocked up all over the musical world. Most of the critics were quite enthusiastic about the work, although reading between the lines it is fairly clear that they found it interesting rather than attractive. John Warrack in the *Sunday Telegraph* was the most disparaging. After what seems a very fair and perceptive analysis of the piece, he suddenly rounds on the composer with: 'Composing madness into the actual technique of music is artistically as self-defeating as portraying a boring operatic character by writing boring music,' and, along with several others, he claims to have felt that the audience were being asked to mock the madman. None of them presented any reasons why they felt this.

The next two new works were heard two months later, in June. The smaller of the two was played second, on the 25th, and was performed by the Pierrots' flautist, Judith Pearce, at the York Festival. It was a fairly substantial piece for flute solo with musical box, titled *Solita*, the name representing a little solo and a sonata. The four movements are those of the classical sonata: a quick first movement in sonata form, a slow movement, a scherzo and a fugal finale, which deliberately recalls Bach. To these Max added a fifth, a slow introduction: and to make a fugue possible for a solo flute, he added a part for obbligato musical box at the end.

The other piece premiered that month was a much greater affair: *St Thomas Wake: Foxtrot for Orchestra on a Pavan by John Bull*; the subtitle tells us that here already is another of the foxtrots which were to become something of a trademark for Max. It is scored for large orchestra, including another interesting arsenal of percussion: the three players between them have, in addition to the usual things, an upright piano with the action removed, police and football referee's whistles, football rattles, 'four metal scaffolding tubes (different pitches)', a 'large biscuit tin filled with glass fragments (shaken)' and another large biscuit tin, this one empty, 'to be struck with fist'.

The work combines three ideas: there is the original pavan by the sixteenth- and early seventeenth-century composer, Bull. This theme appears only at the end when it is played on the harp. The other two themes develop separately, as if in competition: a full-scale symphony is developed by the body of the orchestra, while the pavan is transformed into a series of foxtrots played by a 1930s-style dance band. The two come together at the end in a towering climax.

On one level, the piece is amusing, as usual when Max gets into foxtrots: the foxtrots themselves are really extremely good tunes. That this is not a sustainable way of looking at the piece is evident from the start, however: the other theme, the symphony developing in the orchestra, is decidedly black, ominous and frightening. Against such a background the only way to regard the foxtrots is to contrast the footling vacuity of the medium with what is going on all round. It is surely not an accident that the dance band are seated apart from the orchestra, and wear boaters and striped blazers. The reference to inane young things fooling around in boaters while all around them the heavens fall cannot be missed; Hitler rises unchallenged and Jews are kicked to death in front of their children in the streets.

Max has vivid personal memories of hearing foxtrots on a gramophone while sheltering from air-raids on Manchester in the Second World War. His choice of a dance form that was in vogue in the thirties, and his decision to dress the band in thirties' gear, was surely no accident either: rather, a pointed reference to the financial, political, moral and spiritual bankruptcy of that period, and its paralysis of will, its inability to stop the relentless advance to that war, while the glowering, threatening symphony, with its blaring discords and explosive percussion part, are surely references, too direct to be mistakable, to it.

At the end of the piece, Bull's beautiful little pavan is heard for the first time; but it has to contend throughout with one of the jolly foxtrot jingles on a honky-tonk piano – perhaps a last despairing reference to man's ability to distract himself from frightful reality until literally forced to it, by resort to trifles?

The very last moments of the work are a final refrain from the honky-tonk piano, rising out of the last bangs and cracks from the percussion. The image of dust settling after warfare has raged is difficult to avoid; and of those trifles that man uses to entertain himself as he steels himself to face reality at last in all its horrors, perhaps Max is saying that we should not feel entirely ashamed of needing such things to shield us; or maybe he is saying that man's spirit, helped over the difficult bits by such protections, is sufficiently resilient to survive even the worst that reality can throw at him.

This extraordinary piece, sometimes amusing, perhaps at last faintly hopeful, and throughout deeply moving, was commissioned by the city of Dortmund, and first performed there by the Dortmund Philharmonic Orchestra, conducted by Max, on 2 June. One cannot help wondering if Max did not have in his mind what happened to the city that commissioned the work from him; and maybe he also thought about the carefree, idle days on the Rhine described by Isherwood, Spender and others in the feckless Weimar Republic before the rise of Hitler – days when a nice, jolly foxtrot would have seemed just the thing.

In April *Eight Songs for a Mad King* had been received with shock and not a little horror. But if that work created a stir, it also brought Max a standing ovation. He saved the real shocker for August, and the Proms. On 28 August he conducted the BBC Symphony Orchestra at the Royal Albert Hall in a performance of a work on a titanic scale for full orchestra, on which he had been working as long ago as 1963–4, while he was still at Princeton on his Harkness Fellowship. The piece was *Worldes Blis*, and a measure of its effect was that it provoked a usually restrained southern English audience into behaviour more on the lines of the Paris audience at the first performance of Stravinsky's *Rite of Spring*.

There was a difference, of course: being English, they didn't throw things, and they didn't start a full-scale riot. Instead, they walked out – noisily and ostentatiously. Whenever Max conducts a performance of *Worldes Blis*, he always prefaces it with a brief address to the audience, in which he remarks that at its Prom premiere, 'most of the audience walked out, and most of those who stayed booed'. As with *Eight Songs*, the piece has now been accepted as a wholly legitimate part of the modern concert repertoire, and (more or less) generally acclaimed as a modern masterpiece. At an overwhelming performance by the Royal Philharmonic Orchestra in March 1993, three elderly women walked out, clucking angrily. The remainder of a packed Festival Hall (not a very common phenomenon at the time), including parties from numerous schools, stayed in their seats and heard the piece out in an electric silence right to the end, when it brought the house down.

(As a footnote to these contrasting receptions afforded *Worldes Blis*, it is amusing to record that 1993 also saw a concert performance of Max's Second Symphony – also, by coincidence, at a Promenade Concert – when three or four hundred walked out. Those who left were probably only there for the Beethoven and Schubert in the first half, and stayed on to see what Max's piece was like. In any case, the hall was packed to the rafters, which meant that something close to seven thousand stayed put, so Max can claim to have won heavily, even if only on points. And as Judy Arnold and several others remarked, 'It's good to know he's still capable of doing it!')

Worldes Blis can be assessed on several different levels: the audience at its first performance in 1969 clearly viewed it as incomprehensible noise in the worst traditions of the ultra-avant-garde. Max himself merely says that it is a kind of symphony in which he was trying to make sense of the world about him as he saw it at the time of its composition. It could also, in a sense, be thought of as his *Bolero* – knocking spots off Ravel's, many might feel.

The facts of *Worldes Blis* are that it is a forty minute build-up of tension, as exciting as anything in music. Hence the reference to *Bolero*. But it is recognizably a symphony, in which the orchestration, with braying horn and trumpet calls, carolling snatches of melody from the woodwind and long, infinitely sad *langsam* work for the strings throughout, is eerily reminiscent of Mahler's terrible cry of lament at having to leave the world, in his Ninth Symphony. Indeed, just as great pianists have said that it is possible to hear in late Chopin his anticipation, before the invention of the mechanical means, of the modern concert piano, one is distinctly, and rather creepily, conscious during *Worldes Blis* of hearing what Mahler's, say, 13th might have sounded like.

We have Max's own word for it that *Worldes Blis* was an attempt to sum up how he felt about the world at about this time. It is plain enough that his vision of the world was fairly bleak: there is much violence in this vision, much horror, much of his own anger; but Max, although he is capable of great anger and aggression, is a gentle man: the anger and aggression are always provoked by the injustice, suffering and cruelty that he sees around him. The result is that in this work, as everywhere else in his entire œuvre, the violence and fury are always suffused and eased by a vast and, here, very Mahlerian compassion.

This tremendous build-up of brooding tension, menace, fear and exhilaration is concluded by a climax as shattering as any climax in music – reminiscent perhaps, of the fourth of Webern's *Six Orchestral Pieces*. One has waited just about forty minutes for this final orgasmic release of tension, and when it comes it is everything one has been waiting for: the only time in this colossal piece when the large orchestra, and in particular the huge battery of percussion, are allowed to let it all go. And wonderfully releasing it is. But the stroke of genius is in what follows – for the vast climax is not the end of the piece. After the big bang, when all the tension has been released, there comes a very short coda, a still small voice of calm, in which the last vestiges of sound dribble from the orchestra, and the piece ends softly, fading into silence; but it is not the 'little death' that is said to follow physical orgasm, but rather a mood of profound peace.

All of this makes *Worldes Blis* a glorious, uplifting and tremendously exciting piece of music, however black Max's own world-view may have been at the time when it inspired him to write it. There is nothing at all *difficult* about it: it is Max at his most accessible.

Yet you would not have gained any impression that *Worldes Blis* was easy from a glance at the papers the day after the first performance. Considering that even a music critic is a reporter, under some obligation to report news when he happens to be lucky enough to be present at its making, several of the papers failed in this, their premier function: Robert Henderson, for example, writing a review of the week's music in the *Sunday Telegraph*, observed that *Worldes Blis* 'provoked an unusually vigorous reaction, both for and against', which could mean anything from a spirited discussion in the bar afterwards to a pitched battle between supporters and detractors. Desmond Shawe-Taylor was even more reticent, making no direct mention of any audience reaction at all, but squeezing out a costive 'What puts the listener to a test that many of the large audience found gruelling is . . .'

Colin Mason in the *Daily Telegraph* did notice that the work 'caused a few of the conspicuously large audience to defect' during the performance; Edward Greenfield, on the other hand, in the *Guardian*, either saw nothing of the exodus, which is inconceivable, or chose to say nothing about it.

Only Peter Heyworth in the *Observer* and Stanley Sadie in *The Times* gave the occurrences – which, after all, really were rather remarkable, bearing in mind that this was an English audience – their due weight. Heyworth began by remarking that he had thought English audiences would swallow virtually anything without protesting. One promptly felt apprehensive that the report was going to be vituperatively adverse, and was then equally promptly reassured that it wasn't. In the end only one critic, Stanley Sadie, made the comment that really *had* to be made (and even he put it fairly mildly): 'Many of the audience walked out, which of course they are absolutely entitled to do. But they are not entitled to mutter or to stamp out ostentatiously, as people did, apparently revelling in their closed ears. . . perhaps the BBC should bill such items as "suitable for adult listeners only" . . .'

It was left to the *Guardian* (making up on the front page for Greenfield's non-mention of the walk-out in his music column) to supply necessary though inadvertent comic relief: the eleven-line report tells us of the walk-out, the title of the work and the composer's name, then finally informs us helpfully that 'In it, Mr Davies uses combinations of instruments' – at which revelation the item ends.

When they talked about the work itself, however, the critics were generally pretty much of the same mind: it was difficult, demanding, required more concentration than most works that audiences were likely to hear. Having said all this more or less in unison, they broke off into small solos in which finally to convey their own opinion. Most of them liked it: Desmond Shawe-Taylor ruminated aloud (among generally fairly nice remarks) whether Max had tumbled into 'solipsistic megalomania', and only Heyworth made any serious attempt to analyse the piece in detail.

The last new work of 1969, *Vesalii Icones*, was a ballet for one dancer, supported by the six-piece ensemble of the Pierrot Players, with a big solo part for the cellist. The idea came jointly from Max and William Louther, a black American dancer who at that time was performing as a soloist with the London Contemporary Dance Theatre. Louther contributed the choreography, which he danced himself, to a mixture of scandalized dismay (not least because he appeared practically naked) and rapturous acclaim, in the first performance at the Queen Elizabeth Hall on 9 December of that memorable year.

Max had had the idea of writing a set of dances some years before, when he had bought a facsimile edition of a book, *De Humani Corporis Fabrica* (*On the Construction of the Human Body*), by the sixteenth-century Flemish physician, Andries Van Wesel (in Latin, Andreas Vesalius). The book is illustrated by a series of fourteen engravings showing the structure of the human body in what was, for the sixteenth century, a new last word in accuracy – they were based strictly on Vesalius's own dissections and observations. Nothing came of the idea of the dances, however, until much later, when Max was inspired to superimpose the fourteen Stations of the Cross on the anatomical diagrams. It was this coalescence of two ideas that acted as the direct stimulus for *Vesalii Icones*.

Since there are some of us to whom dance, in all its manifestations, is, like Churchill's description of Russia, a riddle wrapped in a mystery inside an enigma, an account of this work comes best from the person who knows it best. The following brief outline of the work, therefore, is closely based on a note provided by Max himself in the programme book for the Holland Festival at which Louther and the Pierrots performed it.

Each dance starts with the body position of the Vesalius illustration, to the sound of the turning of a wheel of small jingles and bells. The dancer then moves to express the parallel Station of the Cross. The dance is not, however, an attempt to act out either the Station of the Cross or the anatomical illustration with which it is paired. It is rather an abstract from both, in which the dancer explores in terms of his own body the technical possibilities suggested by the Vesalius illustration, in the light of the ritual and emotional experience suggested by the Station of the Cross.

Apart from its value as a description of the piece, this note by Max on *Vesalii* contains one or two characteristically forthright and revealing utterances on religion. In dance no. 6, he says, 'The dancer plays, on an out-of-tune piano, a garbled Victorian hymn (a musical style which I consider almost the ultimate blasphemy) . . .' Later, describing the final dance of the set, in which the story of the Resurrection is altered so that it is the Antichrist, the dark double of Christ of medieval legend, indistinguishable from the real Christ, who emerges from the tomb to put his curse on Christendom for eternity: 'some', Max concedes, 'may consider such an interpretation sacrilegious – but the point I am trying to make is a moral one – it is a matter of distinguishing the false from the real – that one should not be taken in by appearances.'

The echoes here from his earlier work, *Ecce Manus Tradentis*, which dealt with the betrayals of Judas Iscariot and St Peter, and was described by Max as the bleakest piece he had written, are obvious, and become still more so when the full list of the fourteen Stations of the Cross is examined: the agony in the garden; the betrayal of Judas; Christ and Pilate; the flagellation; Christ condemned to death; the mocking of Christ; Christ receives the cross; St Veronica wipes his face; Christ prepared for death; Christ nailed to the cross; the death of Christ; the descent from the cross; the entombment of Christ; the Resurrection; Antichrist.

The music draws extensively on *Ecce Manus Tradentis*; and it finishes, perhaps not altogether surprisingly for such a work at this period, with yet another foxtrot – 'an image', as Paul Griffiths calls it in a perceptive discussion of this work, 'of total corruption'.

So ended the year 1969. The works had flowed out in a torrent, but it was not only the rate of flow that made them remarkable. They were all big works, big in every sense: long in duration, large in conception, ambitious in the questions they asked and the answers they offered. Max himself agrees that 1969 was 'the crossroads'. Steve Pruslin singles out *Worldes Blis* as the moment of Max's coming of age, recalling a comment he had made to Max himself many years later: 'It's your most molten piece – almost it writing you rather than you writing it. You're struggling with an idea so molten that you and the idea are locked in battle.'

Between *Worldes Blis* and *Vesalii Icones*, however, Max had been smitten by a small personal catastrophe. His Dorset cottage, Barter's Town, caught fire and was burned to little more than a shell. It happened while Max was away in York, and was apparently caused by some malfunction in the electrical wiring. He was lucky enough to be able to borrow a house in Bristol from friends, and in September was writing to Eric Guest with a grim catalogue of his property, much of it works of art, and the various states of ruination to which they had been reduced.

Among the worst losses were the manuscripts of the final two scenes of *Taverner*. Max had finally completed this work in late 1968, but had never got round to letting Boosey & Hawkes have these two scenes, so they had to be rewritten from memory. He also lost a small hand-organ that he had greatly cherished. But the loss that left him really heartbroken was the death, presumably by asphyxiation from smoke inhalation, of his cat, Enid. She was a stray he had met at Princeton, and she had adopted him, as cats do. He had brought her back in his sweater from America, missed her greatly while she was serving her six months' quarantine, and was very fond of her.

He began his letter to Guest by saying, 'I've hardly had time to be sorry for myself', and talking about a trip to Poland from which he had just returned. But then, after reeling off the sad catalogue of damages he says:

> I'm still in a bit of a state – it shows itself in constant migraine and tension in my limbs, and my gums bleed most of the time. Unfortunately I've no let up till Jan 23rd – then I have two and a half months with no concerts. I shan't go back to Barter's Town. I

can't imagine it without the organ, and even here I keep imagining
I hear Enid at night.

About a month later he was writing again to Guest, from Vienna. He
was there with Birtwistle and the Pierrots, and had just arrived from
Hamburg, where in two days they had given a public concert, made a
film for television of the *Eight Songs for a Mad King*, and recorded some
tapes for radio ('too much!!!' as Max comments). He says:

> I have lost my desire to possess *objects* as such, but eventually will
> get some necessities when I've at last had time to find a place. The
> loss of Barter's Town has made a difference – it's hard to tell just
> how – but it burned out any desire for 'things'. But I must find as
> soon as possible a practical place to work in, i.e. as noiseless as
> possible, with an encouraging landscape and few people.

He did not know it at the time, but less than a year later he was to find
somewhere that could have been designed to his own specifications.
Before that happened, however, there was another sad note: not a
personal disaster on the scale of the fire, but the beginning of a lingering
piece of unpleasantness that has never completely healed, nor ever been
dragged into the light of day to be fully and properly explained.

The event which occurred is easily enough set down: in 1970 Birtwistle withdrew from the Pierrot Players, who immediately took
another name for themselves and carried on under Max's sole leader-
ship, and went on to be even more successful, make a bigger name, and
carve a more impressive niche for themselves in musical history. All
that is fact; but it is not really an account of what actually happened.
Most importantly, this version of events does not mention that at about
the same time as Birtwistle's breakaway from the Pierrots, there was a
serious rift between him and Max, which has never really healed over –
although it must be emphasized that they do meet, and their meetings
are perfectly civil.

The bad blood between Max and his former bosom friend Harry
Birtwistle has achieved something of the status of a legend among
musicians; yet it is one of those matters that everybody knows exists,
but when one really gets down to serious questions about the when, the
how and most of all the why, nobody actually turns out to know
anything much at all. The issue is complicated by the fact that some of
those whom one suspects of knowing more than most are apparently
reluctant to say anything about it, while, as always, there are people in
abundance who know least of all about it but are delighted to talk
gleefully and apparently expertly about it all day long.

The first question to be decided, if possible, is whether the rift between the two was a direct consequence of Birtwistle's departure from the Pierrot Players. No one is willing to say for certain, but most people with an opinion think that it was. Certainly everybody agreed that the estrangement between them began at the time of the rift in the Pierrots, so it is mostly assumed that the one was consequent upon the other.

Now to the two principals. Max, when asked, is vague. Not reticent, but vague. He claims that he does not really know what caused the difference between them; and he gives the strong impression that he does not really want to know. It is apparent to a questioner that the topic brings him sadness, and to me, at least, it was clear that he was genuinely puzzled, rather hurt, but inclined to dismiss the matter with a shrug and a grimace. I gained a firm feeling that whatever had happened, there was no malice or ill-feeling towards Birtwistle on Max's part, and never had been. I noticed that there were CDs of Birtwistle's music on Max's shelves, and I could not help observing that on numerous occasions, in differing contexts and companies, he never once made a disparaging reference to Birtwistle; indeed, any reference that he did make was distinctly kind and often, even, affectionate. It was still more noticeable that whenever he referred to Birtwistle's music he was unfailingly lavish in his praise.

With Birtwistle it was very different. It took a lot of effort to persuade Birtwistle to talk to me, but when I did he was exceedingly friendly and pleasant, and his hospitality was most generous: I spent two days at his home talking to him. In those circumstances, I wanted to be able to come away with a favourable report, to be able to be even-handed. Unfortunately, that was not possible. For Birtwistle, speaking as late as July 1993, Max could apparently do very little right. Birtwistle is notoriously difficult to interview, and many interviewers have gone away shaking their heads ruefully over the tiny amount of information they have managed to glean. I myself found it difficult to pin him down: he has a habit of giving a very nebulous answer to a specific question, and then following it up, as if in explanation or clarification, with a statement that, on closer inspection, turns out to be even vaguer than the one it was supposed to qualify. Even so, I did glean a clear impression of his attitude towards Max, and a fair amount of hard information to accompany it.

My conclusion is that the break-up of the Pierrot Players was unavoidable, and the bad feeling between Max and Birtwistle was only partly as a result of it, and would have occurred anyway.

To deal with the break-up first: there seems little doubt about why this happened. Steve Pruslin, who was and still is passionate about the group, and Alan Hacker, who to this day gets very emotional and upset when discussing the split between Max and Birtwistle (he was clearly very fond of them both, and felt torn when they parted company) are agreed; so is the more detached Mary Thomas, and so, most persuasively of all perhaps, is Gary Howarth, a hard-headed dealer in common sense if ever there was one. They all say that no small group was ever going to contain two creative geniuses, two personalities so strong and so different, as those of Max and Harry.

It was, then, inevitable that one or other of them would go. Indeed Steve Pruslin says that 'when the crunch came I was surprised that they had lasted the three years they had'. This leaves only the matter of which of the two it would be. In the circumstances it was always likely to be Birtwistle who would do the bowing out. He was a much quieter and more self-effacing character than Max; he was also a much later developer, and a much slower worker. Most important of all, he was already feeling acutely the constraints of working with a small chamber group, when he wanted to write for bigger and more varied ensembles – brass consorts and so forth. The final result of this was that Birtwistle, quite simply, was not writing enough for the group, while Max most emphatically was. This is stated by witnesses ranging from those who are strongly sympathetic to Birtwistle, such as Mary Thomas, through those who were equally fond of both men and fought hard not to take sides, such as Alan Hacker, to unequivocal Max partisans, like James Murdoch, who report it with unconcealed glee. Thus Steve Pruslin (not at all gleefully): 'Harry wasn't providing enough material for them [the Pierrots] to promote him'; and Murdoch: 'As manager of the Pierrot Players, I had a product to sell. Max supplied that product. Harry dried up. I had nothing of Harry to sell . . . We were a music theatre group – the best – and needed music theatre works. Harry didn't write any . . . Simple!'

All this made it certain which of the two would depart, and Harry duly did so. But most witnesses are agreed that this was with some bitterness because he felt that the group which he had helped to found had been to some extent hijacked by the more flamboyant, extrovert, aggressive character. This is backed up by Birtwistle himself: when I talked to him about this, a phrase that occurred and recurred very often in his conversation was one about Max's 'allowing it to happen'. I could never quite get to the bottom of this, and I still do not fully understand what he meant by it in all the varied contexts in which he used the expression. It did seem fairly clear that he felt rather aggrieved with Max – though it is very difficult to see what Max could have done to prevent events from taking their natural course. Maybe Birtwistle just hoped and expected Max to speak up more in his defence, or to appear sorrier than he did.

At all events, these appear to be the true reasons for Birtwistle's departure from the group. Alan Hacker formed another small group with Birtwistle, called Matrix, but it was short-lived, and in any case Hacker always remained a member of the Pierrot Players.

Another strand in the matter that is beyond doubt is that Birtwistle disliked Murdoch, if not on sight, at least from very soon after his arrival. This is almost certainly down to a simple matter of personalities – that, at any rate, is the verdict of Max himself, of Mary Thomas, of Steve Pruslin and others. Harry Birtwistle was quiet, reserved, sensitive and very shy, with easily hurt feelings. Murdoch, I suspect from his way of writing (I was not able to meet him in the course of my research), was none of those things. His prose style is, to say the least, colourful. I wrote to him explaining how Birtwistle had seemed to me, retailing some of the things he said, and asking for Murdoch's side of things. In return I got a letter full of splendidly spirited high–class abuse, most of which I should never dare to reproduce, irrespective of whether it was true or not. But it made it abundantly clear that Murdoch despised Birtwistle as provincial and bourgeois.

It was equally plain from my conversation with Birtwistle that he in turn thoroughly distrusted and disapproved of Murdoch (he was far from alone in this). This was partly undoubtedly on account of Murdoch's flamboyance – the two men were natural antagonists, natural antitheses of each other. The other possibility that has to be canvassed is that Birtwistle was simply jealous of Max's new friendships, especially with Murdoch. While my wife and I were sitting at the dining table with the Birtwistles Harry did make one remark which surprised me, and caused his wife Sheila, in P. G. Wodehouse's memorable phrase, to break the record for the sitting high jump. She had quite clearly never heard him say anything along these lines before. Harry observed that 'my friendship with him [Max] before we fell out was to do with that' – 'that' being Max's homosexuality. When Sheila had finished jumping out of her skin, and Harry had finished calming her down and reassuring her that no, he didn't mean anything like *that*, he changed the subject in the way he has. The explanation for this cryptic remark would seem to be that Birtwistle was quite simply friends with Max, and that when they naturally grew apart there was a bit of jealousy on Harry's part, a bit of resentment, a large dash of genuine anxiety on behalf of his friend when he saw him mixing with someone he felt was dangerous and untrustworthy, and on top of it all a certain amount of bitterness about the hijack, as Harry saw it, of the group.

The one thing that appeared to me to be beyond doubt when I stayed with the Birtwistles was that Harry bears a grudge against Max, and has borne it for a very long time. Birtwistle is a friendly, agreeable man in every other context – shy, certainly, but very funny, and good company. But he could scarcely bring himself to utter a kind word on the subject of Max and Max's music. The contrast between this visible effort to keep the bitterness down to a minimum and Max's easy, unaffected kindness about Birtwistle could hardly have been more marked.

This is as good a point as any to consider another piece of unpleasantness: the rift between Max and Alexander Goehr. As with the estrangement with Birtwistle, this is something that most people have heard about; but whereas in the other case it has been possible to shed at least some light, if only in the form of reasonable conjecture, on the causes of the rift, in the case of Max and Goehr even that little is impossible. All anybody knows is that Goehr turned against Max at some point. Committed Max partisans put it down to simple professional jealousy. Others contend that Goehr has no more reason to be jealous of Max than Birtwistle does. I did on one occasion hear mention of an absurd dispute when both composers were working at the same time on operas (*Taverner* in Max's case) that required an on-stage band, and that there was some deep suspicion that one or other of them might be guilty of plagiarizing the idea. But, quite apart from the fact that an on-stage band is nothing at all novel in opera, one wonders whether two grown-up men could seriously fall out over something so nugatory.

I wrote to Goehr, naturally, asking if he would talk to me when I was researching the book; but he declined. Max quite plainly has no idea why the estrangement came about, and nor did anyone else among the scores of people I interviewed, many of whom know both men very well indeed.

With Birtwistle gone, the other members of the Pierrots felt morally bound to change the name of the group. As before, it was Steve Pruslin who found the new name. His proposal, 'The Fires of London', was accepted by acclamation. It was indeed a very happy choice of name: it did justice to their reputation as a group that was as likely as not to set London alight any time it performed; it was in any case a nice, snappy name, the kind that people would certainly remember; and it carried the connotation – at least in Pruslin's mind – of recrudescence after fire and destruction. This occurred to Pruslin in connection with the Great Fire of London, of 1666. He had discovered that very soon after that devastating catastrophe, a rather stately but wildly invasive pink-flowering weed had taken root and turned the blackened, charred wasteland of destruction into a pageant of bright, colourful life. The same plant performed exactly the same kindly office after the Blitz left London pock-marked with bombed sites in the Second World War. Nowadays better known to the British as rose-bay willow herb, and to botanists as *Chamaenerion angustifolium*, this plant was known in the seventeenth century as fireweed, in honour of its cosmetic work after the Great Fire, and that name was in Steve Pruslin's mind when he rechristened the group.

That year, 1970, they carried on directly from where the Pierrot Players had left off. Four works joined Max's fast-lengthening catalogue, only one of them of any great significance: it was in 1970 that he at last completed the opera *Taverner*. It had been finished earlier but, as we have seen, the final two scenes were destroyed in the fire at Barter's Town, and had to be rewritten. Max was thirty-six in 1970. Taverner and *Taverner*, with their eternal themes of truth and the perversion of truth, delusion and betrayal, had thus preoccupied him for half his life.

An important phase of Max's life now came to its close, and another opened, with a perfection of timing that tempts one to feel that life really does imitate art. In July 1970 he took a holiday in Scotland with James Murdoch (who was very soon to return to Australia to run his own business ventures there). At one point their round trip took them across the Pentland Firth on a ferry, for their first visit to the islands of Orkney; and while they were there they also took the ferry from the little grey town of Stromness, on the principal island of the Orkneys, known as Mainland, to the second largest island in the group, the lonely, hilly, windswept fastness of Hoy.

There certainly was a remarkable series of coincidences in progress that summer Sunday as Max was carried towards Hoy by the island boat, *Watchful*. The first was that among his fellow-passengers was a man named Kulgin Duval, a dealer in books and manuscripts from Fifeshire, on his way to join some friends who were spending a few days' holiday in the remote village of Rackwick. He noticed that Max was carrying a copy of *An Orkney Tapestry*, by the Orcadian poet, novelist and short-story writer George Mackay Brown (which contains, in Mackay Brown's own words, 'a long over-poetical chapter on Rackwick'). Duval introduced himself to Max and, indicating the book, mentioned that he was a friend of the author, and was on his way to meet him, among other friends, in Rackwick. Max, companionable in his turn, produced a flask and poured a slug of Highland Park, Orkney's own whisky, into Duval's coffee, and said that he had been so excited by

Mackay Brown's writing that he had stayed up all the previous night reading the book. He told Duval who he was, and mentioned that he was in search of somewhere quiet and sequestered to live, in order to be able to compose in peace – he had wondered vaguely if there might be such a place for him on Hoy. He and Murdoch had arranged to be met by the island's taxi for a tour of the whole island. Fine, said Duval, and when they had finished their conducted tour, they must come to meet his friends in Rackwick. It was agreed, and for the time being they parted.

Meanwhile, the holiday group at Rackwick was assembling. George Mackay Brown was there, with his friend Archie Bevan, at that time deputy headmaster of the Stromness Academy, his wife Elizabeth, their sons Peter and Graham and daughter Anne. They had been lent a croft house used as a holiday home by the Stromness doctor, Dr Johnstone, a close neighbour of the Bevans. By what was to prove the second coincidence that blustery afternoon, it stood in sight of the spot where the lonely remains of a tiny house faced into the teeth of the gales that rake the thin grasses and outcrop stone of Hoy, looking out over the roaring cauldron of the sea that thunders against its rocky shoulder. Perched high on the crest of a high scarp, this house is the highest of the scattered handful of buildings that make up the village of Rackwick. To this it owes its name, Bunertoon, a transliteration of the local dialect for 'above the town'.

In an unpublished essay, George Mackay Brown himself describes the little ruined stone house:

> One thinks: 'A Rackwick man long ago must have been very poor, very desperate, to set stone on stone in such a place' . . . Perhaps not. This is the fertile sun-smitten slope of the valley. There is turf above for winter fires. There is a water-spring nearby. The fisherman-crofter could see, from the wall of Bunertoon, better than from any other stance, fishing auguries – the movements of tide and wind, birds and clouds.

Inside the doctor's holiday house where the Bevans and their party were gathered there were fire and food and whisky. There was home-made music provided by a friend with a guitar who had dropped in, and their own voices. There were a few books, and stories for the young Anne Bevan, and Kulgin Duval had arrived, laden with sweets for the little girl and malt whisky for the rest.

In the afternoon, two strangers appeared. 'One', says Mackay Brown in his essay, 'was a slight small dark active man with intense smouldering eyes: Peter Maxwell Davies.' They whiled away the afternoon eating curry made by Archie Bevan and drinking his red wine, of which he had brought over a huge glass jar. In a brief interlude of fairer skies they sat outside to drink their coffee. Then it grew darker and fouler and wetter than ever. But at some point the talk must have turned to Max's desire for a remote home in which he could compose, because Archie mentioned a croft called Burnmouth, 'a long beautiful ruin just where the burn empties itself tumultuously among the shore stones' (it is very difficult, with Mackay Brown's words before one, to resist dipping into them). And so, just as the weather worsened, everyone except Duval and Mackay Brown set out in incessant rain to inspect the possibly desirable residence of Burnmouth. ('Kulgin and I sat at the jar of red wine and drank and spoke and laughed . . .')

Eventually the others returned, half drowned; Max had decided that, much though he had admired Burnmouth, he would not try to acquire it. Apart from anything else the beach just beyond it is very popular with holidaymakers in summer, with constant hordes passing the door of the croft on their way to bathing and picnicking – and, more than likely, to knock on his door just to have a look at him – a prescription just about perfect for sending someone of Max's temperament into a decline. But Mackay Brown speculates whether perhaps 'Maxwell Davies may have seen, high on the hill above, a ruin, ghostly in the flung haar, drifted around by a few sheep'.

And so the guitar man sang to them, they drank farewell drams, and the two visitors left to go on board the *Watchful*, five miles away at Hoy pier. Rackwick keened with rain and wind, the sheep huddled under the lee wall of Bunertoon, and indoors the party lit the lamp and wondered if their new friend would find a place somewhere in Orkney. They all very much hoped so, says Mackay Brown: 'We had liked him.'

That was Max's introduction to the desolate, wind-raked place that was to become his true home, certainly his spiritual one; to the poet who was to become his most frequent partner, and an inspirational force in his own right, in his work; to the people who were to rank among the closest friends he had ever made in his life; and, most of all, to the environment: to the lonely fulcrum where sea and sky and bare mountainside meet, which was to change his life in every way. Before a year had passed, this remote, uncompromising fastness would begin to channel his immense creative energy into a totally different, utterly unexpected direction, inspiring a whole generation of music that was as different from the bold, shrieking primary colours of expressionism as it well could be.

7 ~ Years of Plenty

Although Max fell in love with Hoy at the time of his first visit in 1970, the peace that he was to find there was not to come straightaway. In fact the next few years were rather hectic and chaotic as he flitted about from place to place, running different homes simultaneously.

Even as late as 1970, he still slept at Bolsover Street when he was in London, although he had relinquished his formal tenancy some time before. The house there was the scene of many celebration parties for the Fires and their friends after concerts in London; some unusual meals were eaten there, too. Derek Saul remembers cooking spaghetti for the Fires, and Max dressing it with vodka, and another memorable *specialité de la maison* was chicken in chocolate sauce, an invention of Steve Pruslin's.

Meanwhile, since the fire at Barter's Town, Max had been living in the house lent to him in Bristol. Late in 1970, however, he found himself another home. When James Murdoch left the Fires to return to run his business interests in Australia, Max took over the lease on the flat he had occupied in London at 26 Fitzroy Square. This was to be his main residence for four years. Thus he gravitated to the very heart of Fitzrovia, named after the Fitzroy pub at its centre, where Dylan Thomas and his cronies had roamed from pub to club and back to pub on colossal drinking sprees, talking endlessly about art, letters and life, thirty years before.

Orkney was not forgotten, however. It had made a deep and indelible impression on Max – on his soul rather than on his mind – and was never afterwards to lose its hold on him. Certainly he did not keep away for very long after his first visit: his next trip there was precipitated by a quite unexpected approach from the film director Ken Russell. Russell, at that time very much in vogue, was keenly interested in music – then as now, he was known as much for his black and white docu-dramas about the lives of Elgar and Delius, made for the BBC in the 1960s, as for any of the far larger-scale works of later years. Of all directors, therefore, he was the one whom it was least surprising to find commissioning a proper composer to write the score for a film, and that is what he now asked Max to do.

The film was *The Devils*, a luridly bloody, erotic interpretation of Aldous Huxley's novel, *The Devils of Loudun*, and Max enthusiastically accepted the commission to write the music, keen as always to venture down a new and previously untravelled road. Increasingly, however, his lifelong and ever-growing detestation of noise made it impossible for him to compose in London, and he now had no home anywhere quieter. December 1970, therefore, found George Mackay Brown opening a letter from Max, asking if he would find out from Dr Johnstone whether he would be willing to allow Max to live in his holiday house on Hoy for a few weeks.

Mackay Brown passed the request on to the Bevans, who lived very near the doctor. He agreed readily, and in January 1971 Max arrived in Stromness, accompanied by a music student friend and bearing a print of the martyrdom of a medieval saint as a present for George – 'a crude powerful etching', as the recipient said of it.

There was a pleasant evening at the Bevans' and the Johnstones' houses, after which Max and his companion spent the night at the Stromness Hotel – almost the last time Max was to stay anywhere but at the Bevans', as things turned out. In the morning, he bought wellington boots, an oilskin and a sou'wester from Wright's Bootshop, a box of provisions and two bottles of Scotch, had lunch with George and then set off to Hoy in the *Three Boys*, the ferry run by Ginger Brown, predecessor and mentor of Stevie Mowatt (later immortalized by Max in a piano piece), to live and write music for a while.

He stayed in the doctor's house for some weeks, industriously scoring *The Devils* with a metronome and stopwatch, and from time to time flying to London to visit the set and discuss progress with Russell. He found it an interesting novelty to work with film people, and met a couple of people who would work with him later on. On the whole, however, he regarded the interlude as just that, and nothing more – a bit of a blind alley, out of the mainstream of his development as a composer, and having no influence on it.

Having finished the score for the film and presented it, to Ken Russell's great satisfaction, Max very quickly found himself back on Hoy: he arrived at Easter 1971, again staying at the doctor's house, and working on his next job. Russell was so pleased with his work on *The Devils* that he immediately signed him up to write the score for his next film, *The Boy Friend*. This was a nostalgic extravaganza, starring the former top model, Twiggy, and was an adaptation of a musical by Sandy Wilson, which was itself a pastiche of 1930s' musical taste, full of boaters and blazers and bright young things, and musically abounding (and revelling) in sickly bad taste. Max thoroughly enjoyed scoring it,

writing adaptations of the pop jingles and also producing an original
fantasy for a scene in which the heroine of the film imagines a series of
dance numbers, which Max created himself.

This was the end of his brief sideline as a composer of film music,
because, as he explains, it was a back-water. But his work for Ken
Russell, in particular this second score, was remarkable for two things.
The first would never have come to light but for the fact that Ken
Russell himself noticed it in progress. It illustrates very well how
strongly Max has inherited the strain of the conscientious craftsman
from his father. One of the brief pop songs in *The Boy Friend*, called 'All
I do is dream of you', includes some mention of the seasons of the year.
For each word, Max found an appropriate snatch of melody from
Vivaldi's *Four Seasons*, only a bar or two long, and worked these
momentary references into the melody of the song, which was taken
from a fifteenth-century French folk song. Russell found him poring
over it at four o'clock one morning, working and reworking it until it
was just right. As Russell points out, no one could ever possibly know –
except, just possibly, a scholar – what had gone into the little pop jingle,
and few would care. But Max himself would always have the satisfaction of knowing that he had got it just right, and how, and that he had
given as much of himself to the orchestration of a pop ditty as he would
have done to a serious composition of his own.

The second remarkable thing about his composition of the music for
The Boy Friend is that he restricted his work on the score to the
mornings of his stay in Rackwick. In the afternoons he was writing
music, but of an utterly different kind. This was *From Stone to Thorn*, a
rather significant work for two reasons: first, it was the first piece in
which he set words by his new friend George Mackay Brown, and
second, it was also the first work of his to bear the conscious influence of
the Orkneys. As such, it would be noteworthy as a landmark in his
career irrespective of its own qualities. Scored for mezzo-soprano with
clarinet, harpsichord, guitar and the usual hyperactive percussionist, it is
a setting of part of Mackay Brown's cycle of poems *Fishermen with
Ploughs*.

Max and Mackay Brown admit freely that they had never heard of
each other until their fortuitous first meeting during Max's holiday the
previous year; but both agree that they were powerfully drawn to each
other, not only because they took a strong personal liking to each other,
but also because of certain qualities in each other's work and in what
each perceived the other as being in search of. It is true to say that Max
found in Mackay Brown a spiritual partner, a natural collaborator, from
the first moment of his discovery of his work, when he had stayed up all

night reading *An Orkney Tapestry* on his way to the Orkneys, having bought the book out of curiosity when he found that the author was a true Orcadian. The affinity had been instantaneous, and the desire to set Mackay Brown's work – especially but not exclusively the poems – to music had struck Max at the same moment.

Among the several aspects of Mackay Brown's work that exerted this immediate attraction on Max was the fact that he saw in the poet someone who, like himself, needed urgently to examine the meaning of religious belief, religious truth, and the religious impulse in man in general. This will be discussed in more detail later on, but at this point it cannot be emphasized enough that although Max eschews all formal religious faith himself – indeed, he regards it as deeply repugnant – he is profoundly interested in religious music, religious apparatus and procedures and, in particular, religious casts of thought; religious notions of order, serenity, gravity, dignity and grace have always preoccupied him. Many of his friends, indeed, including some who know him extremely closely, are convinced that whatever he may claim, he is in fact deeply religious. This is not the place to attempt to go into this in depth; but it could be persuasively argued that the late Bishop of Woolwich, John Robinson, might well have identified Max as falling within his new definition of Christian. Whether or not he is a Christian must depend to some extent on how we define Christianity; whether he is religious depends similarly on our definition of the larger term. All that is certain is that Max himself dismisses all conventional, organized religion as mere religiosity but, on the other hand, has a fascination with religious belief, a deep spiritual need to probe it deeply. In fact it may be argued that he has spent all his adult life writing religious music in search of a religion, so to speak.

He is also compulsively drawn by schism – by ideas of conflict, especially inner conflict. He is powerfully driven by tension, and tensions of all kinds manifest themselves in his work and in his choice of subjects, ideas and, as with Mackay Brown, partners in that work. Thus the idea of a Roman Catholic poet working and abiding amidst a Calvinist society would stand out like a brilliant spangled banner to Max. The entire notion of Rome, with its whiff of incense and its bright cardinal reds and golds and purples contrasts kaleidoscopically with the pastel yellows and faded greens, the steel blues and slate blues and thrush-egg blues and everywhere the multifarious shades of grey of Orkney. Mackay Brown was a natural soul-mate for Max; and when Max discovered the poem that was to become *From Stone to Thorn*, and found that it dealt with the very Stations of the Cross that Max had himself been so concerned with in *Vesalii Icones*, that put the final seal on the affinity.

The poem in *From Stone to Thorn* relates the Stations of the Cross to the landmarks of the agricultural year, with the singer acting as observer, over a highly lyrical backing from the small ensemble. The piece was commissioned by Jesus College, Oxford, as part of its celebrations of its 400th anniversary, and the first performance was in Oxford in June 1971, by Mary Thomas and the Fires. In all, the piece provides a neat drawing-together of threads at this critical moment in Max's life: the Fires, religious searching and questioning, tension between contrasting, even conflicting, notions but corresponding resolution of tension – in this case, into the stations of the agricultural calendar and natural creation – and most of all Max's future: George, Orkney and the enormous influence they were to have on his music ever after.

On his return to England after this Easter visit to Hoy, Max stayed a couple of nights in Stromness with the Bevans, and set a pattern that has never been broken since. His periods of time on Hoy are always preceded or ended, or both, by a stop-over with the Bevans, who are part of what makes the Orkneys what they are for Max. The friendship between them has grown from strong roots – the Bevans, like George Mackay Brown, took a liking to him on their first meeting – to make up a substantial and enduring part of Max's life, and in particular of the deep-seated links between him and Orkney.

They are ideal friends for him: genial and intelligent, affectionate without a suspicion of gushing. They clearly love him, but in a down-to-earth and unsentimental manner that would be exactly suited to his North country origins. Their house is large, warm and comfortable, with a magnificent view from big bow windows out over the bay. It is a house full of books and learning, but, like Max's own, it is worn lightly. The Bevans revel in the art of conversation, and so do the people they bring to the house – George foremost among them. Their friendship has been solid and enduring for as long as Max has known them, their welcome genuine, their hospitality generous, and their presence there, comfortable, undemanding and dependable. The knowledge that they were there for him whenever he returned has been one of the lynch-pins of the ever-deepening pull the islands have exerted on Max.

On this first occasion that Max stayed with the Bevans, he left them some LPs of his music, which they found interesting. It was their first acquaintance with their new friend's work, and with any music more modern than Britten and Tippett. They were very soon to have a closer acquaintance with it.

From Stone to Thorn was the only new work Max produced in 1971, apart from the two film scores, suites from which were played by the Fires at the same concert at the Queen Elizabeth Hall in December. He also revised an earlier work, the *Missa Super l'Homme Armé*. The following year, however, gave a rich yield. Indeed, it was the first of what may be called the years of plenty for Max.

New works composed in 1972 included the second piece inspired by Orkney and things Orcadian. This was the *Hymn to St Magnus*. It is a very big piece, lasting almost forty minutes, and was written for the Fires' ensemble of six instruments, with an obbligato part for mezzo-soprano. Magnus is the local saint of the Orkneys: he was an Earl of Orkney in the twelfth century and was martyred by being murdered in fairly spectacular style by his cousin, after which he was canonized. The cathedral at Kirkwall, which has made an atmospheric setting for many of Max's works, is consecrated to Magnus. The hymn is in four sections, beginning with a short introduction and concluding with a slow finale, this being a setting of the medieval hymn to the saint which provides the seeds of the work. The two internal sections are large-scale movements in sonata form, in Max's own words, 'permeated by the violence of the martyrdom and the violence of the sea' – the first of many appearances of the sea in Max's work following his discovery of the Orkneys.

The *Hymn to St Magnus* was dedicated to the Bevans, an unmistakable sign that Max was already aware of the crucial role their welcome would play in his adoption of the Orkneys. The first performance was by the Fires in their South Bank season that winter, but the following June the Fires and Mary Thomas travelled to Orkney and gave a complimentary concert, including the *Hymn*, in Kirkwall Cathedral – an event full of symbolism for the future. Max made it clear that the concert was a thank-you to Orkney for making him so welcome; and Orkney received it in that spirit. The relationship was forged, already very strongly.

Other works completed in 1972 included a strange piece, *Blind Man's Buff*, commissioned by the BBC and first performed in May that year, at the Roundhouse, by the BBC Symphony Orchestra under the baton of the orchestra's Principal Conductor, Pierre Boulez – the first time he had conducted a work of Max's. *Blind Man's Buff* is described as a masque, and is a setting of a text by Max himself, concocted from the final scene of Büchner's play *Leonce und Lena* and English nursery rhymes. The orchestra is divided: a septet of wind, guitar, ukelele, harp and percussion plays on stage in courtiers' dress, with a string orchestra in the pit. After an overture, the boy-king, played by a soprano or treble, sings a nursery rhyme on the theme of things not being what they seem; he then asks to know the identity of the jester, played by a mime. The jester responds with a mirror-dance for his twin personae, mime and dancer. These two later remove masks and reveal themselves as a prince and a princess, and the king abdicates and dies. The jester then has a mad solo, accompanied by blindingly bright light, which dazzles the prince and princess but also revives the king as a resurrected ghost.

Another interesting work, though much shorter, less elaborate and less elusive, was the result of a commission from the Globe Playhouse Trust. It was *Fool's Fanfare*, a setting of words taken from the speeches of several Shakespearean fools, including Feste from *Twelfth Night*, Lear's Fool, Touchstone from *As You Like It*, Puck from *A Midsummer Night's Dream* and the Gravedigger from *Hamlet*. A male speaker, introduced by a cracked fanfare on trumpets and trombones, recites the words above an accompaniment from a ukelele, glockenspiel, marimba and other percussion, with comments on his words from the brass.

There were two more realizations of works by earlier composers, the *Veni Sancte Spiritus, Veni Creator Spiritus* of Dunstable and the *Prelude and Fugue in C sharp minor* from J. S. Bach's *Forty-eight*. Max also held an extended dialogue with another of his predecessors in *Tenebrae Super Gesualdo*. This is a dark-toned piece which may be performed in two entirely different versions: in the first, an SATB choir sings Gesualdo's *O vos omnes*, but repeatedly falling silent to allow Max's sextet of low, dark-toned instruments to weave his own four meditations round the original ideas. In the second version of the piece, the *O vos omnes* is sung by a mezzo-soprano (Mary Thomas) accompanied by a guitar. In performances of this work by the Fires, the guitar part was played by Timothy Walker, one of the most frequent guest instrumentalists to play with the group. It so happened that Walker's son was born in this first year of plenty, 1972, and the event was commemorated by a short piece from Max, called *Lullaby for Ilian Rainbow* – the latter two words being the forenames inflicted on the unfortunate and innocent child. The final piece of the year was a puzzle canon, Max's contribution to a collection of musical epitaphs to Igor Stravinsky, published in Boosey & Hawkes's contemporary music magazine, *Tempo*.

One work, finished long before, did not receive its premiere until 1972. This was a giant piece, one of the most significant milestones in Max's career; it represented the end of a phase and Max finally getting out of his system something that had been a preoccupation, very close to an obsession, for over twenty years, since he had been a schoolboy. It was, of course, the first staging, at Covent Garden, of the opera, *Taverner*.

Ken Russell had been delighted with Max's work for him on the two film scores, and the original intention had been for him to direct the production of *Taverner* at Covent Garden – and also to bankroll it. He withdrew, however, having been put off the work, so Max says, by hearing a reduction of the piece for a single voice and piano. In the end, the work owed its performance at Covent Garden largely to Edward Downes, at that time assistant to the Musical Director, Georg Solti.

There was considerable pressure from the Arts Council and other groups for Covent Garden to put on productions of new British operas. Solti, who was interested in little contemporary music and fond of less, was not enthusiastic about doing such works, and was happy to leave it to his assistant. Downes therefore had the freedom to put on operas such as Richard Rodney Bennett's *Victory* and Humphrey Searle's *Hamlet*; but the one he was most keen to stage was Max's *Taverner*. He knew of the opera's existence from Steve Pruslin, who was a friend, and they had discussed it in some detail, Downes had seen the score, and become enthusiastic. He nagged Solti mercilessly about this wonderful new work until Solti finally agreed to hear it – possibly to keep his deputy quiet about it. At all events, in 1971, Max, Pruslin and Downes all went to Solti's house in St John's Wood, where Max and Pruslin played him a reduction of the score of *Taverner* for piano, four hands. 'Solti didn't like it, and that was that,' is Max's terse comment on the day's work.

However, Solti's contract as Musical Director at Covent Garden expired later that year, and he was replaced by Colin Davis. Davis was often sympathetic to new music – indeed, he was a tireless champion of, for example, Tippett's works; at first he wanted Max to write another opera for Covent Garden. But Max offered *Resurrection*, which put Davis right off his music thereafter. However, Downes nagged at him about *Taverner* and showed him the score until eventually Davis agreed: 'OK, so long as you conduct it. I'm not going to.'

So it was that Downes, one of the most adventurous and open-minded of conductors, and a life-long champion of new music, ended up as the conductor of Max's first and largest opera. He had to learn it himself first, and for a good six months before the opening date he was to be found lugging the huge full score everywhere he went. One day he had taken a few minutes off duty to take his small children for a stroll in Greenwich Park, near his home, where there is a bandstand. On this day there happened also to be a band – that of the London Fire Brigade, Downes remembers – playing the usual mix of Strauss waltzes and polkas, ballads and military marches. As they passed, Downes's young son, aged about four, broke away and ran on to the bandstand. There he tugged impatiently at the bandmaster's sleeve and, when the perspiring maestro glanced down in surprise, demanded, 'Can you play anything from *Taverner*?'

A little while later the Downes family travelled to Australia, where the head of the family was conducting at the Sydney Opera House and still assiduously studying the score of *Taverner* in his off-duty hours. One day they went for a picnic in some local beauty spot which happened to be populated by large numbers of emus. These large, flightless birds have very striking eyes, bright blue in colour and with an unblinking, searchlight gaze; in addition, the specimens in the park were quite tame, and would approach picnicking parties in the hope of being fed. One of the Downes children happened to glance up just as the boldest approached close, gave the bird a cursory glance, and announced matter-of-factly, 'Oh, look, it's Max Davies!'

The opera is a setting of a text by Max himself, in two acts of four scenes each. Each scene is one episode from the life of the Tudor composer, and the eight taken as a whole offer a fairly complete account of the most significant events in his life, so far as these are known. In a prefatory note to the libretto Max says that he combed an enormous quantity of documents from Taverner's time, including state papers, letters, contemporary sermons, biographies, diaries, plays and poetry, records of trials for heresy and so forth, 'to give the record of John Taverner as wide an application and meaning as possible'. The text is, indeed, largely made up of direct quotations from such sources, gathered together and spliced into a continuous sequence.

The facts of Taverner's life, or such of them as are known, can be set out very briefly. He was born about 1490. Nothing much is known of him until 1526, when he went to Oxford to be master of the choir in the chapel of Cardinal's College (later renamed Christ Church). Two years later he was tried and imprisoned by the Roman Catholic authorities for harbouring heretical books, but was later freed by no less a figure than Wolsey. This may have been prompted by admiration for Taverner's music, but the words used by Wolsey are at least ambiguous and at worst against such a possibility: he is reputed to have said, 'He was but a musician, and so he escaped . . .' Taverner left Oxford in 1530, and voluntarily brought his musical career to an end, in order to work as a paid agent of Thomas Cromwell in the dissolution of the monasteries.

The first scene of the opera is set in a courtroom, and is, according to the composer's instructions, extremely striking, with the decor, dress and everything else all in bold black and white. The only splash of colour to appear in this scene is provided by the scarlet robes of a Cardinal who enters later.

The scene shows Taverner on trial for possessing heretical books, and takes the form of a kind of kangaroo court, presided over by the White Abbot, with four witnesses – Taverner's father, his mistress, his priest-confessor and a boy of his college chapel choir – giving sketchy 'evidence' against him. Taverner defends himself by way of outspoken assaults on Catholicism, and a chorus, a council of learned men, interjects occasional sententious sentiments, after the manner of the chorus in Greek tragedy. The music follows the dialogue, lightly portraying the characters – there is a slow, yearning melody on the clarinet, for example, for Rose Parrowe, Taverner's mistress, and the comments from the council are accompanied by forthright timpani, perhaps suggestive of the dogmatic nature of their interventions, unqualified by any salutary element of doubt.

The second scene takes place in Taverner's chapel, with a chorus of monks intoning in Latin on his life, in canons based on the *in nomine* from Taverner's mass *Gloria Tibi Trinitas*, and Taverner speculating aloud in English whether to break out in violence against the Church, but eventually deciding in the space of a single line to put his trust in God and to wait and see what happens to him. This very short scene ends with a long orchestral transition, which itself ends with a cracked fanfare which also serves to introduce Scene 3. This shows the King – actually Henry VIII – talking to the Cardinal – actually Wolsey. Taverner is absent, and the orchestra is silent, replaced by a spare, bleak accompaniment from an on-stage consort of viols and lute. The King talks cynically about how a breach with Rome will be a great thing for him, and how it will allow him to appropriate vast amounts of money, get rid of his wife and put his mistress on the throne – while claiming all the time that it is the prickings of his conscience that make him do these things, in the name of protestantism. The Cardinal dithers, but finally decides to try to persuade the Pope to accept the King's pleas. The Jester, behaving like his counterpart in a Shakespearean drama, comments drily on the self-serving deceits of both sides. The scene ends with the Jester, accompanied by high, menacing tremolandi from the consort, stripping off his mask to reveal his true identity as Death, denoted by his having a death's-head for a face.

The fourth scene opens with the Jester, thus revealed as Death, calling on Taverner to confess. As Taverner recognizes his interrogator, we hear for the first time in the opera the Death Chord, which we have encountered several times before, in both the *Taverner Fantasias* and in the *Seven 'In Nomine'*. This chord, of D, F sharp, E and G sharp, now becomes the leitmotif of the Jester in his true persona of Death. Two monks, one in black, the other in white, enter, and the two of them and Death confuse Taverner to a point where he is incapable of telling good from evil. The two monks remove their cowls to reveal their features: the white monk is revealed as a beast, the black as a man of noble

YEARS OF PLENTY · 137

features, emphasizing the ambiguous nature of good and evil. The two monks point out that Christ is irrevocably entwined with Judas, Pilate and the Passion – a metaphor indicating that good and evil are often inseparable and mutually dependent: without evil, how may we measure good?

The music becomes rapidly more and more excitable, with staccato yelps from the brass and a busy side-drum, as Death intervenes to bombard Taverner with statistical data about the Church, to make him realize what is stacked up against him if he takes on the Roman Church. Taverner finally makes up his mind which way he is going to jump, and condemns the impedimenta of Rome as devices of the Antichrist. At the mention of his name the Antichrist itself appears, in the form of a pope with the face of an ape, and declares that it is virtuous to slaughter protestants. Taverner reiterates his hatred of Rome and declares his determination to wage war on it.

Death tells him that this is not enough, but that he must also renounce his own humanity, his beloved music, to prove his sincerity, and calls on Taverner's mistress, personifying his music. She tells him that he is not intended to understand divine nature, except as a simple musician, speaking through his songs. In a passionate, intensely lyrical cameo, counterpointed by ravishing string melodies, she almost persuades Taverner, actually taking his hand and beginning to lead him off to music and peace. But Death will not give him up, and stages a street Passion play, with Death himself playing a figure called Joking Jesus, acting out a macabre parody of Christ crucified, to an accompaniment of single tabla, beaten by a demon. This figure convinces Taverner that his place is as a foot-soldier against Rome on behalf of his new faith; and in this scene Max introduces perhaps his most savage side-swipe against religion in the entire opera, when God the Father appears, offering rewards to those who 'purge our land from heretical filth'. Taverner signs his confession, saying that he repents bitterly having 'made songs to popish ditties in the time of my blindness'. Taverner swears that he is as one reborn, and promises to defend Christ's faith with sword and fire, shouting the tenets of his new faith with the exultation of the zealot.

The second act of the opera opens with another trial scene, this time a deliberate parody of the first scene of Act 1. This time it is Taverner who is the inquisitor, and the White Abbot who is the defendant: Taverner's conversion from Rome was followed, historically, by the English Reformation; in the opera the first serves as an analogy for the second. The witnesses are the same characters in different guises, and the music is based on the same material, but considerably abbreviated and speeded up. This emphasizes the sense of parody, and at the same time heightens the effect as the same kind of kangaroo court hustles the Abbot through the proceedings to his sentence to burn at the stake. At the point where the Cardinal intervened to pardon Taverner in the first act, a Cardinal enters now; but he has no face, symbolizing his total loss of power. The scene closes with Death manipulating the wheel of fortune, and the chorus setting out one of the pivotal questions of the whole opera: St Michael warred with the serpent, and cast it down; but who can tell the difference between the two? Death howls ironical congratulations, and the act closes with a tremendous orchestral climax, the first in the work so far.

The next scene is another confrontation between the King and the Cardinal. It begins with the Cardinal informing the King that his second marriage is forbidden on pain of excommunication, and that his cause is forbidden to all members of the true Church. The King replies with a denunciation of the Roman Church, claiming that this is being done in the name and interest of the people. As his denunciation proceeds, Death gradually strips the Cardinal of his regalia, and replaces it with that of an Anglican archbishop, who promptly delivers to the King everything he wants.

With Taverner absent, this scene between King and Cardinal, like its counterpart in Act 1, is accompanied by the consort of viols and lute, with the orchestra silent. As the first scene of Act 2 parodies the first of Act 1, and the parody is reflected in the speeding up of the music, so in this scene the music of the consort here reflects the contrast between the parallel scenes in the two acts. Thus in the first scene between the King and the Cardinal (Act 1 Scene 3) the music was spare in the extreme, with much of the dialogue in unaccompanied recitative. In this counterpart scene the music is livelier, with a patina of superficial brightness and optimism, echoing the hypocrisy and cynicism of the real reasons underlying the great changes being effected in the religion of the country and the new relationship between the Church and the State.

Scene 3 is set in the chapel, in which the condemned White Abbot and his monks are saying Mass in Latin, with several references to the betrayal of Christ by Judas Iscariot. Taverner enters at a point neatly associating him with Judas, and immediately damns the Church of Rome for its excessive concern with material wealth and for its corruption. The Abbot and monks continue to celebrate the Mass in quiet dignity. Then the King's soldiers burst in and proclaim the dissolution of the monasteries. Their captain snatches the communion wine from the Abbot's hand and pours it on the floor, while the monks sing one of Taverner's own most celebrated settings: the Benedictus from *Gloria Tibi Trinitas*.

This gradually fades and is engulfed in Max's own music, violent, strident and dominated by a thunderous chorus of bells, as the orchestra play a colossal transition into the final scene of the opera. This takes place at Boston, Lincolnshire, with the Stump in the background, and depicts the final condemnation and burning of the White Abbot at the stake. There is no reprieve: at the end the faggots are lit and the Abbot burns – the freshly converted zealot being shown to be more perfectly merciless in the Lord's work than even the established order; or an illustration, perhaps, of the old adage about the convert being more Catholic than the Pope.

In the final moments of the opera the Abbot uses his dispensation to say his last words before burning to issue a warning that one day there will be no need for burnings at the stake to punish heretics. But this is no hopeful prophecy of a time of freedom of thought: there will be no necessity for the stake, he says, because the simple pressure of public opinion will be so powerful that unorthodoxy, even of thought, will be quite simply inconceivable. So in this defiant prediction, the Abbot in his last words on Earth makes a mockery of the very irony of his own words in opening the same last statement: 'I am fell into the hands of those who, preaching free thought, do burn me for opposing it' – and Max, we may feel, has added to this great edifice the final trowelful of his disgust at the spiritual repression at the heart of all religions made by man. Finally, Taverner kneels in prayer beside the pyre. Rose Parrowe comes and stands behind him, looking down on him sadly; but her love for him is gone for ever: she does not touch him, but sings that 'The Lord . . . has made thee a stranger, drunk with wormwood.'

The music in these final terrible minutes is for the strings, and is the most searchingly beautiful in the entire opera: deeply tragic, filled with pity, fear and lamentation. Like *Worldes Blis*, which dates from the same period, this music is strongly reminiscent in spirit of the great lamenting Adagio that closes Mahler's Ninth Symphony.

Given the general shortage of known facts about Taverner, and the episodic nature of the opera, it is clear that Max's work is true to such facts as we have; but it would be fatuous to regard it as an opera 'about' Taverner, or 'about' the English Reformation – or even 'about' the appalling transformation in Taverner's soul brought about by religious fanaticism. It is plain that the opera uses Taverner as an analogy, perhaps even an allegory. It speaks, or seeks to speak, through the character of Taverner and what happened to him in his time, of the perversion of religion by men and the perversion of men by religion – all men so perverted, and all religions so perverted. It is also clear that while Max was careful to ask no direct questions, and even more careful to answer none, his whole opera is in fact a single enormous question: religious faith does this to people. Why?

This is the question that lies at the heart of Max's lifelong fascination with religion. We have discussed elsewhere, and shall discuss again, the striking contrast between Max's strong personal distaste for and distrust of religion and his perennial fascination with it. This opera is certainly the largest, and one of the most vivid, expressions of this conflict in his work.

Apart from the obvious swipes at religion in the text – the Jester's ironical comments on the self-seeking nature of both players in the King-versus-Church divide in Act I, Scene 3 and so on – the opera is replete with references to the anti-intellectual cast of mind of the Church, but also, more importantly, of religion itself, as filtered through the minds and souls of its adherents, its hostility to intellectual advance and questing for knowledge by the individual. The Church's attitude that knowledge is better undiscovered if it casts doubt on established dogma is clearly in the composer's mind when Death remarks (in the Boosey & Hawkes libretto of the opera, page 20): 'Your assiduous study and learning from hidden books gave you scruples about the validity of your religion . . .'; and shortly after this, Death again the speaker, there is an extended reference to 'the indestructible heritage of the Church', followed by the great catalogue of things that will be piled up against Taverner if he takes on the Roman Church: 'the fourteen articles of faith . . . the ten commandments of the Law, two evangelical precepts of charity, the seven works of mercy, the seven deadly sins, the seven opposing virtues, and the seven sacraments of grace' – symbolizing the dead weight of dogma, ideology, ideas anchored in concrete, and the face set resolutely against all change, however rational it may be.

A short while later in Act I, Scene 4 Taverner is forced to reject his father and his mistress, the latter clad to represent Music. This is perhaps the most poignant and moving scene in the opera, because it shows the main character, at least, in a more human light than elsewhere. But it cannot be other than a savage indictment of the intemperate, insensate and obsessive core of religion, its fundamental unreasonableness, its belief in and portrayal of a world in which all is black and white, where there is no compromise, no worldliness, no measure, no balance: no reason.

All this is surely symbolized and epitomized by one telling stroke of inspiration in the casting: it can be no accident that it is the character of Death who has to administer Taverner's religious instruction: religion equals the death of thought, the death of the human virtues of measure, balance and so on mentioned just now.

The appearance of God the Father in the same scene in the person of the bloated, hypocritical priest-confessor is too obvious to need comment; but it was surely a swipe at conventional notions of the godhead to portray God the Father by a high, querulous counter-tenor. And near the end of this scene, just before Taverner rises, converted, and ecstatically proclaims his joy in his born-again state, the cynical Death has a short speech, one of the most telling in the entire opera, in which he says:

But the unclean spirit, when he is gone out of a man, passeth through waterless places, seeking rest, and findeth it not. Then he says, I will return into my house whence I came, and when he finds it empty, swept clean, he enters and dwells there with seven other spirits, more evil than himself, and the last state of that man is worse than the first.

This must surely be a counter-blast against the notions of conversion, missionary proselytizing, 'one convert is worth a dozen saints', and most of all the zealotry of the born-again – a direct reference to what follows next in Taverner's own speech as he rises and declares himself a loyal foot-soldier of the Lord.

Max is equally hostile to the equation of the Church with the State, as shown by the remark on page 28 of the libretto that 'In great matters of state it counts little who we are or what we feel . . .' For Max, clearly, when religion equals the State, he wants no part of it in either guise. Both bodies are guilty of the cynical subversion of the individual – and, by implication, of the individual *conscience* – to the expediency of the State.

Perhaps the most appalled view of religion and clerics is on page 33 of the libretto, when the Archbishop says, 'England is our storehouse of delights, a very inexhaustible well, where much can be extracted from many.'

If that is the most cynical view of religion, itself at its most cynical, the most paradoxical aspect of the whole opera is that the character of Taverner is convincingly sincere throughout. There is nowhere any ground for suspecting him of being merely a cynical hypocrite. Both during his own trial in Act 1, Scene 1, and later when he is himself hunting with the hounds, he carries authentic conviction at all times. This is clearly the question Max asks most urgently of all: how can a man behave this way? How can he behave like this and live with himself? How can he behave this way and remain sane? What is it about religious faith that twists people into doing this kind of thing? What is it about people that makes them need religion so much that they are willing to be twisted this way, if that is the price religion costs? The chorus asked the question: 'St Michael warred with the serpent, but who can tell one from the other?' Max asks us to ponder the question: 'How can religion enable a man to swear one thing at one time, and then, a brief moment later, to swear the opposite with equal vehemence, *and be equally sincere in both?'* All the intense black and white imagery of the set designs, which were stipulated very precisely by Max himself, rather than being left to the whim of individual designers and directors, serve this fundamental paradox, the one overwhelming question, of a man almost literally swearing black is white and white black. This is Max confronting religion with its alter ego, the religious faithful with their worst nightmares: if religious faith, potentially uplifting, can do to its adherents the things it clearly can do, who is to say whether it is good or evil?

It is significant that Max nowhere offers any hint of an answer to any of these questions, but merely leaves them for us to consider. The one thing he does make clear is his own response: an excoriating dislike of organized religion, of religiosity and of the established Churches. The ferocity of his distaste for these things is in no way diminished, but, on the contrary, rather highlighted and concentrated, by his scrupulous avoidance of overstatement in the opera.

Taken all round, Max was not very happy with the production of *Taverner* when it was staged at Covent Garden. Certain details were awry as a result of decisions being taken over his head. As the most flagrant example, the band of on-stage musicians was off-stage instead, in order to make room for the enormous set; but the effect was to destroy the contrast intended in those scenes in which Taverner himself is absent.

Max says, mildly enough, that 'Theatrical people tend to think that they know how things should be done, because they've always been done that way.' He admits to the feeling that the last thing anyone to do with the production was interested in was the music; but then, this would accord with the general attitude at the Royal Opera House, not least among the audiences: genuine music-lovers were then a relatively uncommon species in and around the purlieus of Covent Garden.

Taverner was very successful with the opera-going public at any rate, both in its first run, in July 1972, and later in the same year, when it was revived. It was revived again at Covent Garden in July 1983, when it was once again a great success and a near sell-out; and it has proved equally popular in Stockholm, where it was produced in 1984, and Boston, where it received its American premiere in 1986.

Meanwhile, life with the Fires was settling down into a pleasant pattern. Max wrote work after work for the group; meanwhile, they continued to commission pieces from new composers – the aspect of their work that many of the personnel of that day, including Steve Pruslin, for example, regard as among the most valuable of all. This work was helped by a grant from the London Orchestral Concert Board, chaired by Sir William Glock, which enabled the Fires to put on a regular annual series of three concerts at the Queen Elizabeth Hall. The full list of contemporary composers, most of them young, who received commissions from the Fires, makes very impressive reading.

By this time – mid-1972 – Max had already started discussions with his friends in the Orkneys about the possibilities of restoring Bunertoon, the little croft that he had glimpsed in the rain during his first visit to Hoy. Then it had been a roofless ruin, open to anything the elements chose to hurl at it – 'just walls, with sheepshit up to here', Max described it, extending his arm at shoulder-height – but it was wonderfully situated, looking out over the boiling cauldron of the Pentland Firth. Max could see both its potential as just the lonely, utterly off-the-beaten-track hideaway he was seeking as a place in which to compose, and its actual virtues: it might be in a ruined condition, but what remained of it was built in the manner of Hoy: three feet thick and *solid* – very necessary to keep out the ferocious winds coming off the Atlantic.

At that time the ruin, although it was on land farmed by Jack Rendall, was owned by the Laird, one Malcolm Stewart, an absentee landlord who could not really afford to maintain the buildings on his substantial estates. Shortly afterwards he made it over to the Hoy Trust, of which a number of local dignitaries, including some of Max's friends, were members. In 1976, however, Parliament passed the Crofting Act, which enabled sitting-tenant farmers in Jack Rendall's position to purchase the land they farmed and any buildings that happened to be on the land. Bunertoon was among the properties bought from the Hoy Trust by Jack Rendall. By the time the Act was passed Max had already taken advice, decided that Bunertoon was potentially renovatable and habitable, and taken out a lease on it. With the passing of the Act, he simply stopped paying his rent to the Hoy Trust and paid it directly to Jack Rendall instead – and continued to do so until a very satisfying day in July 1985, when he bought it outright for £2,500. From the moment when he had first expressed an interest in coming to live in Rackwick, Jack had, of course, been quietly giving Max the once-over on behalf of the rest of the very close, tight-knit little island community, where a newcomer who did not fit in, especially if he was an *arriviste* from the mainland or, even worse, England, would be a potentially explosive nuisance. The fact that Jack sold Max the croft readily and without a moment's hesitation indicates clearly that Max had passed the test.

All the same, the renovation took over two years to complete. Archie Bevan's two sons, then aged about fifteen and thirteen, did the really strenuous part, shovelling out the huge quantities of droppings left inside by sheep taking temporary refuge over many years in the standing walls from the colossal winds off the Pentland Firth. Then Max called in a friend from England, David Nelson, and between them they began to turn the ruin into a habitable cottage. Nelson did the difficult parts such as the woodwork; as Max wryly puts it, 'I was relegated to jobs like pointing walls.'

The work proceeded slowly but steadily. A new roof was put on – after Max's ancient gramophone had been lowered in through the hole where the roof was to go: the horn was so enormous that there was no other way of getting it into the building. Eventually the little house was complete, and ready for human occupation for the first time in many decades. Max moved in in 1974, and was delighted with his new home from the first day. It was always comfortable enough, though in the early years he had no electricity there. Instead he would compose by the light of oil lamps, and keep himself and the cottage warm with an open fire, on which he burned driftwood, gathered in huge quantities off the beach in the nearest cove, and coal, which he lugged up to the cliff-top from the nearest point of delivery – Jack's farm, a mile away.

Since then he has had electricity installed (in 1980), and the little home now boasts a CD player, an iron stove to replace the open fire, and storage heaters to back it up. The lavatory, which in the early days had been a chemical affair, now has a proper soakaway, and there is an electric shower unit as well, both of them in a shed, as stoutly built as the croft itself, reached from the cottage door by a series of stepping-stones leading through the garden, across a chattering little burn that bubbles and chuckles its way beside the croft and down the almost vertical cliff-face beyond. The only minor drawback with this arrangement is that the shed is roofed with a sheet of corrugated asbestos, and the corrugations make a perfect series of small entry points for the wind, which whistles eerily as it finds these entries and comes howling gleefully through them into the shed. Max's one concession to this is that in the winter he restricts his showering to once per two days, instead of once a day.

The most important thing about Bunertoon is that it provides what Max chose it for: peace, solitude and quiet. He does not get disturbed by holiday trippers; there are still very few air-force planes hurtling across the sky with their short-lived bolts of nerve-shattering sound; he looks out through his little window in its immensely thick embrasure, over his small plot of potatoes and a few other extra-hardy vegetables, then across a short sward of tough, curly, springy turf, and finally, over the lip of the steep cliff and straight out over the Pentland Firth. This ensures that although Max certainly has the quiet he needs, it is not silence. The Pentland Firth is one of the two roughest areas of sea in the world, alongside Cape Horn; a hundred feet or so below Max's cottage there thunders, all day and all night, all year round, a seething crucible of boiling sea, swept in by five tides and out by four more, churned and whipped by the vast winds of the region, and counterpointed by nothing except the lonely cries of birds. These are things that have become the very stuff of Max's music over the last couple of decades. To Max himself, they have become the daily stuff of life itself.

In the eventful year of 1972, Max had bought himself yet another home, once again in his favoured county of Dorset. This was Eccliffe Mill, near the small town of Gillingham. The mill was in need of a lot of work to make it habitable, and this proceeded throughout the next few years. The complicated saga of Max's various homes comes to a reasonable degree of resolution in 1974. In that year the renovation of Bunertoon was completed, and Max was able to move in, relinquishing his lease on 26 Fitzroy Square. He did manage to live in the mill for periods while it was, strictly speaking, still under renovation: he spent a part of 1973 there, writing a major work for the Fires, *Miss Donnithorne's Maggot*, at very high speed. But the mill was to serve its real purpose later on.

The Fires, meanwhile, were serving their original purposes, providing an outlet for Max's creativity, an opening and a glimmer of hope in the arid musical landscape of Britain for young aspiring composers, and generally operating at the cutting edge of contemporary music. They had now been in existence, in their earlier incarnation as the Pierrot Players, then as the Fires, for over five years, and they had remained remarkably constant: they suffered a couple of hiccups over the percussionist, Tristan Fry, having dropped out in the first year, and his replacement, Barry Quinn, in 1971. But with the arrival of Gary Kettel to replace him, the line-up was complete, and was not to change again until 1976.

The manager had changed, however, to noticeable effect. James Murdoch, flamboyant and inspirational, a born salesman, publicist and entrepreneur, had flown the group by the seat of his pants, and done so with brilliance and flair. On his return to Australia the group found Louise Honeyman to take over the helm, and her style, though as different from that of Murdoch as it could have been, was vastly effective and probably, by the time she took over, very necessary. She was efficient, able to deal with bureaucrats and bureaucracy, unflappable, in short, the ideal manager. Her capable management was a god-send during this period, because it was now that the Fires first began to tour extensively, both in the provinces and abroad. Touring to the British regions was made possible by grants provided by the Contemporary Music Network, a newly-formed off-shoot of the Arts Council; the foreign trips were mostly paid for and run by festivals or other private sponsors.

Despite all the moving about and his busy life as a member of a well-travelled concert group, Max still managed to turn out five new works during each of the next couple of years, and seven in 1975. The most striking thing about this period is the marked increase in the number of pieces with an Orcadian influence. Thus in 1973, among a number of new realizations of early music, he produced also a delightful set of *Renaissance Scottish Dances*. These, though not of strictly Orcadian provenance, still marked the powerful influence of Scotland and things Scottish on Max, which was to become more and more important to him as time went on. They are rumbustious pieces, full of the sounds of folk fiddlers and bagpipers. But that year also saw two major pieces with distinctly Orkney origins. *Stone Litany* is a cross between a symphony and a song cycle, and has been described as the most powerful evocation of Scotland in music since Mendelssohn's *Hebrides* Overture. *Fiddlers at the Wedding* is unequivocally a song cycle, settings of more poems from George Mackay Brown's *Fishermen with Ploughs*, from which Max had set his first work with an Orkney flavour, *From Stone to Thorn*.

Stone Litany is subtitled *Runes from the House of the Dead*, and is quite literally a setting of runes carved, as graffiti, on the stone walls of a prehistoric edifice on the Mainland island of Orkney. This mysterious place, called the Maeshowe, is a burial chamber designed and constructed with quite incredible ingenuity. It has an inner chamber, reached by a tunnel, and this is so laid out that there is only one day of the year – the winter solstice, the shortest day – when the sun is able to shine straight down the tunnel and bathe the chamber with light.

The piece is full of strange sounds, helped by the presence in the large range of percussion of a flexatone, a device that makes a weird whistling sound, not unlike an ondes martenot, and a glass harmonica, consisting of wine or brandy glasses filled to set levels to give each glass its own key. These glasses can produce a great variety of eerie, uncanny effects, from a sustained mooing like a lightship to a high-pitched ringing sound. The array of weird sounds helps to suggest the mystery and bone-chilling antiquity of the Maeshowe; but the piece is also full of the sounds of the sea and the ever-present wind, and thus in some ways foreshadows the First and Second Symphonies that were to come a few years later.

The runes set in this work are thought to date from the twelfth century AD, hundreds of years after the construction of the astonishing chamber itself, and were carved as graffiti by invading Viking soldiers, bored as sentries have been since time immemorial. The piece is in four purely orchestral sections and four for voice and orchestra. Max chose to set them in Orkney Norn, the original language of Orkney, etymologically a variant of Old Norse; so it is clear that the words are not intended to be of any importance in listening to the piece. It is, however, pleasing to hope that his choice of precisely which bits of this ancient graffiti to set was influenced at least a little by the last, which reads simply, 'Max the Mighty carved these runes'. The strangeness of the sounds and the utter unfamiliarity of the words contribute to the overall effect of other-worldliness of the piece as a whole, and the voice is to be thought of as another instrument of the orchestra, contributing its own eerie effects which combine with the rest. These are especially noticeable in the opening, purely orchestral section, full of low tones, with much atmospheric work for the clarinet, and the eerie sounds of the flexatone wonderfully evoking the high wind keening in the scanty grass of the islands, and in the final section, in which the mezzo-soprano soloist intones 'Max the Mighty . . .' in a tremendous parabola of pure sound over an expressive accompaniment of mainly harp and the tuned wine glasses to convey at once the vast open skies and the deep, self-contained and private mystery of the place.

The other large-scale piece with an Orcadian background from the same year (1973) is a much simpler affair: *Fiddlers at the Wedding* is a setting of a further selection of poems from George Mackay Brown, these being put into the mouth of an itinerant tinker, who sings of the harsh, uncharitable life he leads, dealing in nothing but the barest essentials. The cycle, like *From Stone to Thorn* before it, has the shape of individual songs interspersed with interludes for the unusual and pleasing instrumental group, which consists of alto flute, mandolin, guitar and a most unorthodox group of percussion. The latter includes a set of tuned brandy snifters, this time placed on the skin of a medium-pedal kettle-drum. The overall effect of this highly ingenious instrumentation is extraordinary, radiant and sweet-toned.

The following year saw a stronger invasion still of influences from Scotland in general and Orkney in particular in Max's music: *All Sons of Adam* and *Si Quis Diligit Me* were realizations of early Scottish motets, and a Church of Scotland version of Psalm 124 was another, more substantial one. The major work with Orcadian background, however, was a piece inspired by a tragedy on Hoy, in which the last two children born in the village of Rackwick were drowned, leaving the village almost depopulated. The poems, 'The Drowning Brothers' and 'Dead Fires', by Mackay Brown, were set on either side of a brief solo for the accompanying instrument, a guitar.

The most important new work to appear in 1974, though, was another piece, composed for the Fires and Mary Thomas, and given its first performance by them in March, in the Town Hall of Adelaide, where Max had been Visiting Professor and through which they were passing on tour.

The new work was *Miss Donnithorne's Maggot*, and was a particular source of pleasure for Max because it offered him the chance to collaborate once again with his old friend Randolph Stow (known to all as Mick).

Miss Donnithorne is almost always thought of as the mad king's other half, so to speak. They are paired on record, and very frequently in concert performances as well. There is nothing surprising about this: they are natural companion-pieces. They are about the same length, and together make up a nice symmetrical concert programme. One is for a male, the other for a female singer; and they are complementary in other ways, too. But the contrasts between them, and the very real differences, are more significant than the evident similarities.

To get the similarities out of the way first: they are both portrayals of madness, albeit of very different manifestations. Both require a supremely agile voice, neither being a piece for conventional singing. Their words and music are written by the same team. And there the similarities end. The differences are much more interesting. In the first place, *Miss Donnithorne* is a much simpler, more straightforward, piece than the *Eight Songs*. Miss Eliza Emily Donnithorne was an Australian woman whose sad story formed the true-life prototype of Dickens's Miss Havisham, the old lady in *Great Expectations* who was jilted at the altar, and whose house remained ever after exactly as it had been made ready for the wedding reception and bridal night that never happened. Miss Donnithorne was engaged to be married to a naval officer, was jilted like Miss Havisham, and fled into the same kind of fugue, letting her wedding cake decompose, wearing the rags of her wedding dress for years and living as a hermit in her house, talking through a crack in the front door on the occasions when it could not be avoided.

The two biggest differences between the two works are, first, the musical style, in particular that of the singer, and second, the attitude towards madness adopted by the writer of the words.

The role of the mad king requires a voice of extraordinarily extended range, and the result can scarcely be called singing at all. Miss Donnithorne, by contrast, is a comparatively 'normal' part. The influence of *Pierrot Lunaire* is very strong indeed, not altogether surprisingly, since Max conceived the piece as a vehicle for Mary Thomas's extravagant vocal and histrionic gifts, and Mary's greatest success had long been her triumphant rendering of Pierrot. So, although the part entails plenty of squawks, squeals and other special effects for those who like them, it is far closer to *bel canto* than to the extended-voice requirements of the other piece. Although it is not the *Sprechgesang* of *Pierrot*, it sounds very much like it.

As for the poet's approach to his subject, the *Eight Songs* are presented as unrelieved tragedy and pathos. There is no humour at all in the piece. Miss Donnithorne, by contrast, is very funny indeed throughout. She is also often exceedingly rude, in a pleasing and amusing way, as for example when, affecting old-maidish shock and fits of the vapours, she actually takes an earthy (in Steve Pruslin's word, an 'unladylike') interest in sexual obscenities hooted through her window by a couple of youths; and the work ends with a large sexually explicit pun.

None of this is to say that there is no compassion for the sad figure of Miss Donnithorne herself; it is present in the sensitivity of the in-strumentation, and still more, perhaps, in the alternation in the mezzo part between tormented cries and whimperings and the straight sung parts, closer to conventional *bel canto*. The words themselves clearly show the vast compassion felt by the poet for his pitiful subject, as the music does for the composer through the sensitivity of the instrumenta-tion. The difference between this work and the *Eight Songs* is that in *Donnithorne* the compassion is offset by the rich opportunities for humour and satisfying, earthy crudity. The work was commissioned by Anthony Steel for a series of performances at the 1974 Adelaide Festival of the Arts, and was first performed there in March of that year. Since then, it has become one of Max's most popular and most frequently performed works.

By the end of 1974 this period of transition was coming to a natural and peaceful conclusion. The renovation at Eccliffe Mill was not yet complete, but Bunertoon, which was much more important, was now ready, and Max at last had the sequestered retreat that he had dreamed of. In 1975 this produced results: of seven new works produced that year, six were Scottish-influenced; and no fewer than five of them were directly inspired by Max's Orkney surroundings.

My Lady Lothian's Lilte was a short dance movement for the Fires with an obbligato part for Mary Thomas's mezzo-soprano, based on an anonymous Scottish original. Then there were three short and very beautiful pieces for solo instruments, all based on phrases taken from poems by George Mackay Brown: *The Kestrel Paced Round the Sun* was written for Judith Pearce, the Fires' flautist, *The Seven Brightnesses* for Alan Hacker's clarinet, and *The Door of the Sun* for Duncan Druce on viola. *Stevie's Ferry to Hoy* commemorates Stevie Mowatt, protégé and successor of Ginger Brown, who pilots his tiny vessel, *Scapa Ranger*, expertly between Stromness and Hoy jetty every morning and afternoon, often with Max aboard. Like the other three, it is a very brief but highly evocative piece, this time for piano solo, and aimed at young learners. It was written for Anne Bevan, who was learning the piano at the time.

Max wrote one other piece in this year of 1975, unique in his enormous output so far, and the only one dating from this year that was wholly without any specific Scottish flavour or influence. This was *Three Studies for Percussion*, written for the pupils of Gosforth High School, Northumberland. It is a short piece (five minutes' duration) for eleven percussionists, and features four xylophones, two glockenspiels, bass and deep bass variants of a mysterious instrument called a metallophone, a small wood block, temple block and suspended cymbal. Max describes it as 'bristling with technical difficulties', but adds that children have a great natural feel for rhythm, which is still largely untapped.

Just one other work was composed that year; but it was a major one, and an extraordinary one. *Ave Maris Stella* was written in response to a commission from the Bath Festival, and is inscribed 'In memoriam Hans Juda', the much-loved treasurer of the Fires of London, a lifelong devotee of chamber music, and a true friend of the Fires from their beginning.

The piece is an extended meditation on a medieval plainsong of the same title, set by several early composers, including Max's favourites, Dunstable and Monteverdi. It is a highly atmospheric work, with much of the character of a nocturne about it. It begins with an evocation of morning, with unearthly sounds growing out of the silence just before the dawn. A slow, quietly dignified lament on the cello is gradually augmented by the other instruments until the clarinet portrays the crowing of the cock. Then comes the feature of the piece that makes it unusual, and anticipates the symphony that was to follow: the marimba, a mellow-toned member of the tuned percussion, joins in the delicate interweaving of the melodies, and gradually becomes more and more prominent. In the piece as a whole it is at least as important as any of the other instruments, and indeed takes a dominant role throughout much of the piece.

The whole piece is composed around a device that was to become more and more central to Max's compositional techniques from this point onwards: the so-called magic square. This is a mathematical device which offers the composer a wide variety of ways to manipulate a basic stock of pitches and note-lengths: it serves the composer, rather as the palette serves the painter.

Magic squares are well documented, and this is not an appropriate place to discuss them at any great length: like many other such devices, they are of central importance to the composer, but of little to the listener.

The magic square may perhaps be said to stand in relation to the finished piece of music as builder's scaffolding stands to a finished building: the building could not have been created without it, but by the time the outside spectator – or listener – comes along to appreciate the result, the scaffolding has served its purpose, and both it and its influence on the complete work of creation are invisible. The piece of music is there to be heard and to speak for itself: the aids to its creation are things that the listeners do not need to know about and the composer does not want them to know about. This really ought to go without saying, but it is something that many pundits and self-styled experts on modern music forget.

The piece proceeds through a series of developments on the plainsong, which is not itself heard until near the end of the work, as happens very frequently in Max – for example, in *St Thomas Wake*, *Worldes Blis* and many other pieces built round plainchants or other ready-made musical sources. The work ends as it began, with a movement of eerie, unearthly quiet, which breaks out at the very end into a single great plaintive cry on the flute, backed heavily by the others, and then fades into the silence from which it was born.

There are two other things of note about *Ave Maris Stella* – apart, of course, from its stature as a masterpiece of modern chamber music: first, it was composed with the intention of being performed without a conductor. This makes the point most emphatically that, big-boned though the piece is, clearly though it anticipates the towering orchestral works that were to come, it is unequivocally a work of chamber music. Second, the score is prefaced by a short Greek epigraph. This sets out a message to the reader – and, by implication, the listener – to pursue wisdom and to fight against philistinism. This will, as we shall see, be an increasing preoccupation of Max's, including in a political context. It also highlights an aspect of his personality, as expressed through his music and in other ways: he is, and always has been, an intensely moral man and composer.

Ave Maris Stella represents a crossroads in Max's career in many ways. It looks back over the Fires' lifetime, celebrating the virtuosity of the group as it lovingly recalls its dedicatee, Hans Juda, who had been with them all along the way. It is based on a plainchant of the same name; but the plainchant is less immediately evident to the listener than in many earlier works. It is a big piece – in many ways, a huge one: it is chamber music, but it is writ large; as such, it anticipates by a year Max's first symphony, which he once described, provocatively, as 'nothing more than chamber music writ large'. Most important of all, it was the first major piece that Max actually composed in Bunertoon, often sitting gazing out over the Pentland Firth, and, at night or during the evenings, poring over the paper by the gentle yellow light of oil lamps. In this it marked the opening of an era, a phase which is still in progress, and is probably the most important in Max's life so far.

Ave Maris Stella also, particularly in its birthing in Bunertoon and its anticipation of the first symphony, acted as a staging post on the way to the year 1976. And if 1969 had been the *annus mirabilis* of Max's youth, the crucible in which all his experience, his long and rigorous apprenticeship and his overflowing talent were heated to the white-hot temperatures of *Eight Songs, St Thomas Wake* and *Worldes Blis*, 1976 was perhaps the year when he advanced into his maturity, if not with a swagger, at any rate with a pronounced air of confidence. In 1976 Max came into his own, and not only in a musical sense.

8 ~ Pax Orcadiensis

Towards the end of 1975, then, Max was settled happily on Hoy, with Bunertoon established as his principal residence, but also, which meant much more, as his home. He still needed a pied-à-terre in London, however, having vacated the house in Fitzroy Square. So, in October, he bought 151 Queen Alexandra Mansions, Judd Street, near King's Cross Station (and so handy for when he got off the train from Inverness after coming south from Hoy).

This coincided with another change that was to be of great significance later on in his life: Judy Arnold arrived to take over the management of the Fires. She was Max's first visitor at his new flat in Judd Street to discuss the possibility with him that October, and remembers that there was not a stick of furniture in the place, and they sat on the carpeted floor.

Judy Arnold had been on the musical scene for some time. She counted many musicians among her friends, including Alfred Brendel, who often stayed at her house for weeks on end on his frequent visits to London. Another was the fine pianist André Tchaikowsky, who also lived with the Arnolds for three years, and for whom Judy acted as agent-cum-manager for a while. In 1968 John Amis invited her to Dartington to look after the artists 'as a sort of holiday job'. He repeated the invitation in 1970, and it was then that Judy met Harrison Birtwistle. He asked her to consider acting as his manager, doing for him what James Murdoch was doing for Max – as we have seen already, Birtwistle neither liked nor trusted Murdoch, and was in any case already beginning to contemplate parting company from the Fires.

Judy thought about it, and indeed gave it a try for a short period; but after about a month she decided that the relationship would not work. Before she abandoned the idea, however, she had been given a formal introduction to Max. Nothing in particular happened for some time, but then in 1975 she was asked to take over the group of supporters known as the Friends of the Fires of London, and it was very soon after this that she was sitting on the floor of Max's bare apartment, being asked to take over the management of the Fires themselves, and to act as Max's manager. The original suggestion emanated from Steve Pruslin, who was already a friend of Judy's. She took the job, and has remained with Max, his most loyal supporter, advocate, champion and shield ever since. At the same time her husband, Michael Arnold, a non-practising barrister and a formidable businessman, took over Max's finances, handling the sale and purchase of all his subsequent properties, his tax affairs, and so on. For many, Judy has been a dragon in the path to Max himself; from the beginning of their association with Max both the Arnolds have always been highly controversial figures, with a capacity for arousing high passions in the people with whom they deal.

Thus 1976 began on a note of starting afresh. It was to prove quite an eventful year, apart from the musical developments it was to usher in.

First, the renovation work was completed at the mill at Eccliffe, and Max's parents took up residence there. They had continued to live at their old address in Wyville Drive, Swinton, as long as Tom Davies was working. He had retired in 1964, however, and, like many from the great conurbations of industrial Lancashire, the Davieses had migrated to the quiet of the East Anglian coast and taken a bungalow in Cromer, which they named 'Wyville' in honour of their old road. Now, however, they moved into the converted mill in Dorset, and were to remain there until almost the end of their lives.

Max was composing fluently and well. Works completed in 1976 included three voluntaries for organ, a delightful realization of a dance by the sixteenth-century Scottish composer William Kinloch, *Kinloche His Fantassie*, and something of an oddity: *Anakreontika*, a setting of five brief lyrics in the style of the poet Anakreon from the late Hellenistic period, a warm, sultry evocation of the time and place, full of Mediterranean sunshine and romance, and something of a maverick among the newly released works glimmering in the pale pastel shades of the Orkneys.

A big, important piece from 1976 was *The Blind Fiddler*, yet another loving setting of George Mackay Brown's poems, this time from his collection, *A Spell for Green Corn*. For the third time the fourteen Stations of the Cross are represented (it should not be forgotten that Mackay Brown is a Roman Catholic). The piece also entails the seven deadly sins and the seven last words from the Cross. The seven songs are put into the mouth of a blind itinerant Orcadian fiddler, and are interspersed with seven dances. The instrumentation, for an ensemble of, again, seven, complements the songs, mutating from a dark, eerie beginning through a series of emotions, some lighter, some tense and frenetic, some deathly, to a final unearthly calm.

The Blind Fiddler fits comfortably into what may be thought of as Max's Orcadian canon – words by Mackay Brown, and the familiar religious undertones. The next work completed, his Symphony No. 1, did not fit into any scheme yet defined: it was a new departure, and one of the most significant of Max's career. Max had written a few works for full orchestra up to this point: the *Second Taverner Fantasia*, *St Thomas Wake*, *Worldes Blis* – the last being a symphony in all but name. But he had waited until his late thirties before embarking on this, traditionally the most challenging of all musical forms, but the result was worth waiting for. The piece was commissioned by the Philharmonia Orchestra, who gave the premiere – although that was not to be until a good deal later, in February of 1978. It marked a new beginning in Max's development as a composer: a shift in emphasis away from pieces which, however large they may have been in conception and in breadth of imagination, were essentially ensemble pieces, written mostly with the Fires in mind, to altogether bigger works for full orchestra. It also marked the first step in what Paul Griffiths has since proclaimed 'the most important symphonic cycle since Shostakovich'.

Max once declared, at some time during his expressionist period when he was pouring out a torrent of chamber and music theatre pieces for the Fires, that he did not think he would ever feel it necessary to write large-scale works for full orchestral forces. He was wrong, and this first symphony was the first work to demonstrate the fact. It is a mighty piece, almost an hour in duration, and follows the conventional symphonic plan of four movements. The second is a scherzo, which heaves itself from a slow, churning beginning like some monstrous sea beast emerging from beneath the surface of a heavy swell. The third is a magnificent and majestic adagio, in which the influence of Mahler is clearly audible throughout. The first movement and the finale are both giant seascapes, magnificent evocations of the sounds Max hears every day from his front garden at Bunertoon: we hear the waves in all their moods, splashing happily on the flat grey rocks in the bay below, crashing thunderously against the walls of red rock, slapping and gurgling through honeycombs of holes and flumes; and always there is an accompaniment of the scream of the wind off the Pentland Firth and the plaintive cries of seabirds. By this time Max had already written a substantial body of Orkney-influenced works, but most of them had had the words of George Mackay Brown to support them; in this colossal piece he produced for the first time an extended piece of 'pure' music to represent his island home, and it is a triumph. With the first symphony, it may legitimately be felt, Max came home.

This seminal work was also the first fruit of a new direction taken by Max in *Ave Maris Stella* the previous year, in the prominence given to the tuned percussion. This symphony is scored for a large orchestra, though not a huge one; but its percussion section is unusual, in that while there are no drums, conventional cymbals or other instruments commonly found there (apart from the timpani, which are most emphatically present, with a very prominent part), there are several tuned instruments, all with their own highly distinctive sounds. These are the marimba that had been used to such high effect in the earlier piece, tubular bells, the flexatone that Max had used once before, in *Stone Litany*, glockenspiel and crotales, which are brass or bronze discs with central domes, giving off a delicate ring of definite pitch: they are sometimes called antique cymbals. All of these have their moments, throughout the giant work.

In all, the Symphony No. 1 is full of the sounds of the sea, and its colouring is distinctive: it is all flashing iridescence, all silvers and quicksilvers, flashes of brass and gold and bronze and pewtery glints, with just an occasional hint, as if reflected in water, of the subdued pastels and greys of the place that inspired it. The lurid primary colours of the expressionist works are nowhere even hinted at.

In a radio interview some years later, Max described this symphony, gigantic construction though it is, as 'chamber music writ large', and one can certainly see what he means, at least in the slow prelude to the second movement, which is a plangent evocation of the play of light on a calm sea. That the same piece can encompass also the overt, yearning sensuality of the Mahler-like chorale in the third movement is a fine indication of the conflict, or tension, that is an essential ingredient of Max's music – a factor pointed out, for example, by the composer Gerard McBurney, who knows Max and his music very well and is an exceptionally acute and articulate commentator on it. Here, he says, is the conflict between baroque sensuality and North country puritanism: an extreme down-to-earthism, coming out in the distaste for bright colours.

No doubt there is something in this; but it seems equally legitimate to view the tension as the essential piece of grit necessary to produce the pearl; and there seems no reason why the lack of primary colours should be ascribed to a distaste for them. Nor does there seem to be any reason why we may not feel that the sea, which directly inspired much of this symphony, simply generated a different range of brightnesses, more metallic and gleaming, rather than a bright and gaudy matt finish.

Max had been working on this symphony, on and off, for five years before he completed it in 1976. No one would have expected him, then, to start work very soon on another – but that was what he did. In 1979 he was commissioned by the Boston Symphony Orchestra to compose a large piece for their centenary celebrations in 1981. A particularly pleasing aspect of this commission was that although there were to be several other works associated with the centenary, Max's was the one that was to be taken to major cities in the USA as a showpiece for the virtuosity of the orchestra. When Max and Judy Arnold met Seiji Ozawa and the orchestra's manager, Tom Morris, in Edinburgh, Judy asked why Max had been so honoured. Morris replied that the choice had been easy, because his name had been top of every member of the advisory panel's list of possibles. On receipt of the commission, Max immediately began the first sketches for his Symphony No. 2. A good deal else was to happen, however, before it was finished.

The next significant event in Max's life came with a commission from the BBC. This was for a large-scale work to be performed as part of the celebrations for Queen Elizabeth II's Silver Jubilee the following year, 1977. Unusually, the BBC did not stipulate that the piece must be first performed by BBC forces, or on BBC premises. Max decided that the work would be an opera. It would not be on the same large scale as *Taverner*, but rather a chamber opera, for it would be for performance by the Fires; it would be on an Orcadian theme: that of the betrayal of the patron saint of the Orkney Islands, St Magnus; and it would be performed, he decided in a sudden flash of inspiration, in the cathedral dedicated to that very saint, St Magnus's Cathedral, Kirkwall. Thus the St Magnus Festival was conceived.

Max had already expressed his thanks in music more than once to the Orkneys and their people for taking him to their hearts, but it was this tripartite decision, he says with certainty, that clinched his relationship with them. He took his idea straight to the Bevans, his closest friends in the islands. How did they feel, he asked, about a festival, right there on Orkney?

The Bevans were all for it. As the obvious next step, they took it to the local Arts Club committee, fully expecting them to hurl themselves into the project with the same enthusiasm with which they were already fired themselves. This was indeed the response of one member of the committee, Norman Mitchell, then the music master at Kirkwall Grammar School and organist at the Cathedral. The rest of the committee, however, unanimously turned up their noses. At first sight this is an extraordinary reaction to such an idea, especially when it was suggested by such an illustrious figure, who would be able to lend prestige to the festival. Max, however, explains it away simply enough: he assumes that they were snooty about the idea because they had not thought of it themselves. This seems likely enough. It sounds as though Max was dismissed as a typical pushy arriviste, trying to shoulder his way into a position of central importance in his adopted home. But Max himself throws another light on it when he reveals that most of the committee were themselves not Orcadians, but outsiders. Presumably no one hates an arriviste more fervently than another arriviste who happens to have been in residence a little longer.

The result was that Max, Mitchell, the Bevans and George Mackay Brown decided straightaway to put on the festival themselves. They spent hours sitting in the Bevans' house, endlessly discussing it over pints of Archie Bevan's home-brewed beer. The festival already had an assured centrepiece with Max's planned opera, and the decision was quickly taken: Max and Mitchell were elected the first co-directors. Satisfied and very pleased that he was going to be able to express something of the sense of homecoming that the Orkneys had given him, Max went away and began work on the opera which was to become *The Martyrdom of St Magnus*. The work went well and quickly. He finished the opera during 1976, and conducted it, triumphantly, at the first St Magnus Festival the following June, standing beside a pillar in which the skull of St Magnus was walled up, cleft almost in two by the axe used in his execution.

Before that historic occasion, however, there was another important event, this time a rather sad one. The Fires of London broke up after ten years together.

The first to go was one of the founding members, the clarinettist Alan Hacker. He left the group in mid-1976, and in his case there was a single, clearly identifiable cause for departure. By this time the Fires were spending a good deal more time on foreign tours than in earlier years, and 1976 saw them embarking on an arduous – though very successful – five-week tour of North America. These tours were something of a triumph of organization for Judy Arnold: she expended vast amounts of her exuberant energies on organizing them, and although she was much criticized for certain aspects of the planning by the members of the group – and indeed still is, when one discusses those days with the former players – the tours were still considerable victories against all the odds, in particular financial odds: money was always extremely tight, and the 1976 tour was no exception.

Since 1966 Hacker had been 80 per cent paralysed, and was permanently confined to a wheelchair. It was virtually impossible for the other players to take care of him adequately in the rigorous conditions of touring, so his eldest daughter looked after him. In his own words, 'I was put in the position by Judy Arnold of accepting an American tour not only without a fee for my daughter but [with] the need for me to pay her expenses myself.'

This is not quite fair to Judy Arnold, whose version of the events is rather different. She inherited the tour from her predecessor, who had

Joyce Palin, aged about fourteen   Eric Guest, aged eighteen

The Manchester Group, 1956. Front, left to right: Alexander Goehr, Audrey Goehr, John Dow; back, left to right: Harrison Birtwistle, John Ogdon, Elgar Howarth, Max

Max and the original Fires of London. Back: Max, Louise Honeyman (manager), Timothy Walker (guitar), Gary Kettel (percussion); centre: Jennifer Ward Clarke (cello), Judith Pearce (flutes), Duncan Druce (violin), Steve Pruslin (keyboards); front: Murray Melvin (actor, speaker) holding Ilian Rainbow Walker, Alan Hacker (clarinets), Mary Thomas

Max and the crew of *Taverner*, Covent Garden, 1983. Above: Ragnar Ulfung; below, left to right: Edward Downes, Robert Ornbo, Max, Michael Geliot, Ralph Koltai

The Fires, second generation. Left to right: Rosemary Furniss (violin),
Jonathan Williams (cello), Greg Knowles (percussion), Judy Arnold
(manager), Steve Pruslin (keyboards), Philippa Davies (flutes),
David Campbell (clarinets), and Max

A scene from *The Lighthouse*. Left to right: David Wilson-Johnson,
Michael Rippon, Neil Mackie

Outside the renovated and habitable Bunertoon

With George Mackay Brown

In the kitchen at Bunertoon, with the monster gramophone

Aboard Stevie's ferry, the *Scapa Ranger*

Max and his parents outside Buckingham Palace after his award of the CBE, 1981

With his neighbour, ally and friend, David Hutchinson (Hutch), Rackwick, 1993

Children of North Walls School performing *Songs of Hoy*, Hoy, 1992

Class of 1993: with the young composers of the Hoy Summer School. Co-instructor, the eminent composer Judith Weir, third from the right

With György Pauk and the RPO rehearsing the Violin Concerto

Max at his desk in Bunertoon, looking out over the Pentland Firth

negotiated an overall fee for it, and at the same time she inherited a substantial operating deficit. This made it impossible, on simple financial grounds, for anyone to accompany the tour to look after Alan Hacker. In addition, however, Judy says that she had in any case spent much time pleading with Hacker not to attempt the tour at all, because it would be so gruelling that he would not be able to stand the strain of it. The schedule necessitated catching planes at six o'clock virtually every morning, and Hacker had to rise two hours earlier than everyone else to get ready. For these very reasons he had not accompanied the Fires on their tour of Australia in 1974, and, as Judy adds, a tour of Australia is nothing like as gruelling as one to the States.

Some of the others then got very protective of Hacker, and suggested that the Fires was only the sum of its members, and that if any one of them wanted to go on a date – or, *ergo*, a tour – and couldn't, the date should not be accepted. This, Judy reckoned and still reckons, was a bit thick, since one of the members proposing it had not gone on an earlier tour because of pregnancy, and Hacker himself, as mentioned, had not gone on the previous tour of Australia. At this point, however, Max made a decisive contribution: the Fires, he said very quietly, would go to the States; they would go under the name of the Fires of London, and they would take whatever players were agreed on by the group's Council of Management. Shortly afterwards Alan Hacker solved the problem of what to do about him by accepting a teaching job and thus becoming the first of the old brigade to leave the group.

By the end of the tour to the USA several of the others had also made their decisions to leave. One had spent the entire tour desperately missing her infant child, and had already declared that she would never again undertake such a tour; another was already mulling over an offer of a teaching post, and yet a third had already, before the tour, decided to leave when they got home from it, because of domestic problems.

There is thus some conflict between the versions of the story told by Judy Arnold and the members of the group. Max himself, when asked about the incident, is in no doubt whatever. He says, simply and flatly, 'There was no money. Judy couldn't conjure money out of thin air any more than anyone else.' This is only one example of a phenomenon that was to be seen more and more frequently as time went on, with one or other member of the Fires or their auxiliary forces complaining about their treatment at Judy's hands; but in almost every case Max, if questioned about the incident, is found to back Judy's side of the story without hesitation. Judy was often unpopular with the Fires; but, as Steve Pruslin points out, very often the griping member of the group would be strolling in Vienna, or Bogota, or New York, or some other interesting or exotic place as he got his gripe off his chest, and the truth was that without Judy's formidable organizing skills the player in question would simply not have been there to moan about her. Furthermore, Judy would never have dreamed of taking a major decision, such as the shedding of a player, without getting clearance from Max himself. In other words, Max used her, all the time, as a hatchet man to do his dirty work for him, and as a protective shield for himself – in short, he used her to do precisely the jobs that a good manager should do.

Whatever the rights and wrongs of the case, it so happened that just as he was encountering this difficulty over the Fires' tour, Hacker was offered a job by Wilfrid Mellers in the Music Department of York University. Understandably, he took it gratefully, though with a good deal of sadness, feeling that he had very little choice.

He was quickly replaced by David Campbell, and the tour then went ahead. It was a triumphant success, though also a gruelling ordeal for all concerned. Mary Thomas says that there were many moments during the five weeks when she thought she was going to expire overnight – especially, for example, when the itinerary took them in the space of three days from a balmy Los Angeles to frozen Vancouver, then back to Santa Barbara.

The group carried on with substantially the original line-up until January 1977, which was the last time they played together. There was then an interval until their next tour in April. It was another five-week blitz, this time of South America, and by the time they set off there were only two of the original Fires left, apart from Max: the ever-loyal Steve Pruslin, and Mary Thomas.

No one could suggest any immediate cause for the sudden exodus. The most likely explanation is that suggested by Mary Thomas: most of the original line-up had now been with the group for close to ten years, and they had become stale. Certainly some of them were getting a little restive at playing virtually nothing professionally but Max and very young composers who had impressed him. Some of the group were keen to branch out in the direction of, for example, Boulez, whose work was hardly ever considered; others, for example the cellist Jennifer Ward Clarke, wanted to try a move towards early music. *Tout court*, it was probably a case of all good things having to come to an end.

Among the new faces David Campbell had been joined in the interim by Sebastian Bell on flutes, Beverley Davison on violin and viola, Lesley Jones on cello and Gregory Knowles as percussionist. Of these only two,

Campbell and Knowles, were to last for any great length of time, so the second line-up was distinctly a caretaker affair.

However, the Fires took on the intimidating prospect of the tour of South America and Mexico with a will, and despite the usual kind of difficulties associated with travel in exotic parts of the globe, managed to turn it into another very successful adventure. The only really unpleasant mishap was the serious illness of the new cellist, Lesley Jones. At some point they all went down with a stomach upset, but mostly they shrugged it off. The unfortunate cellist, however, suffered a serious attack of dysentery in Mexico, early on the itinerary, and was unable to play again on the tour. For a time Max worked rapid miracles, sitting up at nights rewriting *Miss Donnithorne*, among other pieces, for performance minus the cello part, until they could issue a Mayday for a replacement cellist when they arrived in Bogota. The replacement, Marilyn Sansom, behaved with admirable stoicism – not to say heroism – in the circumstances. Max's desperate phone call woke her at about five in the morning. 'Can you come to Bogota?' he asked urgently. She asked no unnecessary questions, and was on the plane at nine that morning.

The trip was not without other incidents. Max wrote to Eric Guest from Bogota about a bomb that had just gone off at a political meeting round the corner, and to say that they were all confined to their hotel, it being census day, with the streets full of soldiers with machine-guns. 'But', he added, 'it's been a marvellous trip.'

There were only two more trips on this scale: in 1980 the Fires spent five weeks in Australia and New Zealand, and in 1985 they returned to North America for their last big tour. There were numerous shorter tours to Europe, plus any number of visits for individual concerts, which took them, all in all, to almost every country west of the Iron Curtain, and to at least two on the far side of it.

These tours were all successful, in that the audiences were appreciative and avid for more wherever they went. They were also uniformly exhausting. Suffice to say that the trips were a predictable mixture of minor and occasionally major health worries; of rising at appallingly early hours of the day and hundred-yard sprint records broken as everyone ran for planes; of bureaucracy, bloody-mindedness and obstructionism, problems with contracts and protocol in Iron Curtain countries.

There were also little local difficulties rather more specific to a travelling percussion department. One piece, for example, requires a plunger with a rubber suction-head; used with a bucket of cold water, this can make a very satisfying slurping noise. It was vital, however, that both the bucket and the head of the plunger were of the correct size, otherwise they produced altogether the wrong kind of slurp. Another awkward special requirement was for a bicycle wheel, which had to be spun against something like a ruler to produce a fast rat-a-tat-tatting noise. Obviously, a bicycle wheel was of no use for this purpose unless it was attached to a bicycle, so they had to scour the crew and anyone else who happened to be about to scrounge the loan of someone's ancient boneshaker for the performance. The most demanding part of the exercise was explaining, usually to someone who spoke nothing but demotic South American Spanish, and in a heavy local dialect at that, precisely what the bike was wanted for.

On one occasion, again in South America, a day began with their British Council minder upending a large cup of coffee in Max's lap. Quite apart from the agony this caused, it necessitated a quick emergency change to a reserve pair of trousers. This achieved, everyone boarded the plane to go on to the next destination. The flight was bumpy. Judy Arnold, who was sitting beside Max, succumbed to the stomach upset that had been doing the rounds of the group, and passed out; but not, alas, before being suddenly and spectacularly sick – in Max's lap. Whether he had a third pair of trousers on hand is not recorded. Nor, probably mercifully, is what he said.

There were other incidents to enliven the tours and any account of them. Once, in Hungary, when they were to perform in some remote small town miles from civilization, among the instruments required was a harpsichord. Their local contact, who was organizing the concert, assured them that such an instrument would be found and would be waiting for them on arrival. They bumped and jolted their way to the venue over roads like cart tracks, and, to their great and gratified surprise, found everything waiting for them – except that there was no harpsichord, but a large and unwanted harp.

Perhaps the most extraordinary incident took place during their tour of Australia in 1980. Among the works they took with them was *Le Jongleur de Notre Dame* which, very briefly, concerns a juggler who ends up by becoming a monk. On the tour in question the part was played by a genuine juggler who rejoiced in the name of Rhubarb the Clown. Rhubarb was married to an Australian, and had been a member of a troupe of jugglers in Australia several years before.

One of the Fires' performances of the work was to take place at the Adelaide Festival, and the whole place was thronged with vast numbers of people. Judy and Rhubarb were struggling through the crowds, trying to get to the rehearsal, when Rhubarb bumped into someone. He turned to apologize, and found, to general dumbfounded amazement, that the woman he had accidentally jostled was a former member of his juggling troupe, who had since left to join an order of nuns. She had only just completed her training period, and this was her first day outside the convent. So here she was, a juggler turned nun, bumping, literally, into a former member of her own troupe on his way to play a juggler who turns monk. They had no difficulty in persuading her to attend that night's performance, which, apparently, she thoroughly enjoyed.

It must be stressed that such incidents were only occasional light relief from the dour routine of touring. In general, tours were unrelenting hard work, but rewarding both for the opportunities they offered to see some pretty exotic places and for the wild enthusiasm of the audiences everywhere.

Meanwhile, irrespective of changes of personnel, the Fires were still continuing with their policy of taking risks by commissioning works from very young composers, of whom Judith Weir is a good example. The Scottish composer was then quite unknown, just another student in her final year at Cambridge with a few performances of her works by University musicians to her credit, when she received, completely out of the blue, a letter from Judy Arnold offering her, at Max's direction, a commission to write a piece for the Fires. It was her first professional commission, and coming from a group with a truly international reputation such as the Fires, it left her dumbfounded.

Not unnaturally she accepted the commission, and her piece was duly performed by the Fires at the 1977 St Magnus Festival. As Judith Weir herself freely admits, the piece itself was 'utterly impractical: it had parts for just about every percussion instrument known to man'. But Max never once said, 'This is unconductable . . . you should have done this . . .' Rather, he murmured, 'You ought to have a try at conducting this piece yourself, you know . . . gives you a new perspective on a piece . . .' The recollection is true to Max, both in the tact it shows from the man and the gentle method from the teacher.

Centring on Max's new opera, *The Martyrdom of St Magnus*, the inaugural St Magnus Festival of 1977 was a conspicuous success.

The opera is scored for very economical forces: one mezzo–soprano, one tenor, two baritones and one bass, all of whom take several roles. They are backed by the normal Fires ensemble of flute, clarinet, viola, cello, keyboards and percussion, plus several guests: a guitarist, who in particular backs the character of Blind Mary, a double bass, and two trumpets and a horn. The latter are required for the fanfares, and also represent the blind, brute forces of war.

The story of the opera is based on actual Orcadian history, as recorded in the *Orkneyinga Saga*, and as subsequently filtered through the mind of George Mackay Brown, for the work is ostensibly an adaptation of his historical, factually based novel, *Magnus*. It recounts the life and death of Earl Magnus of Orkney, a very unusual figure among twelfth-century Vikings in that he was a pacifist. He is ridiculed and tempted, and at last murdered by the decree of his cousin, Earl Håkon. He is promptly canonized, and the opera closes with the cast taking the role of a chorus of monks, quietly adding Magnus's name to the list of saints.

Neither Mackay Brown nor Max, however, saw the story as merely history. Characteristically, both could see only too much contemporary relevance in it; and as a result, the work becomes a political allegory, with Magnus standing for the eternal prisoner of conscience, the eternal lonely voice speaking for sanity and bloodied, suffering humanity, and getting precious little but ridicule, contempt and ultimately, when the patience and the desire to play cat-and-mouse games wear thin, suffering and death for his pains. This contemporary, or rather perennial, relevance is marked by an abrupt change in the time-setting of the opera in the seventh of the nine short scenes: from the twelfth century we are suddenly jolted right up to the present day, with the cast transformed into reporters, all rushing round hunting Magnus out and jabbering absurd journalist's clichés. The next scene has Magnus's cousin Håkon dressed as a contemporary officer, whom we are to presume is a member of the secret police, while Magnus, now internationalized and eternalized, represents the figure of the political prisoner. There is some cynical dialogue between the butcher who is ordered to carry out the execution and the officer, after which Magnus/the prisoner goes quietly to his fate.

The parallels between this storyline and that of *Taverner* are obvious enough: the scenes of Magnus's temptation, the utterly cynical attitude of the anonymous, international secret policeman in Scene 8, the devious self-deceptions and the easy surrender to expediency, both by Earl Håkon in his twelfth-century guise in Scene 6 and by both the secret police officer and the reluctant cook-butcher, who has actually to carry out the execution in Scene 8, are strongly reminiscent of the earlier, larger-scale opera.

Perhaps because of Mackay Brown's involvement, *The Martyrdom* is, however, a much more affirmative and prescriptive piece than *Taverner*. Where that work was content to ask enormous questions and leave them hanging awkwardly and reproachfully before the audience, this one asks them, but also essays answers. This is made clear by the much more pronounced distinction of good and evil – in *Taverner*, the two were represented as inseparably intertwined, and the main character of Taverner himself was uncomfortably sincere and human. Here in *The Martyrdom* good and evil are much easier to identify, and the triumph of good is represented by the final scene in which Magnus is canonized and rewards Blind Mary (who has done duty as a kind of prophetess figure) by restoring her sight. The simple message of the piece is stated quite openly at the end by Mary, her sight restored by Magnus and now confirmed as a seer-prophetess rather than a scruffy gypsy fortune-teller: looking with her new-found sight at the audience, she asks, 'Who else will die, who among you will be sacrificed, among the blind, hungry mouths; who the victims, who the persecutors; the sacrificed, the slayer?' And then she simply pleads with the new saint: 'St Magnus, keep us from a bedlam of sacrifice.'

The Martyrdom of St Magnus is thus a considerably less complex work than its predecessor, and this is manifested, as much as anywhere else, in the sparse, austere scoring. Much of the music is based on the Gregorian chant which St Magnus himself would have known; and the textures are lean and economical throughout. There are some moments of great violence, however, such as the outburst on the timpani and heavy percussion between Scenes 7 and 8. There are moments, too, of great lyrical delicacy, for example, the tender, elegiac accompaniment on the brass to Magnus's soliloquy on death in Scene 5, when, though he has received an omen of his cousin's treachery and his own destruction, he resolves to go on none the less; or the two are juxtaposed, with the blaring, crashing chords marking the execution followed by a wonderful moment of calm, with tuned percussion adding a soft heartbeat-tick, set amidst a magical array of eerie, outer-space effects to suggest the passing of time – and by that very device, paradoxically, the timelessness of the lessons that have been put before us.

The highly successful production set the tone for the St Magnus Festivals over the next few years. This was not only because of the quality of the centrepiece; it owed much also to the commitment of the entire cast and crew; and in the case of the latter, at least, it represented a considerable tribute to their dedication, for there were unexpected strains.

The director chosen was Murray Melvin, a very experienced actor who had worked with the Fires before, including at Dartington in the early 1970s. Stage manager was Kris Misselbrook. He too was an experienced theatrical hand, and had heard of the forthcoming festival the year before on the theatrical grapevine. He had then, by sheer chance, met the Bevans' elder son Peter while taking a hiking holiday in the Orkneys. He was introduced to Max at Bunertoon, and they spent the whole of that first day together, getting to know each other, talking politics, on which they found themselves in agreement – both were of the Left – drinking red wine, gathering driftwood off the beach of the old wreckers' cove below Bunertoon, and, in general, striking up an instant friendship. This suggested a good working rapport, and Misselbrook duly got the job.

The problem was largely one of different perceptions of their respective roles on the part of Max – and, to some extent, the Fires also – on the one hand, and the professional theatricals on the other. The Fires had never worked with professional directors, stage management, and so on before, and the experience rather put them off their normally very assured stroke. Murray Melvin in particular did not get on well with Judy Arnold, and he regarded everything he had done with the Fires as theatrically amateurish. He also had sharp differences of opinion with Max over details of the staging, especially the lighting.

This again raises the question of who has the final word in such disputes in works combining music and theatre. As before, the theatrical side tended to regard matters of stagecraft, lighting and so on as their domain, and felt that a composer who insisted on writing highly explicit and precise details of such matters into his stage directions was impinging on their territory. Max felt – and still feels – that it is his vision that gave rise to the piece as a whole, and his rights in it are indivisible. If the composer, or any creator for that matter, holds this view very strongly, as Max does, there is little more to be said. Without him the piece as a whole quite simply would not exist to be put on the stage: he is, because he must be, the king-pin.

The musical side of the operation tended to support Max strongly in this. Melvin very sensibly refused to make an issue of it, concluding any difference of opinion with something to the effect of, 'Well, you're the boss, I only work here.' However, the situation did impose a considerable strain on the company, and also acted as a disincentive to someone such as Melvin, with a mind of his own, to work with the Fires or Max again. This said, the same team did continue with *The Martyrdom* for a while, taking it straight from Orkney first to the Proms and the Roundhouse (the former railway shed in Camden, North London), where it scored a spectacular triumph, and then on the road for a tour of English cathedrals. After this unusual and delightful-sounding tour, there was a flurry of letters between Max and Murray Melvin, in which they fairly effectively argued out their differences. As theatrical rows go it was a pretty damp squib, and its true significance in the career of either protagonist can scarcely be understated. Certainly, though both recall the disagreement with a wry grimace and a certain amount of evident discomfort, there is nothing remotely resembling ill-feeling. All the same, it had been yet another unhappy experience for Max at the hands of theatrical people, one more in a long line stretching back as far as *Taverner* in 1972. He was eventually to find something close to an ideal director in David William, who directed the first performance of *The Lighthouse* and other productions of Max's works; but until his arrival Max had fair grounds for complaint at his treatment by the theatrical profession.

Soon after this series of performances of *The Martyrdom*, Max and the Fires were off on tour to Hungary with Kris Misselbrook, who observed that in the generally happy atmosphere Max was on the whole chirpy and confident: he enjoyed being on the road, practising his languages. However, Misselbrook also thought he perceived in Max an element of unusual self-doubt below the surface glitter. He recalls, as an example of this, an evening in a restaurant in Budapest when Max and Steve Pruslin had a tremendous shouting match. This was, Misselbrook thought, because Max liked to be the life and soul of things, and he could not easily accept someone else being just as bright and cocky at the same table.

This is a questionable judgement, even from someone as perceptive and as sympathetic to Max as Misselbrook. Max's ego is large, undoubtedly; but that goes with the territory – creative people need large egos, for obvious reasons. His self-confidence is not invincible, either: everyone is vulnerable, Max as much as anyone else. However, the further implication in Misselbrook's assessment, that Max has a compulsive need to be the centre of attention, seems unjustified. According to Judy Arnold, Max and Steve rowed all the time. It was just part of the relationship. She stresses that Max has never sought to monopolize the limelight, a view with which most of those who know him would concur.

It is extraordinary that a year as frantically busy as 1977 still saw no fewer than six new works from Max. Three of them were very short: a motet, *Our Father Whiche In Heaven Art*, for six instrumentalists, based on an early Scottish composer, John Angus; and two carols, 'Ave Rex Angelorum' and 'Norn Pater Noster'. The latter is a novelty: a setting of the Lord's Prayer in Norn, the form of Old Norse that was the ancient language of Orkney.

The other three works completed this year, however, were much more substantial, including at least one of Max's greatest masterpieces. This is *A Mirror of Whitening Light*, another evocation of that tremend-ous crucible of the sea, the Pentland Firth, whose every mood Max surveys from his lonely eyrie at Bunertoon. The piece was commissioned by the London Sinfonietta – something of a rarity, because although the Sinfonietta was formed, and existed, principally for the advancement of new music, collaborations between it and Max were rare, mainly because Max was preoccupied with his own group. On this occasion however, they did ask him to write for them, and he gave of his very finest. The work is a twenty-minute chamber symphony for an ensemble of fourteen, a dazzling kaleidoscope of different kinds of light in the crystal-clear air of Hoy playing on the waves in all their attitudes and guises. As with all Max's strongly Orkney-influenced pieces, there is nothing difficult about it: all one has to do is to relax, open the ears and listen, and allow the imagination to do the rest.

Runes from a Holy Island is also a symphony, in miniature, indeed in microcosm: the five tiny movements together make up a piece of ten minutes' duration. The holy island is not Lindisfarne, otherwise sometimes called 'Holy Isle', but Hoy; and the piece is a loving, highly atmospheric evocation of Max's ever-more-cherished home, with tuned percussion, and especially the marimba, playing a prominent part.

Finally, *Westerlings*, a commission from the University of the Swedish town of Uppsala for the quincentenary of its foundation, is a setting of four songs by George Mackay Brown at his most sumptuous and evocative, recalling the Viking past of the islands, interleaved with four orchestral seascapes, and brought to a conclusion by a prayer – the same Pater Noster in Orkney Norn as Max had set before.

These three works are all, in their own ways, masterpieces of contemporary music: atmospheric, evocative of the lonely, windswept but beloved place that gave them birth, and of a consistent quality of inspiration and musical craftsmanship that proclaims a master at the height of his powers. It might be said that it was with these three evocations of his adopted homeland that Max took his place in the long line of truly great composers. Like any such proposition, it is highly arguable; but while every devotee of Max's music will have his own short-list of favourite pieces, and many will have favourites that reign as such only until they hear something else, the stature of these three pieces is surely undeniable. Together they make 1977 a landmark year.

The flow of large-scale pieces continued. The following year saw Max working on a big commission from Flemming Flindt, a star of the Royal Danish Ballet, and their Ballet Master for twelve years. The result was *Salome*, a big, colourful, at times highly erotic ballet on the well-known biblical theme. Lasting a full two hours, in two acts of five and four scenes respectively, it allows Max full scope for his adept use of all the colours of the orchestral palette, and in that alone makes for an exotic contrast to the pastels and metallic tones of the Orcadian music – the symphony, the three major works of the previous year and others – that had flowed from Max over the previous year or two. The work was a triumph: Flindt put the ballet on as a show in the Circus building of the Tivoli, which holds 2,000 seats. There it ran for an astonishing sixty consecutive performances, every one a sell-out.

Both the other two big works of 1978 were music theatre. One was *Le Jongleur de Notre Dame*, which, we saw earlier, occasioned a remarkable coincidence on tour in Australia. The piece is a gentle comedy: the juggler seeking admission to a monastic order is played by a mime; the Abbot who admits him alone has a vocal role. The juggler is set to perform various menial tasks – sweeping up, cooking, washing clothes – by a series of monks, each represented by solos on different instruments, and each little 'duet' of solo music and mime engenders a lot of amusing antics. The monks then offer their skills to the Virgin, in the form of instrumental solos of great virtuosity. The juggler too offers his humble skills, accompanied by dances on the piano and cello. The others are scandalized and treat him fairly contemptuously until the Virgin appears, represented by a graceful figure on the violin, and makes it clear that his own magic is as valid as the others', just different in kind. The juggler is accepted, and the piece ends with a rollicking tune from a children's wind and percussion band, representing the outside world.

The other piece was yet another opera, with a difference: this one, *The Two Fiddlers*, was written for children. As we have seen, right from his days at Cirencester – and, we can fairly confidently feel, from long before that, with his own musical education having been such a tormented and obstacle-strewn affair – it has been an article of faith with Max that children are quite capable of making music, in the fullest sense, both by composing it and by performing it; and that they should – indeed, if they are to reach anything like their true musical potential, they must – be not merely allowed, but encouraged, to do so. He put this central musical conviction into action in *The Two Fiddlers*, which is a pretty substantial piece in its own right.

The story is based on a version in short-story form by George Mackay Brown of a well-known folk tale. Two fiddlers, played by boys (though all the roles, including the two principals, can be played by girls), who have to be reasonably accomplished violinists, are on their way home from a wedding at which they have performed, when they fall among trolls. One, Gavin, escapes, but his friend, Storm, is taken underground by the trolls and made to play for them. They are so taken by his performance that they offer to grant him a wish. He chooses freedom from work for his people, and they grant it; but then they refuse to let him go, keeping him for twenty-one years.

During Storm's captivity Gavin marries, has children and grandchildren of his own, and becomes wealthy. When Storm finally returns, the two reunited friends go to a party, and Storm is horrified to discover that the effect of the gift he has secured from the trolls on his people's behalf has turned them into couch potatoes, good for nothing but television, pop music and everything that Max despises and thinks responsible for the vacuity of much of today's society. Storm plays a new tune, which breaks the spell and reinvigorates the people, putting the spark of individuality back into them. A haggis is ceremonially piped in, and a final chorus drives the moral home.

It is not by chance that it is in a work for children that Max for the first time explicitly sets out his own private nightmare: the spiritual death inherent in entertainment that requires no contribution from the person being entertained. A loathing of trash entertainment, in which everything is reduced to the lowest possible level of appreciation, is an abiding preoccupation with him.

There is nothing intellectually snobbish about this: Max is not a snob. Far from being ashamed of his own background, he is proud of it, in as much as he has any emotional feeling about it, so he is not an inverted snob either. His own tastes are almost entirely what would commonly be described as highbrow; but no one ever stood up more fiercely for the individual's right to choose than Max, and this stance of his is not in any way that of the highbrow looking down his nose at the pastimes and interests of the less gifted. Rather, it is the appalled reaction of someone who has always hurled himself into everything he enjoys, and expects people to do the same in their appreciation of his own creations, to the kind of bland, pap diet of cheap trash thrown to the proles in Orwell's *Nineteen Eighty-Four*, and in real-life societies that are coming increasingly to call that nightmarish vision to mind. Max's belief is that almost all children possess the potential for creativity, and that the main problem is extracting it from them. He feels that if their creativity can be tapped while they are young enough, they will never be satisfied with the kind of pap satirized here, but will demand stronger fare, requiring a distinct contribution, and a distinct effort, on their part as well. If further demonstration were needed, this illustrates very well the point made by Gerard McBurney about Max's being a highly *moral* composer.

Fortunately for those destined to perform *The Two Fiddlers*, Max also understands clearly that the artist, be he novelist, composer or whoever, who sets out to ram a moral or a message down his recipient's throat, rather than aiming to entertain, is courting certain failure. He will have achieved an article of propaganda, he may have written a very fine sermon; but he will find his reader clapping the book shut on page 2, or his audience walking out of the theatre after five minutes. People do not like being preached at, even if they agree profoundly with the theme of the sermon. They can detect propaganda a mile away, and will junk it in seconds. Max, being well aware of this, sensibly makes his little opera (it lasts under an hour) great fun to perform or to watch, and allows the message to speak for itself.

The Two Fiddlers was premiered at the second St Magnus Festival, in June 1978. Kris Misselbrook visited Max again that year, spending time with him at Bunertoon, going for walks, gathering firewood off the beach and collecting black-backed gulls' eggs for tasty breakfasts. He stage-managed the opera, and the dominant impressions the experience left in his mind were how well Max wrote for the local community, and how perfectly his mind interlocked with that of George Mackay Brown: the two, he says, were made for each other. Misselbrook was also involved with *Le Jongleur*. He recalls that after producing the virtuoso solo arias for each of the instrumentalists representing the monks, Max asked him how he could write a virtuoso piece for stage manager. Judy Arnold had already written that part, Misselbrook replied, in the touring schedule.

The remark may have been made only partly in jest: a couple of months before the festival Misselbrook had spent a season on the Continent with the Fires, in Munich; and a couple of months *after* it, in September, he was off again, this time to Max's beloved Italy, with the party of schoolchildren from Kirkwall Grammar School who had performed *The Two Fiddlers*. This they performed, to wild acclaim, all over north Italy. They were greeted and garlanded everywhere like a conquering football team. The trip must have been memorable indeed for the Orcadian children: most of them had never been out of the islands before, with the result that they were vastly intrigued and excited by all manner of commonplace things – lifts, for example, and trains, which they had never seen before. How exotic Italian cities must have seemed to children from such a cold country of wind and thin grasses is easily imagined.

It was a very different story the following year when the German premiere of the same opera was to be staged in Bonn, with an all-German cast. Max went out to attend the first night, and agreed to give an interview to the local newspaper that morning. He had not managed to get to the rehearsal the previous night, but the journalist who arrived to interview him had. At one point in the interview the reporter asked, 'What kind of people are in this opera?'

'Children,' said Max unsuspectingly.

'Well,' said the reporter, 'I was at the rehearsal yesterday, and they certainly weren't children then.'

'Oh?' said Max, sitting up suddenly and taking an interest. 'What *were* they, then?'

'Adults,' said the reporter innocently. And he pulled a copy of that day's issue of his own paper from his jacket pocket and proffered it to Max. There he saw a large photograph, showing his opera in progress, replete with muscular young men in their twenties and thirties. There was not a child in sight.

'I'm going home,' said Max, and rose to his feet, looking, according to Judy Arnold, who witnessed the incident and tells the story, fully as if he intended to do exactly that there and then.

'You can't go home,' Judy wailed. 'Everybody knows you're here. Besides, we're having lunch with the British Ambassador.'

'Well, he's a diplomat,' snorted Max. 'He can use his diplomatic skills and sort this out!'

And so it turned out. Judy somehow managed to coax the still incandescent Max through the remains of the interview with the bewildered journalist, and got him as far as the British Residence. There the door was opened to them by a gentleman who peered down on Max from a height of about six feet eight. 'How do you do?' he asked courteously. Judy's trepidations were not assuaged when she recognized him as being none other than the Ambassador himself, Sir Oliver Wright.

'Trouble!' cried Max dramatically, setting the tone for what Judy Arnold says was one of the more fraught luncheons she has attended. The Ambassador was not the senior career diplomat he was for nothing, however, and behaved impeccably throughout. They gave Max quite a lot to drink, and in time he calmed down a little.

Not even Sir Oliver at his most urbane, of course, could salvage anything from the German performance of the opera. All Judy Arnold remembers of it is the sight of the brawny young men, all singing as if they had the lead in *Siegfried*, such lines as '*We're* not frightened. *We're* real *men*!'.

After the ordeal Judy, not unnaturally, went for the Festival organizer tooth and claw. 'You knew it was for children', she roared at him.

'Well, *ja*', he said, taking an involuntary step back. 'But we showed it

to our expert, and he said it was impossible for children to sing. Look,'
he added, clutching a copy of the score, 'take this passage, for instance.
Look at it . . .'

He showed her a passage in which the queen of the trolls has to sing,
indeed with full coloratura, a passage reading 'Ha-ha-ha-have a
cu-hu-hu-hu-hup of tea-he-he-hea!'

'But . . . but . . . it's a *joke!*' Judy spluttered, almost as beside herself
as Max had been the day before to see the self-evident so comprehensively
ungrasped. 'It's a JOKE!'

'Ein yoke?' gasped the uncomprehending organizer. 'Ein yoke? Was
ist das yoke?'

Judy gave up. When, some years later, Max's later opera for children,
Cinderella, was performed in Paris, she went along well in advance in
the hope of forestalling any such mishaps. Her efforts to explain to the
French translators the significance of the name of the character Sir
Wellington Bombast-Blimp are best left to the imagination. When they
arrived at the expression 'Shiver me timbers', even Judy's optimism and
resourcefulness gave out. To this day she is incapable of recounting the
story without going into uncontrollable convulsions of laughter.

The next few years saw Max putting down ever deeper roots in
Orkney, growing more and more profoundly attached to the people of
the islands, and receiving the same growing fondness from them.
Again, the works reflected this; the very next year, 1979, saw a looming
threat to the place he loved that drew an impassioned response from
him, and bound him yet more closely to it.

Like all small island communities in the last quarter of the twentieth
century, the Orkneys were under perpetual threat. The world was very
rapidly realizing the appalling threat posed not to mere communities,
but to the entire planet Earth, by global, man-made pollution. But what
was for others an intellectual concept, a subject for impassioned debate,
a cause to be fought for in parliaments, or on the streets in demonstra-
tions, was for the inhabitants of remote communities like the Orkneys a
terrifyingly real everyday menace. The most frequent source of such
nightmares for the Orcadians was the ever-present peril of oil spillage
from the giant tankers and supertankers that plied the sea-lanes round
their islands. In 1979, however, for a change, the threat came from the
land. Beneath a place called Yesnaby, no more than a couple of miles
from Stromness, a large deposit of uranium – large enough to be worth
commercial exploitation – was discovered.

International regulations decree that no uranium mine may be
excavated closer than thirty miles from any human habitation. With

Stromness so near to what would be the core of the putative mine, the result could only be one of two: either the mining would never be done, or it was goodbye Stromness. In the merciless, economics-driven morality of the age, the British government (then in the hands of the Labour Party) gave its licence for exploratory mining operations to go ahead.

The response from the islanders was instant, and as ferocious as they could make it. Max's contribution was *Black Pentecost*, a symphonic setting for mezzo-soprano, baritone and orchestra of extracts from George Mackay Brown's novel, *Greenvoe*. The novel is a fictionalized account of a brief period in the life of a thinly disguised Orkney, in the course of which the island is subjected to a sudden, unexpected and terrible threat from outside. In the novel the threat is of some unspecified industrial kind, but Max had no difficulty in fitting it to his theme of the outrage of the local population at the prospect of losing their home – to an extent that can probably not be truly grasped in its full enormity by anyone who does not inhabit an island. *Black Pentecost* is a work of enormous power, in which the female singer sings lyrically of the beauties and simplicities of the islands, while the baritone roars in outraged, ferocious protest at the proposed legal rape. The orchestra, meanwhile, provides a graphic portrayal of the Orkneys in the style of so much of Max's recent work, and a commentary on both strands of the vocal part.

Black Pentecost was not the only piece in which Max made his personal protest about the uranium mining. In the same year he composed *Solstice of Light*, a song cycle for four-part choir, tenor soloist and a simple organ accompaniment to words, needless to say, by Mackay Brown, at his most lyrical. The piece was written for the St Magnus Singers, the resident choir of local people who perform every year at the festival; and Max also had in mind Neil Mackie, the young Scottish tenor who had taken the role of St Magnus in *The Martyrdom*.

Mackie sang the tenor solo part at the first performance of *Solstice of Light* at the 1979 festival. The piece is a series of miniatures making up an episodic history of the islands, and it is among the most sumptuous that Max has produced. The songs are interspersed with extended solo interludes for the organ, a comparatively rare instrument in Max's enormous output, but the writing is as assured and idiomatic as if the composer was himself a virtuoso on it.

The words of the poems all resonate with the peculiar, unmistakable power of Mackay Brown's poetry – simple yet lofty, with a mysterious effect drawn from words such as 'ice' and 'water', colours, words relating to the movement of water, air, wind and rain. The last of them is titled 'Prayer for These Islands: New Troves', and it, and the work, end with the line, 'St Magnus, pray for us.' At the time, the meaning could not possibly be misunderstood, at least by anyone aware of the threat. It appears that St Magnus heard the appeal, and answered it, because uranium was soon found elsewhere, in greater quantities and accessible at lower cost. The uranium mines on Orkney were never bored, and, for the time being at least, the islands, and the islanders, were spared. But it is an ever-present threat: the idea could be revived at any time on any politician's or businessman's whim. The Orcadians can never forget, or relax completely.

Before the threat receded, Max produced another piece of work in 1980 which was unlike anything else in his catalogue: *The Yellow Cake Revue*. The 'yellow cake' of the title is a common name for uranium ore, and the piece was conceived and presented at the 1980 St Magnus Festival as a cabaret entertainment, based on a cycle of cabaret songs performed by Eleanor Bron. They are light-hearted and amusing, and everyone – the singer, Max playing the piano accompaniment and the audience – had great fun at the first performance; but the words were also savagely bitter, and assailed the uranium project and the people behind it much more openly, with correspondingly greater effect. The songs are not heard these days (though they have been performed occasionally since the first performance, mostly by Mary Thomas accompanying herself on the piano), but two small but very beautiful piano interludes have survived: they are 'Farewell to Stromness' and 'Yesnaby Ground'. Both are plaintive, deeply sad little tunes, and are among the most popular pieces of music in Max's output. The second piece contains a typical Max pun: Yesnaby Ground is of course the site of the planned mine; and the piece is also a musical ground.

Two of the three remaining pieces dating from 1979 were written for children. *Kirkwall Shopping Songs* is a cycle of six songs by Max himself for young children to sing and accompany on recorders, about a shopping expedition. There are three interludes for school percussion and a pianist. They were premiered at the 1979 St Magnus Festival by pupils of Papdale Priory School, conducted by Glenys Hughes, who was later to become a moving force in the festival and ultimately one of the two joint Artistic Directors.

The other two works were both operas: *Cinderella* was for children; *The Lighthouse* was for adult performers, but its appeal is to anyone – especially anyone fond of a ripping yarn, in this case a ghost story. Consistent with Max's strong feelings about the absolute necessity for children's music to be as genuine as any other, and about categorically never composing down to children, the opera for them is as rigorously crafted and composed as anything else he has written: Steve Pruslin, indeed, places it among the half a dozen finest pieces Max has ever written.

Cinderella loosely follows the well-known story, with modifications. Cinderella is an au pair girl who arrives at her place of employment by train. There are three ugly sisters, who all meet a just fate by marrying three characters not in the original tale, the chiefs of the three armed services. Field Marshal Sir Wellington Bombast-Blimp, who caused Judy Arnold to collapse in hysterics, is, of course, the head of the army. His naval and air force colleagues are Lord Admiral Sir Nelson Drake Victory and Lord Delta-Wing Vertical Take-off respectively. The opera takes the form of a series of songs, choruses, dialogues and dances, suitable for eight- to twelve-year-olds, and all the instrumental parts – recorders, a trumpet, piano, two violins, an optional viola, a cello and a double bass, plus a large percussion section for six players – are written for non-specialist schoolchildren of the same ages. The work has been performed many times by just such forces, and amply vindicates Max's lifelong belief that children can perform real music provided that it is tailored carefully to their needs, their size, and so forth.

The other opera of 1979, *The Lighthouse*, was a commission from the Edinburgh International Festival. The story is taken from a real-life mystery. In 1900 the Lighthouse Commission boat arrived on its normal run at the lonely lighthouse on the Flannan Isles, in the Western Isles, to bring provisions and the relief crew. No one was waiting eagerly as usual, and on investigation they found the lighthouse deserted. Everything was in good order, and the light had been kept perfectly maintained; but of the three-man crew there was not a trace. The light had been seen shining as it should have been the night before. It has never been discovered what happened, and the incident rivals the celebrated case of the *Marie Celeste* as one of the great unsolved mysteries of the sea.

For his opera, Max set the story in a fictitious island, Fladda, to avoid, as he says, giving offence to the surviving descendants of the missing crew. There are only three singers, a tenor, a baritone and a bass, who take two or perhaps three roles each. The music follows the action closely, and is for the most part made up of recitative, relieved by the three songs which are at the heart of the opera, and are discussed in detail later.

In a Prologue the three appear as the three officers of the relief boat, testifying at the court of inquiry in Edinburgh, giving their answers to calls from a solo horn, which represents the questioners from the Board. We are very quickly taken in flashback on board their boat, and mystery soon appears: all three officers see or hear various chillingly inexplicable apparitions. They arrive at the lighthouse in one piece, however, and we are brought abruptly back to the Board of Inquiry, where they testify, in horror, to finding the lighthouse deserted except for a plague of rats and a horrible smell. In response to the horn, they all testify in turn to the condition of a chair that they found thrown aside, and a broken cup, as if someone had risen from the table in a great hurry. As a touch of realism, they all give slightly conflicting accounts, just as witnesses in real trials often do: one says the chair was on its side and the back leg was broken, another that it had been thrown forward and had a broken front leg; one says the cup was on the table, another that it was on the floor, and so on. At the end of the Prologue the court brings in a verdict of death by misadventure, and the three officers sing in chorus of how the light is now automatic. We shall be reminded of this later.

The second and longer of the opera's two parts is called 'The Cry of the Beast', and opens with the three singers now playing the three crew members on the lighthouse, sitting at table chatting after their meal. One of them, Arthur, is a religious fanatic, and is clearly getting on the other two's nerves. There is a typical piece of the word-play that Max is fond of, in which all three, innocently and in quick succession, make use of the words 'the beast'. While Blazes and Sandy start a game of cribbage, Arthur, now taking the part of a 'voice of the cards', intones nebulous and mystical warnings of unknown horrors, with references to the Tarot. He resumes his real identity and preaches at the other two, and they continue generally to get on one another's nerves. Someone proposes a sing-song.

Each now delivers a song. Blazes sings a coarse and lurid song of his youth as a street thug, and tells of how he stamped a miserly old woman to death for her secret cache of gold. Sandy, who is generally got up to appear the young, innocent, rather pretty one of the three, sings a ditty of sexual delight, very thinly disguised behind some very convincing bad-poet's imagery. This is the most adroit of the three songs: on the surface it is cloyingly sentimental, but actually it is splendidly obscene; it is enlivened by some magnificent Max puns, and at the end, when all three men sing snatches of it in sequence, there are some hilarious double-entendres achieved by judicious juxtapositions of words in different voices. When it comes to Arthur's turn, needless to say, he sings a frightful hymn in the worst traditions of Moody and Sankey, all about the destruction of the Golden Calf by a righteously avenging God.

These three songs represent a considerable coup for Max as librettist: the use of the words is extremely clever. So is the choice of appropriate accompaniment in each case. Blazes' street ballad is accompanied by a street fiddle, banjo and bones; the doubly bogus sentimentality of

Sandy's is perfectly captured by a cello and a slightly wonky upright piano; and Arthur's awful hymn by a parody of a Salvation Army band, with clarinet, horn, trumpet, trombone and – the master-stroke – a tambourine.

After the songs it is almost over. All three see something coming through the door: all see in it a memory of ancient horrors. For each man harbours a terrible secret, of which he is desperately ashamed, but which he has thrust far out of sight into his unconscious. Now it comes to claim him. For Blazes, it is the old woman he kicked to death 'with that streaming face'; Sandy turns out to be somewhat less innocent than he appeared: in his stuttering terror as he beholds his version of the beast, he blurts out that as a boy he debauched not only his own sister but also apparently either a choirboy or, more likely, the son of his local parson, and then betrayed them both; and Arthur turns out to have been false to the God of whom he makes so much – and all his religiosity is revealed as nothing more than attempts to cover up his apostasy.

Gradually their different visions draw them inexorably towards the door, out into the cold and the sea, led by Arthur, still acting out the part that has become second nature to him, singing another absurd hymn. At the door they metamorphose instantly into the three officers from the Lighthouse Commission boat, encountering the plague of rats. They leave hastily and send in the relief crew. The crew members turn out to be spectral versions of the original three, and promptly start repeating the dialogue between Sandy, Blazes and Arthur with which the Act began. The opera ends with the music over which the words 'The lighthouse is now automatic . . .' were sung to close the Prologue.

This splendid tale was an enormous hit at its premiere at the Edinburgh Festival in 1980 (with at least one direct descendant of one of the members of the real vanished crew of the Flannan lighthouse in the audience – apparently she thoroughly enjoyed the entertainment). It has since gone on to become one of the most popular and frequently performed operas by any composer of the twentieth century.

The opening run at Edinburgh was remarkable for a couple of the extraordinary coincidences that seem to follow Max around, and also, sad to say, by a couple of disasters. The first coincidence was that on the opening night of the opera, the automatic light that has for decades replaced a human crew in the real Flannan lighthouse unaccountably went out. It had been performing perfectly, when it was examined no reason whatsoever could be found for its sudden failure. A helicopter had to be sent the next day to get it put right and restarted. Another unexplained mystery.

The second, which included the worse of the two disasters, was that a couple of days before opening night the production crew were discussing possible alternative backdrops for various points in the action. As they were talking about one possibility, which was an open seascape with three bodies floating in it, a message arrived for one of the discussion group, David Wilson, the road manager. It said simply that his brother, a merchant seaman, had just been washed overboard from his ship off the coast of Nigeria and drowned.

The other disaster, though it did not involve anything as grisly as this death, was agonizing enough for Max. As starting time approached for the second performance of the opera's Edinburgh run, no one had seen the horn player. Starting time arrived, and still there was no sign. Half an hour went by. Eventually Max, in a state more easily imagined than described, climbed on to the stage and explained, with profuse apologies, that some members of the band were missing. He made all the right noises and managed to disguise his feelings. Privately, no doubt, he was reviewing his lifelong opposition to the death penalty.

At length, three-quarters of an hour late, the horn player came reeling into the pit, and the performance started. It was, of course, a disaster. Everyone else did all they could, but nothing could conceal the fact that the horn player, with a demanding and mercilessly exposed part, was hopelessly drunk.

For the next couple of nights Judy kept an understudy on hand, but there was no need for his services. Then, on the following night, the opera was being recorded for later broadcast by the BBC – and it was this night that the errant horn player, this time with the trumpeter in tow, decided to turn up for the performance as drunk as a lord. The result was a chaotic performance. The other players were overwhelmed by anger and shame, and the BBC broadcast was out of the question. As a result everyone lost their broadcasting fees. Afterwards Judy Arnold was so incensed that she even briefly contemplated suing the two for damages, before quickly realizing that neither of them would be worth powder and shot, since they were both regular offenders. One of the two culprits found work hard to come by after this. A while later he opened a bar in Greece, and not long afterwards succumbed to the effects of being his own best customer. The other eventually underwent a drying-out cure, has rehabilitated himself and is still playing.

There were few new works in 1980. We have already looked at *The Yellow Cake Revue*. There was another in the long sequence of explicitly Orcadian pieces, *A Welcome to Orkney*. This was a short and boisterous allegro for an ensemble of fourteen, written for Chetham's School of Music in Manchester, for performance during their appearance at the St Magnus Festival that year. Then there was the *Little Quartet No. 1*.

This was the first time Max had written for strings since the String Quartet of 1961; before that, the only other extant piece was the *Quartet Movement*, written when he was an eighteen-year-old schoolboy, in 1952. Yet, oddly enough, the string quartet is a form that has exerted a special fascination for Max all his life. When he was the castaway on *Desert Island Discs* his single most essential selection from the eight works he chose to accompany him to the celebrated desert island was the *Grosse Fuge* of Beethoven, in its original form, for string quartet. As recently as late 1993 he said, when asked what his future held, that the one thing he was especially keen to do was to write some more string quartets. The *Little Quartet* is in fact not as minor a piece as its name suggests: it is indeed little in mere dimensions, lasting only eight minutes, but it is technically quite difficult, though not at all difficult to listen to – on the contrary, it is a joy, gentle, austere and mellifluous. It is in three movements – slow, fast, slow – played without a break.

There was, however, one colossus among the works completed in 1980: his Symphony No. 2, commissioned by the Boston Symphony Orchestra. This work, though not quite as long as the first symphony, is scored for a very similar, biggish orchestra and, like its great predecessor, has very prominent parts for tuned percussion. It is another vast Orcadian seascape, perhaps the purest sea-picture of all Max's works, with the outermost of its four movements particularly evoking visions of the sea below his croft in its most cauldron-like ferocity. The second movement is a beautiful adagio, as monumental and serene as anything Max had written to date; the third, a quicksilver scherzo, the sea in its most playful moods, all splashy wavelets and water rushing and gurgling through the myriad blowholes and crannies in the ancient rock. The finale, as magnificent as anything in his canon, follows the slow movement of the first symphony in beginning slowly and ominously, gathering momentum to a tremendous climax of pure sea noise before returning to a serene calm. Poseidon, the Ancient Greeks' god of the sea, was known among other sobriquets as 'Earthshaker'; rarely in music can the awesome, unimaginable power of the sea have been better portrayed.

The premiere, given by the Boston Symphony Orchestra in February 1981, under the direction of their long-time Principal Conductor, Seiji Ozawa, was hailed everywhere as a triumph, both in Boston for the premiere and everywhere else the orchestra subsequently took it.

Alas, the British premiere was a very different affair. Although an unusual amount of rehearsal time had been allocated (unusual, that is, given the extraordinary conditions in which British orchestral musicians are expected to work and compete with the rest of the world), the conductor, Gennadi Rozhdestvensky, none the less skimped the rehearsal of the work (as he was wont), with disastrous results. Soon afterwards, however, the BBC Northern Philharmonic and Edward Downes gave the piece the kind of performances it deserved.

The activities of the year were rounded off by a further successful St Magnus Festival and the five-week tour of Australia and New Zealand by the Fires. By this time, however, things were beginning to change on the home front. Towards the end of the 1970s Max had made it clear that he wished to reduce his commitments to the Fires. This caused a certain amount of friction, particularly between Max and Steve Pruslin: Archie Bevan, for example, recalls at least one fairly acrimonious row between the two of them taking place in his living room, looking out over Stromness Bay. (Oddly, neither Max nor Steve remembers any such argument, though both have reliable memories. Neither, of course, disputes Archie's word.)

The truth is that Max, despite his rash declaration twenty years before that he thought he would never 'find it necessary' to write for large orchestral forces, was finding that that was precisely the way his creative powers were leading him, willy-nilly. One suspects also that his ever-growing attachment to the Orkneys and their people and his ever-increasing fertility of invention under the islands' benign influence were also considerable forces in detaching him from the essentially London-based Fires. He was well advanced on a process of forging closer ties than he had ever managed before, and of achieving a degree of much needed serenity, and he was very reluctant to allow anything to interfere with the process.

In 1980, therefore, Max asked John Carewe to take over as principal conductor – not as Artistic Director: that position Max never relinquished. Carewe was a veteran champion of new music, and had conducted early works of Max's as far back as the late 1950s. He had had a lot of contact with the Fires and the Pierrot Players before them, but had rather disappeared from sight when he accepted the Principal Conductorship of the BBC Welsh Symphony Orchestra in 1972. He now began to work with the Fires on the same basis as the players: that is, he had first refusal of any dates offered.

Sadly, the new relationship was not a great success. In the end the conclusion was that the players of the ensemble felt that they could only really be happy with greater freedom of choice of conductor, rather than having a full-time principal conductor. In the end matters came to a head, and the connection between Carewe and the Fires came to a somewhat acrimonious end. From that point until their final dissolution the Fires worked with numerous conductors on an *ad hoc* basis. As for

Max, he never lost touch with them, or ceased to work with them; but he was able at last to spend less time worrying about touring, conducting and, not least among his considerations, writing pieces for them.

In 1980 the Fires themselves underwent a second large-scale metamorphosis, ending with what was in effect their second long-standing line-up: Philippa Davies (no relation) took over as flautist in 1978, David Campbell was already securely in possession as clarinettist; Rosemary Furniss joined to play violin and viola, and Jonathan Williams on cello, both in 1980; Gregory Knowles was already the regular percussionist, and Steve Pruslin remained on keyboards until the end. He, in fact, was the only one of the group, apart from Mary Thomas, who was present throughout from the founding of the Pierrot Players in 1967 to the end of the Fires twenty years later. It was a truly remarkable achievement, by a remarkable musician and a man of exemplary integrity and loyalty.

Having partly shed one lot of heavy responsibilities in this way, Max had meanwhile undertaken another set. In 1979 Sir William Glock finally relinquished his post as Director of the Dartington Summer School of Music, after no fewer than twenty-six years in the position. Max was a Dartington regular over many years. He had attended as a student in his teens and early twenties, had provided a running translation of Luigi Nono's lectures just after his return from his year's study with Petrassi, and had many works of his own performed and premiered there. As one of Glock's favourites he had often gone back throughout the intervening years to give classes in composition and musical analysis, and Glock had had him in mind as his successor for many years.

Max accepted the post with a firm commitment to develop the educational aspects of the annual event, but it has to be said that in that direction his tenure was not a great success. The event had traditionally been a mixture of established and aspiring professional musicians, teachers, passionate amateurs, concert-goers and plain music-lovers who appreciated congenial surroundings and an intensely musical ambiance. Max was unequivocal in his desire to turn Dartington into something much more like a serious musician's forcing house. Indeed, he more than once expressed the desire to restrict attendance to professional musicians seeking higher tuition.

In this aim he could hardly have been more at odds with the Trustees of the Dartington Trust. Their objective was to make the concern as lucrative as possible, to which end they had recently raised the rents sky-high. The result was that almost no serious students could afford to attend any longer, and the event was left to make the best of the wealthier groups of concert-goers and amateurs. The Trust thwarted

Max and his objectives throughout his five-year tenure of the Director-ship; but then, with two such diametrically conflicting aims, that was scarcely to be wondered at. He was greatly embarrassed one year when he had to ask all the visiting artists and teachers to accept a 20 per cent reduction in their agreed fees. In all, it was not a happy venture, and he was glad to bring it to an end when he resigned in 1984.

To return to 1981, however: the Fires had none of those lengthy, arduous tours over the next couple of years. With that and the reduction in the time he had to devote to them, Max was able to turn out a steady stream of work. A very weighty and difficult piano sonata, a second *Little Quartet*, a Sonatina for Trumpet, a brass quintet, two sets of songs, *Seven Songs Home*, commissioned by the International Kodály Society for the centenary of Kodály's birth, and *Songs of Hoy* and a music theatre piece, *The Rainbow*, for the children of Orkney schools, were the result of a surge of freshly released activity during 1981. *Hill Runes* was a tough, sinewy piece for solo guitar, written for Julian Bream, which took the instrument a very great distance from its regular sunny haunts and introduced it to the chilly, windy atmosphere of Orkney. *The Bairns of Brugh* was a short piece for sextet written for the Bergen International Festival, and continued the stream of sombre but accessible portrayals of Orcadian landmarks.

There was also a piece to commemorate a very notable event in Hoy, specifically in Rackwick, the scattered hamlet where Bunertoon was situated. Before Max's arrival in Rackwick, the last two children of the village had been drowned, thus almost completing the depopulation of the place. At its lowest point the village was reduced to a single inhabitant, the much-loved farmer Jack Rendall. He, however, at over fifty, had taken everybody by surprise by marrying a visitor from England, and in 1981 he and Dorothy delighted everyone in the islands by producing the first child born in Rackwick for thirty-two years. George Mackay Brown commemorated this truly happy event with an acrostic poem, the first letters of the eleven lines spelling the name 'Lucy Rendall', and Max set it to music for mixed chorus in *Lullaby for Lucy*. It is a sweet-toned, gentle piece, and utterly delightful.

The other work dating from this fruitful year was *The Medium*, a ferociously demanding piece, described as a monodrama, for Mary Thomas, which she premiered at the 1981 St Magnus Festival. She portrays a fairground fortune-teller, and goes off into a wild succession of fantasies, all the time growing more extravagant, both conceptually and vocally. This was among the last pieces Max wrote for this outstanding virtuoso singer and musician, and it was probably the stiffest test of her great gifts.

And so we come to 1982. This and the succeeding couple of years were to be highly eventful, and marked by some deeply sorrowful incidents. But by and large Max was now as contented as at any time in his life to date. The title of this chapter, 'Pax Orcadiensis', is taken from that of an article he wrote for *Tempo*, Boosey & Hawkes's quarterly magazine devoted to contemporary music, and it aptly describes his state of mind at the point we have reached. His roots were going deeper, his friendships growing closer. The serenity mentioned earlier was not illusory. Bunertoon spoke to the very depths of his soul: just as Max and George Mackay Brown were made for each other, as Kris Misselbrook observed, so Bunertoon and Max were a house and its occupant in perfect harmony.

But none of this should be taken to suggest that he had lost any of his enormous, bounding nervous energy. Serene he might be while he planted vegetables in the little plot of garden in front of Bunertoon, or sat composing under oil lamps at the table before the little window; but he still radiated vigour and energy, and a good thing too, in view of what was coming. Momentous events lay ahead, which neither Max nor anyone else could possibly have foreseen.

9 ~ *The Eternal Triangle*

In 1981 Max was awarded the CBE for services to music. He was gratified, and proud of the honour, in a moderate sort of way; but on the whole he makes fairly light of it, making it clear that he regarded, and still regards, the award as an honour for the profession as a whole. The award of a CBE is nothing especially remarkable in a profession which, on balance, receives its fair share of such awards; but it derives an altogether greater significance in the light of things that were to happen only a few years later.

The following year was marked by a sudden flurry of small pieces written for brass instruments. There were arrangements of two motets by Gesualdo and four voluntaries by Tallis, and an original march, *Pole Star*, all for a quintet of two trumpets, horn, trombone and tuba, and a substantial, very beautiful virtuoso piece for horn solo, *Sea Eagle*, a majestic and sonorous evocation of the flight of the great sea-bird. There was also a long and taxing Sonata for Organ, something of a rarity among Max's works, as previously noted. This piece was first performed in June 1982 at the St Magnus Festival by Richard Hughes, husband of Glenys.

The other two pieces completed in 1982 were the most important, and one of them was to light the powder trail that was to lead to a new stage of his career not long afterwards. *Image, Reflection, Shadow* is a massive chamber piece for a sextet, or, more accurately, for three pairs of instruments: flute and clarinet (both doubling other members of their families), violin and cello, and piano and cimbalom. It is often thought of as a companion piece to *Ave Maris Stella*, but the prominence given to the marimba in that work now passed to the more plangent tones of the cimbalom; and certainly it has some important factors in common with the earlier piece: it is roughly the same length – a bit longer, in fact, at about thirty-eight minutes to the other piece's thirty-two; it is a piece of the most demanding virtuosity; and it was composed with the explicit intention that it should be performed as true chamber music – that is, without a conductor. We have seen that Max was beginning to distance himself just a little from the Fires by this time, but this piece was written for them, and the demands it makes on the players is itself good evidence of the affection in which he still held his group.

The piece is in three movements: an eerie, intensely atmospheric adagio, then a brisk, clangorous allegro and a final movement in which the closing allegro grows naturally out of a gentle lento, which itself swells gradually out of a poignant and desolate cimbalom solo. The whole piece has a distinctly oriental feel, full of Japanese gong-like sonorities, with the piano and cimbalom being treated unequivocally as percussion instruments. It also represents an audible return, for a while, to the sound-world of Schoenberg; but the desolate harmonies of the Debussy of the last three sonatas can be clearly heard as well. The title of the work is taken from three lines of a stanza of a poem by the runic scholar, Charles Senior:

> Image: content in still air.
> Reflection: true upon still water.
> Shadow: living on still weed and rock.

This poem speaks of an island, a gull, its reflection in the water of the sea and the movement of its shadow along the sea floor. But in important ways it is something of a retrospective glance for Max, in that it carries none of the overt references to the Orkneys which had increasingly come to characterize his music over the past few years; instead, it offered a fairly emphatic return to an earlier period in Max's composing life. It was also a diversion away from another growing tendency, towards the writing of large works for full orchestral forces. It can probably be said that this would not be the best piece by which to introduce someone to Max's work, especially if the newcomer was suspicious of modern music: it is not the easiest or more immediately accessible of his œuvre.

Putting it another way, *Image, Reflection, Shadow*, magnificent specimen of sustained chamber music though it undoubtedly is, is something of an aberration, in the literal sense of the word – a wandering off. Max's return to the main road was achieved by way of three compositions which together make up a large and powerful trilogy: the *Sinfonia Concertante*, which was the final piece from 1982, and two of the comparatively sparse output of 1983, *Into the Labyrinth* and the *Sinfonia Accademica*.

The first part of this trilogy was the *Sinfonia Concertante*. It was commissioned by the Academy of St Martin-in-the-Fields and first performed at a Promenade Concert in the 1983 season, conducted by Sir Neville Marriner. The third part, the *Sinfonietta Accademica*, was a commission from Edinburgh University to commemorate its 400th anniversary. It was premiered at the University by an orchestra with which Max had not worked before, the Scottish Chamber Orchestra, conducted by Edward Harper. The middle leg, *Into the Labyrinth*, was commissioned by the same orchestra, and although it formed the central third of the trilogy, it was in fact the first to be played, in the St Magnus Festival, in June 1983. The soloist was the tenor Neil Mackie, who had first come to Max's notice when he auditioned for, and got, the part of St Magnus in *The Martyrdom*, and for whom Max had since written the lovely *Solstice of Light* and the parts of Sandy and the first officer in *The Lighthouse*.

The *Sinfonia Concertante* is a generally quiet, sombre work, with much use of the now familiar Orkney sounds. It is scored for a classical wind band of flute, oboe, clarinet, bassoon and horn, with strings. There is a distinct acknowledgement, both in the instrumentation and in the way the wind band interacts with the strings, to another work of the same title, attributed, somewhat doubtfully, to Mozart, as his K297B. That work too is scored for wind band, minus the flute. Max's work, however, anticipates his later big works for full orchestra, especially the Symphony No. 3, in giving the timpanist a very prominent part. He opens the piece, and has a dominant role at the outset of the finale.

The first movement is a big, vigorous allegro molto, but it is preceded by a slow introduction of almost equal length. The allegro, with a main theme on horn and strings over a whippy, tootling accompaniment from the other soloists, is a sustained piece of typical Max wit and warmth, which breaks up at the end into a soft wind-based lead-in to the second movement, andante. Here the Orcadian influence is at its strongest, with the usual soft colours and lyrical feel. The work closes with a movement with the uncommon marking of 'flessibile'. After a ruminative introduction there is a timpani solo followed by a splendid duet betwen timpani and a double bass, pizzicato. Tension mounts, and then the movement turns, in quite dramatic manner, Orcadian, soft, mysterious and reflective.

If the first of this trilogy is sombre in tone, *Into the Labyrinth* is darker still. It is the only one of the three pieces based on words, adapted as usual by Max himself, from George Mackay Brown's play, *The Well*, and muses on the effects of mankind and modernity on the fragile lifestyles of a small, remote and tightly knit society. The words are limpid and very beautiful, with Mackay Brown at his simplest and most lyrical, including such lines as 'How should we merit this gift of water? It is so beautiful a thing, only the mind of God would have imagined it. It is the seven oceans, it is the single jewel of snow on the window. It is the loch and the burn. It is the palace of fish. It is the cloud tangled on the hilltop . . . '

The work begins with a short slow movement for tenor soloist and strings alone, speaking solemnly of the endlessly self-repeating rituals of island life. Next comes a spirited invocation of the four so-called elements (three compounds and a plasma), earth, air, fire and water, followed without a break by a short instrumental interlude. Then comes the heart of the work: four sections, each complementary to one of the four elements in the last movement, and all except one gloomy and resigned. Fire has a reference to the shrivelling of the peat cuttings, air talks of the islanders sailing off to the fishing grounds, but 'then came engine and oil. We turned our backs on that presence . . . '; and earth brings a reference to the rusting of the plough. The exception is water, which speaks apparently happily of turning into whisky. From this point on the words get more and more oppressively black and pessimistic, followed faithfully by the music. All in all it is one of Max's grimmest and heaviest works.

The *Sinfonietta Accademica* is another of Max's Orcadian pictures. The word *accademica* is something of a misnomer: it does not refer to the character of the piece, which is not academic at all, but to the fact that it was Edinburgh University that commissioned it. It begins with a rollicking, drunken Orkney tune, which Max was to use again soon afterwards, and would become his best-known tune by far. This gets the opening allegro off to a fine start: one wonders what its effect must have been on the audience when it was first heard, for it must have been utterly unexpected in a piece from a composer still widely, however erroneously, regarded as rather stern and 'difficult', written to celebrate the 400th anniversary of a university for which the word 'august' might have been specifically coined.

However, this mood does not last too long, and for most of its length, the piece paints portraits of the Orkneys and their inhabitants. Max himself has said that the piece came into his head after he had visited the ancient ruined church on Hoy, and then played the harmonium, as he often does, at its large, draughty Victorian replacement. The harmonium can be heard distinctly during the work, represented by various orchestral effects. One other point of interest is that Max was still (as he has continued to do to this day) using plainchant as the basis of some of his works: this piece employs the *Dies Irae*, dealing, of course, with the Day of Judgement, from the Mass for the Dead, and another, *Victimae Paschali Laudes*, dedicated to Easter Sunday and the Resurrection. However, Max was by now already making extensive use of magic squares, and in this piece, as he had done for the first time earlier, in *Ave Maris Stella*, he combined the two compositional techniques.

After the drunken opening tune, the first movement is gentle and contemplative. The central movement of the three is a Max sea-scape; and the finale blends a hymn-tune, representing the church, with sounds of wind and sea, and a final wheeze from the breathy old harmonium.

The common point in these three big works was the involvement of the Scottish Chamber Orchestra: having given the premieres of the second and third, they soon took the first into their repertoire also; and it was the SCO which was soon to provide Max with the opening into a phase of activity which may come to seem his greatest service to British musical life. Before that happy collaboration, however, there were some very unhappy times just round the next corner.

We have seen how Max began to edge himself away from his long-standing preoccupation with the Fires, with first John Carewe and then a variety of conductors taking over the reins. This brought him relief, taking off a lot of pressure and freeing him to spend more time in the Orkneys, where he was spiritually happiest, composing big-boned music for large-scale orchestral forces, which had by now become the area of composition in which he felt musically happiest.

The Fires, too, were more relieved than anything else. According to Mary Thomas, the increasing tension that was creeping into relations between the group and Max was beginning to affect the others. It was a relief, she recalls, to have an outsider taking over – albeit an outsider who was in reality a well-respected and very familiar old friend. The truth of the matter was, almost certainly, simply that the group were suffering the kind of strains that any group would almost inevitably suffer after being together so long: Max, Pruslin and Mary Thomas had of course been there from 1967, ten years longer than anyone else.

The new relationship was commemorated by Max in the only other piece he wrote in 1983, *Birthday Music for John*. The John in question was Carewe, the birthday his fiftieth, and the piece a spirited little trio for flute, viola and cello. Unfortunately the new amicable spirit did not last long. As we saw earlier, the new arrangements were not to the liking of the group, who were getting restless, and before long, the ostensible immediate cause being a row about money, contracts and arrangements in general over the first performances of Max's new work, *The No. 11 Bus*, Carewe and the Fires parted, never to be reconciled.

The following year, 1984, saw six new works added to Max's catalogue. Among them were two with very happy associations: a carol, 'One Star, at Last', was a setting of a poem by George Mackay Brown for the celebrated service of Nine Lessons and Carols performed every Christmas Eve by the choir of King's College, Cambridge, and broadcast by the BBC all over the world on Christmas morning. The other was the little Sonatina for Violin and Cimbalom, written for two members of the Fires, Gregory Knowles the percussionist and Rosemary Furniss the violinist, who had married the previous year. The piece was both Max's wedding present to the couple and, in its closing lullaby, a celebration of the birth of their son Christopher.

The estrangement between Max and Carewe was a sad end to a relationship. John Carewe has vivid memories of being at the famous New Music Group Manchester concert at the Arts Council in 1956, and of being electrified in particular by Max's Trumpet Sonata. He had been associated with Max's music, and an energetic champion of it, since then, and actively involved in conducting it and bringing it before the public since 1958. But if this was saddening, something else was to hit Max much harder in 1984.

His parents were still living in the old mill at Eccliffe, where they had been since 1976, but they both wanted to move. His mother, Hilda, was now in her eightieth year, his father, Tom, his eighty-third, and both had become very frail. Tom had driven his car for as long as he felt it wise and safe to do so, but he had finally felt compelled to stop. Max had made arrangements with a local taxi-driver to collect them and run them about whenever and wherever they wished, but they had refused to take advantage of this: a last residue of defiant working-class thrift and independence, but one which had the effect of more or less confining them to the mill. They both wanted to move back from the depths of the countryside to a town, where they would more easily be able to do the shopping and anything else requiring them to go out. Accordingly the mill went on the market in mid-1984. But, alas, in August, before a buyer had been found, Hilda Davies suffered a very severe stroke. She was taken to hospital in Shaftesbury, where she was to remain, rarely regaining her lucidity, to the end of her life almost two years later.

This was distressing enough, but there was more grief to come. The loss of his wife in this way was devastating to Tom Davies. They had always been a happy and stable couple, deeply fond of one another and deeply affectionate, in the reserved manner of their time. But there was another problem: Tom had never done any housework, cooking or any of the other things that were regarded as women's work. He was left pretty well helpless, but in any case he was already beginning to go into a gentle but rapid decline: he was literally pining away. The need for a move to something more practical immediately became vastly more urgent. A buyer was swiftly found for the mill, and pleasant sheltered accommodation was found in Shaftesbury. Max bought it, and in November 1984 the removal van came to the mill. Max, the Arnolds and Hilda's brother-in-law, Les Walden, were all there to help, and the apartment in Shaftesbury was carefully made ready.

Tom Davies was fetched and shown in. He took one look around and passed out where he stood. The doctor was summoned in a hurry, and Tom was taken straightaway to the same hospital in which Hilda lay. He never recovered, and on Christmas Eve 1984, aged eighty-three years and three months, he died. Whatever the medical profession may say about the non-existence of such a cause of death, Max and everyone else who had any close knowledge of Tom's last days all say the same: he died of a broken heart.

Hilda lingered on for another eighteen months, and died on 18 June, 1986. Max suffered enormous anguish throughout this time, plus considerable physical and practical hardship, having to make frequent long and arduous journeys from Hoy or London to Dorset. But life, and work, had to go on, and these sorrowful couple of years were as productive as any. One way in which Max sought relief was totally unexpected: he composed the piece that has taken an unchallenged place as his funniest, most famous, most popular and most frequently performed: *An Orkney Wedding, with Sunrise*. It was commissioned by the Boston Pops Orchestra and their conductor, John Williams. But it was also a response to his own grief, and his recognition that he must find a way of emerging from it.

Just as Max had commemorated the birth of Lucy Rendall with *Lullaby for Lucy* in 1981, it was with her parents' marriage much in mind that he composed *An Orkney Wedding*. It is also the piece in which the rollicking Orcadian tune that opened the *Sinfonietta Accademica* comes into its own. It is a vivid – not to say lurid – portrayal of the guests fighting their way to get to the reception through typical Hoy weather – a ferocious tempest of rain and a howling hurricane off the Pentland Firth. Once indoors they revel in the conviviality provided by a band of village fiddlers, and take full advantage of Scotland's most celebrated product. The party becomes more and more riotous, then gradually peters out as the guests slip more or less gracefully beneath the tables. And then comes a truly magical moment, as the sun rises above the eastern horizon. It is represented by a noble *maestoso* theme played on Highland bagpipes. In concert performances they are always played by a piper in full Highland regalia, beginning as he enters the auditorium from the side or the back, and swelling as he advances majestically through the hall, mounts the stage and makes his way to his place between the leader and the conductor.

In performance the piece is often accompanied, if the conductor is a kindred spirit, by much horseplay with a bottle of Scotch, which the conductor passes round the leaders of the string sections who bear the brunt of the rustic fiddlers' parts. Certainly it found such a sympathetic soul in Andrew Davis, who conducted it in 1992 when it received the accolade of being performed on the last night of the Proms. When it was played at the Lucerne Festival it was lubricated by a bottle of Schnapps. Max doesn't greatly like horseplay, and does not now indulge in it in his own performances of the work – though he makes no attempt to stop others from doing so. The piece can survive the slapstick, because although it is most certainly light-hearted and fun, suitable for the Pops Orchestra that commissioned it, it is also a proper, through-composed piece, as Max himself remarks.

An Orkney Wedding is many things: it is yet another loving portrait of Max's adopted home, and its colourful, earthy people. It is another faithful picture in music of its wind, sea, weather and its bluff, uncompromising landscape. It is a reminder of Max's skittish, off-centre sense of humour, but also of his consummate skill as an orchestrator, and his outward-looking inventiveness with instrumentation. It is a monument, too: not only to the Rendalls but also to his parents; to his homage to them in his grief at their sickness and death. Most of all, perhaps, it stands as an enduring reminder of the strong artistic strain that Max inherited from his mother and the craftsmanship, the gritty, obstinate determination to give full value for money, that he took from his father. It reminds us that however deep the roots may become that he puts down on Hoy, there is among them one tenacious tap-root that reaches down all the way to Manchester.

An Orkney Wedding was completed in 1985. But numerous other pieces were written during the sorrowful couple of years 1984 and 1985: a short motet, *Agnus Dei*; an equally short piece for a dark-toned quintet of alto flute, bass clarinet, piano, viola and cello, *Unbroken Circle*, in homage to Sir William Glock; a pretty little Guitar Sonata written for Julian Bream but, in the end, not played by him. It was performed instead by Timothy Walker, the regular and frequent guest guitarist for the Fires, who premiered it at the 1987 St Magnus Festival. Then there are the big pieces, all of them interesting, several representing departures in yet new directions for Max. It is a tribute to his everlasting adventurousness and resourcefulness, if ever there was one, that he should find it possible to go off exploring new pastures at a time of spiritual contraction, when most people find refuge and comfort in familiar things.

The first of these was *The No. 11 Bus*. This was the piece which brought about the breach between Max and John Carewe. It is also something of a bone of contention between Max, on the one hand, and practically everybody else, on the other. For although Max vehemently asserts that he regards this as one of his very finest pieces, he appears to have the opinion largely to himself. Even as loyal a supporter as Steve Pruslin tends to grin indulgently when this notion is put to him, and to murmur, 'Ah, yes, well, that's Max being protective,' which is probably as succinct a way of explaining away the difference of opinion as any. Max does indeed have a tendency to be protective of those of his works that are least well received by others: this work and the opera *Resurrection* are two good examples of this.

All that said, *The No. 11 Bus* is very funny at times. It is a music theatre work for a mime, two dancers, three singers and the normal Fires ensemble of six instrumentalists, playing flute (piccolo), clarinets, violin, cello and piano (celesta), and the usual manic percussionist, who has a formidable array of special effects to play with, including such exotica as a lion's roar, sleigh-bells, a saucepan and the famous rubber suction plunger and bucket of water which caused memorable problems in South America and elsewhere. Everyone is involved in the stage action, so everyone appears in costume, coming on-stage one after another, each arrival greeted by amusing antics from the mime – such as polishing Steve Pruslin's little bald spot.

The work traces the actual London No. 11 bus route, with the various personnel all taking parts – a policeman, a bus conductor, a ticket inspector, passengers, a charwoman, a bag-lady, two British Movement thugs who beat up the bag-lady, two punks wearing ghetto-blasters on their shoulders in the approved manner, and so on, in an extended sequence of songs and dances, with the ubiquitous mime getting up to all kinds of antics around them. As one might expect with Max, there is rather more to it than this: the various characters all have secondary significance as figures from the Tarot pack of cards, or for what those figures represent – death, commercialism, and so on. The music provides a continuous commentary on the action, until at the end, when the bus reaches Hammersmith, the terminus of the real No. 11 route, all the characters exit one by one until only the ensemble of six instrumentalists is left. Then they too get up and leave with their instruments one by one, as in Haydn's 'Farewell' Symphony, until only the pianist and the percussionist are left playing. The percussionist and the mime converge on the pianist, the former gives him a tremendous roll on the side-drum, the lights go down, and the auditorium is left in total darkness and profound silence.

This entertaining piece was given its premiere at the Queen Elizabeth Hall in March 1984, by the Fires with Mary Thomas, Donald Stephenson and Brian Rayner Cook. The dancers were Anne Dickie and

Tom Yang, who had much earlier performed the dancing part in *Vesalii Icones* with great aplomb and distinction. The central role of the mime was taken by Simon McBurney, brother of the composer Gerard, and the performance was conducted by the young German conductor, Günther Bauer-Schenk. It brought the house down, which is odd considering that it has never since established itself, in Britain at least, as a favourite piece of Max's music with the public, or even with his close admirers. On the Continent, though, it has become quite popular, being performed fairly often in Germany in particular.

The reasons why certain pieces of art or entertainment become popular or fail unaccountably to become so usually defy analysis. *The No. 11 Bus* is probably one of these, although it is possible that the piece is over-long, at almost an hour, and the double significance of the various characters is perhaps too obscure.

In many ways 1985 was a vintage year: it was the year that saw *An Orkney Wedding* burst on the world, and there were four other substantial pieces. *First Ferry to Hoy* is one of Max's new departures. It embodies four songs and five instrumental interludes for an ensemble of fourteen players, depicting between them a ferry ride at dawn from Stromness pier out to sea, where whales are spotted at play. Its novelty is that for the first time Max deliberately combined roles for children's amateur forces in the choirs and a children's band with professional ones in the instrumental ensemble. Thus the five interludes for the ensemble are brilliant and demanding, while the songs, to texts by the composer, and the parts for the children's band of recorders and percussion are simple enough to enable them to rehearse them separately, yet blend them fully and naturally into the texture of the piece in performance. Commissioned by the London Sinfonietta, it was first performed by them in November 1985, with the Youth Choir and Children's Band of the Inner London Education Authority, conducted, it is pleasant to note, by Max's old friend Elgar Howarth, who was by now making a considerable name for himself as a conductor.

Later in the year Max produced one of his longest and most impassioned pieces for choral forces, *The Peat Cutters*. The direct source of inspiration was a fell fire that raged across the heather-clad hillsides of Hoy, terrifyingly close to Max's own little corner at Bunertoon. It prompted him to return to a theme on which he had expatiated in music before, and to which he would return still more passionately later: the miraculous self-renewal of nature. Hand-in-hand with that are the fragility of nature in man's custodianship, and the over-riding responsibility on him to value and safeguard it. The piece has five moments, all but one slow, the exception being the second, sub-titled 'The Fire', which gives a graphic depiction of the fire roaring across the unprotected and helpless heathland. It is for children's and youth choirs, with an accompaniment, subtly and delicately scored, for brass band.

The other two works of this year were both on the biggest scale, and both were major musical events in their own right, but in the future they may both be seen to have been significant as much for what they presaged as for themselves.

The first of them was Symphony No. 3, and it confirmed the gathering power and confidence Max was gaining in this medium. He now added another work of colossal force and weight to the already impressive first and second symphonies, which also enhanced his authority as symphonist by taking a completely different direction from those vast works.

It was commissioned by the BBC to mark both European Music Year (1985) and the fiftieth anniversary of their own BBC Philharmonic Orchestra, and it was dedicated to that orchestra and to its long-standing Principal Conductor, Edward Downes. In fact, that dedication was at least in part a reward and a thank-you from Max to Downes and the orchestra: they had, it may be recalled, performed something of a rescue operation on Max's second symphony, by giving it its first decent performances after its disastrous British baptism at the hands of Gennadi Rozhdestvensky.

With such solid musicians as Downes and his Mancunians in charge there was never any danger of a similarly chequered infancy for the new symphony, but even so there was one vertiginously uncomfortable moment. When Downes received the conductor's score of the third symphony from Boosey & Hawkes, he stared at it for a long time, riffling through it in gathering incomprehension, utterly unable to make head or tail of it. This went on for several days, with Downes getting more and more mystified and panic-stricken. Then all of a sudden he happened to glance for the first time at the numbers at the bottom of a couple of pages, and light dawned: the copy he happened by ill chance to have been sent had been bound with the pages (a *lot* of pages) all higgledy-piggledy, impossibly out of sequence. A few minutes' work was enough to unscramble them, and after that there was no trouble. It is tempting to wonder if one illustrious musician might have looked at the page numbering of his copy of the second symphony.

Symphony No. 3 differs from its two predecessors in not having a large percussion section, or, in particular, a very prominent part for the tuned percussion. Max made up for it, however, by giving a very important, almost obbligato, part to the timpanist. As with the first two symphonies, it is amply designed, once again over fifty minutes in length, and in the traditional scheme of four movements; like them, too, it is a work of awesome power.

Max himself has said that he expects the piece to be listened to, and considered, purely as music, without outside influence, which is more easily done with this symphony than with either of its predecessors, in which the Orkney sea, sky and wind are so graphically depicted. It begins with a titanic first movement, lasting a full eighteen minutes. As purely musical pointers, Max is still deriving material from plainchant: this first movement draws on one, 'Sancte Michael Archangele, defende nos in praelio'; but it is not by any means distinctly heard. The profound influence of Mahler, however, which has been a constant undertone in Max's large-scale orchestral music since *Worldes Blis* and before, is clearly audible throughout, especially in the deeply elegiac music for the strings and the brass, complete with choirs of whooping horns. The movement is also mildly reminiscent of *Worldes Blis* in being a mighty, extended build-up of tension, ending, however, on a note of gentle and unexpected quiet, with unmistakable birdsong on the high registers of piccolo, flute and violins.

The internal movements are both scherzos. In the second of them the material of the first scherzo appears slightly mutated, as if in a distorting glass. The first scherzo in particular contains distinct hints of Sibelius, Max's other great acknowledged orchestral influence, most clearly in the throbbing strings. The movement is a series of sad processionals for the brass, also very reminiscent of those found everywhere in Gustav Holst's music. They alternate with short, rosy, passionate melodies in the strings, with an accompaniment throughout of a chattering dialogue between the woodwind.

In the third movement (the second of the scherzi) there are a couple of especially magical moments: first Max creates gaps, or 'windows', as he calls them, through which we can hear an advance trailer for some of the material of the huge final movement. In one of them there is the unmistakable cry of a lone sea-bird, and it is a heart-stopping moment, repeated, *diminuendo*, after a brief silence. According to Max there is no Orcadian influence at all in this symphony, but this cry really can be nothing but the mew of a gull, the loneliest and most desolate sound imaginable. Possibly Max was unaware of having placed it there.

The final movement is as long and weighty as the first, and up to a point mirrors it, making use of some of the same material. There are more sad processions in the brass and many more long, sad melodies for the strings, heaving and throbbing with very Mahlerian yearning. The movement ends with a long, endlessly drawn-out cry of anguish, of heartbreak, perhaps of resignation, perhaps of all of them, on the violins, with knockings on the door from the timpani almost to the end. This soft, terrible cry brings the enormous structure to conclusion, and the effect, though it could hardly be more different from the thunderous climaxes of the first and second symphonies, is perhaps even more shattering for being so calm, resigned and deathly. Whether it was consciously an elegy for his parents, one recently dead and the other clearly on the threshold of death, Max has never said; but it is difficult to avoid the conclusion that, conscious or not, it was his musical representation of coming to terms with death and grief. If so, he triumphed over both, by immortalizing them here.

All this is quite clearly to be heard by anyone simply sitting down and listening to this deeply moving music, and it requires no elaborate analysis of the catalysts to its compositional techniques. However, since Max himself has made mention of such sources they had better be mentioned here. So, whereas the first two symphonies were big Orkney seascapes, this one is influenced by the architectural proportions and perspectives of the Renaissance architects Alberti, Piero della Francesca, Leonardo and, in particular, Brunelleschi. To be more precisely accurate, it is founded on the mathematical calculations behind their architecture.

That may sound alarming to the large percentage of those who admire Max's music but have never heard of Brunelleschi, did not know architects employed mathematics and could not follow the equations if they were shown them. But that is beside the point – and Max is the first to agree cheerfully. As a matter of fact, the mathematical substructure of Brunelleschi's architectural theory is formidable. But in the second symphony also, there was far more than mere sloshing on of orchestral colour to represent a big Orkney sea-and-skyscape. In fact, at the time of writing that symphony Max was greatly exercised by the mathematical equations to do with different kinds of wave-form. Looking down from on high to the fiercely contesting cross-tides and channels in the Firth below, he observed that there were waves in which the wave form was what moved, while the water molecules stayed more or less in the same place, going up and down rather than along the surface of the sea. But there were also other waves in which the wave form itself was static, while the water actually moved from place to place.

He found the appropriate mathematical works in which to read up on this, and spent a long time doing so. Then he took the equations and theories out with him on his daily tramps across the hills of Hoy and paced out different distances, using the ever-changing gradients of the hillsides to lay out these wave-form equations on a physical medium. The result, he will assure anyone who inquires, is there for all to hear in the music – for all to hear, that is, who can. But if he is asked, 'Well, what if I can't hear any of that?' his reply is instantly and completely reassuring: 'Doesn't matter in the slightest,' he says quite cheerfully. 'Nobody could be expected to hear all that.' He immediately goes on to elaborate: 'These are things that are of enormous interest to composers, and of none whatsoever to listeners.' The same, precisely, is true of the architectural–mathematical base underpinning the third symphony: it is of great interest to composers, and of none to the average listener.

Max cites a telling parallel. It was very recently discovered, he says, that Debussy, in *La Mer* and elsewhere, made use of the mathematical concept of the Golden Section, or Divine Proportion, Fibonacci Series and other such arcana. All this had come to light in a recent book (*Debussy in Proportion* by Roy Howat, Cambridge University Press, 1984). The important thing, Max points out forcefully, is that the use of mathematical devices was not realized until the appearance of this book, sixty-six years after Debussy's death. During the interim nobody had realized that Debussy had made any use of the concepts whatsoever – and nobody's enjoyment of his music had been affected in the slightest by the lack of that knowledge.

The significance of architecture in this symphony is also of interest for entirely different reasons. We have seen that certain ideas, or themes, have lain dormant for as long as twenty years or more in Max's mind before finally making an appearance. Here Max composed a symphony, based on architecture, in the 1980s, finishing it in early 1985, when he was a few months past his fiftieth birthday. Twenty-two years before, it may be remembered, he had written to Donald Mitchell from Princeton: 'I am making an architectural film with Jonathan Mansfield – architect, also on a Harkness Fellowship – and as the musical and visual shapes are related absolutely, we are working out . . . a notation which involves *all* the experience. I don't know quite how this will work out . . . ' We know now.

The remainder of 1985 was taken up largely by two projects: one was the writing of the final piece completed that year, and the other was the last major foreign tour by the Fires, this time to the United States. It lasted five weeks and was a triumphant but shatteringly exhausting experience, like all the later Fires tours.

The last great work of a good year was the Violin Concerto. This had been commissioned by the Royal Philharmonic Orchestra for the fortieth anniversary of their founding by Sir Thomas Beecham, and was to be played at its premiere by no less a soloist than Isaac Stern. As he usually did, Max rose to a big occasion and, tailoring the writing of the piece specifically to the playing style of the intended soloist, delivered one of his most golden, romantic and lyrical scores.

It is modelled on the Violin Concerto of Mendelssohn, which Max says is his favourite of all concertos, and this in itself tells us a good deal about the work. Among the ways in which it pays its respects to the Mendelssohn is the fact that the three movements are played without breaks – Mendelssohn composed his concerto this way because he detested the contemporary custom of applauding between movements.

The opening movement is long – over half the entire length of the work. It begins with mysterious, autumnal colours from the woodwind, the bassoon especially prominent, heralding the opening line from the violin, which comes in and simply sings for the rest of the movement. This extended cantabile is all lazy, golden late-summer, faintly elegiac and wistful in tone. There is one especially arresting passage in which the solo violin shimmers above a soft, dramatic accompaniment on strings and timpani, which have a prominent part throughout the concerto. The movement ends with a languorous and beautiful melody for the clarinet, which dissolves into the second movement. This is an adagio, and displays the powerful influence of Scottish music on Max. In his own description, it

> is characterized throughout by unhurried melodic unfolding, based on a Highland bagpipe tune I wrote called 'Mor Fea', conjuring up the near-silent expanses of still, lonely moorland, with its characteristic sea-reflected silver northern light, where cries of moor- and sea-bird, wind in the heather and the distant wash and boom of the Atlantic are the only sounds.

The third movement begins with shimmering high strings and a delicate pizzicato in the lower ones. The soloist enters with a gay, dancing theme, and the woodwind perform little carolling arabesques among themselves. Some dramatic work for the timpanist follows, and the brass make a late entry for the first, muted climax. The cadenza which follows is shared by the soloist and the timpani. It is a sultry, atmospheric episode, with distant-thunder effects from the timpani. Finally, the soloist plays a little peasant dance tune, merry and yet at the same time wistful, over more dramatic coloration from the busy timpanist; the brass come in one more time for the last climax of the work, once again restrained but with some exquisite writing for very high trumpets, and the concerto ends with the solo line fading into nothing and one final, soft drum-beat.

The concerto was given its premiere at the following year's St

Magnus Festival – the tenth – with Isaac Stern and the Royal Philharmonic Orchestra conducted by André Previn. The shape and dimensions of St Magnus Cathedral posed a few problems, mostly to do with the physical deployment of the orchestra, but they were all overcome, thanks largely to Previn's skills and imperturbable good humour. Stern himself observes that the atmosphere of the place, soaked in centuries of Norse and Orcadian history and the essence of Max's music, gave the work a special poignancy that affected everyone profoundly. He immediately went on to perform the work again in London, Los Angeles and New York, and made a fine recording of it for CBS the same year.

Stern's judgement of the work is straightforward: he was in regular contact with Max while it was being written, and says:

> It soon became clear that this was to be a major work of this century . . . The piece challenges the total technique and sensibilities of both performer and orchestra. It is not easy to play but has a haunting beauty, with most effective writing for both orchestra and soloist. In a time when so much contemporary music has a homogeneity, where one composer sounds so much like another, Sir Peter has managed to carve out for himself a clearly personal musical identity, recognizable as only his. I believe it is a work that will continue into decades to become a standard work to be performed by many colleagues who appreciate both challenge and beauty in the works they choose to play.

This view is shared in all essentials by another eminent violinist, György Pauk, who has taken the work into his regular repertoire, plays it often and loves it. Yes, he says, it is difficult, certainly. Much of Max's music is, and 'the most difficult aspect of it is the rhythms. They're logical, but they're very difficult to read, and very difficult to keep. However,' he continues, 'the really unusual thing about the concerto is that it's perfectly written for the instrument – for the violin. That's very unusual in a composer who doesn't play the instrument. It's written as if by a violinist – and a very good one.'

For all the rival claims of Pinchas Zukerman, Itzhak Perlman and a good many others, Stern is an almost legendary figure, for many simply *the* violinist, and his agreement to come to Orkney lent enormous cachet to the St Magnus Festival. There were lighter moments, however, most of which seem to have been uncovered by Michael Tumelty, a columnist on the *Glasgow Herald*. Writing in his 'Orkney Diary' after the festival, he revealed a mischievous sense of humour in the great man.

Before his celebrity recital in Stromness with pianist Bernard Pommier, Stern felt a twang of nerves and a call of nature.

The two men, searching for relief, discovered that they must join the queue at the outside loo which serves the hall. When we recognized our distinguished fellow-sufferers, we, of course, gave them priority.

Stern went first. He then held the door open for Pommier, closed it firmly behind him, looked at the queue, grinned and said, 'For once I get to set the tempo,' and scuttled off to the hall.

Tumelty goes on to reveal the great sock shock, in which Max had to conduct the RPO but inadvertently left his black socks on Hoy. Compelled to borrow a pair from Richard Hughes, he found that they had been on Hughes's feet for two days, and also that they came from two different pairs. Nor was this all. He also had to borrow a white jacket to conduct the orchestra, and, in Tumelty's words, the one he managed to find 'must have belonged to a long-armed trombonist'. Max's hands almost disappeared into the voluminous sleeves, and this, coupled with his non-use of a baton, made for considerable problems for the orchestra.

They were not the only ones, either: among other little local difficulties that Ian Maclay, then General Manager of the orchestra, had to cope with, were the fact that the airstrip at Kirkwall, the islands' only airport, cannot land aircraft big enough to accommodate a symphony orchestra or its instruments, and an alarming shortage of hotel rooms. However, these obstacles were more than compensated for, Maclay says, by the joie-de-vivre that suffused the whole event.

At some point during this especially memorable tenth festival Max got into conversation with Mike Newman of BBC Scotland. More to make conversation than with any serious expectation in mind, Newman said he needed a piece for the signature tune of a television series he was to make shortly on the history of chamber music, called *Music in Camera*. However, he was then either lucky enough or subtle enough to play his fish very cleverly: it would, he went on, have to represent 'the history of music in forty seconds'. Max was incapable of resisting a challenge like that, and, according to the delighted Newman, 'the piece arrived in the post within a week. He'd knocked it off in forty minutes. It begins with a plainchant, and advances every bar.' Not surprisingly, Newman is among the large number of people who will not hear a word against Max.

The collaboration with the Royal Philharmonic was to have repercussions later on. For the moment, however, something else was bearing unexpected fruit. We have seen that the period June to October 1983 saw the premieres of no fewer than three major works by Max, all of them Orkney-influenced, and two of the three having some strong Scottish connection. They were the *Sinfonia Concertante*, the cantata *Into the Labyrinth* and the *Sinfonietta Accademica*. We saw also that the Scottish Chamber Orchestra premiered two of these three works, and rapidly took the third as well into their repertoire. None of the three works, however, was conducted at its first performance that year by Max himself. The orchestra had a young and innovative Managing Director, Michael Storrs, who found Max very exciting and galvanizing in his effect on the orchestra. He quickly invited Max to accept a few conducting dates with the orchestra, directing his own works; and Max, very nervously, accepted.

The following year the orchestra appointed a new Managing Director in the person of Ian Ritchie. He was very much in Storrs's mould: dynamic and immensely energetic, and, most of all, full of ideas, and young and adventurous enough to want to try them out. Among his first actions as MD was to create a new position in the management stratum of the orchestra, Development Manager. This job title normally translates to mean 'fund-raiser-in-chief', but Ritchie had something entirely different in mind. It was intended to generate income for the orchestra, to be sure, but not in any obvious way, and not in any way substantially for perhaps twenty years. The job of the Development Manager here was really to develop new ways for the orchestra to go, new ways of working, in particular new ways of working with the local community, thus integrating the orchestra fully into that community, and, ultimately, of giving the community a sense of civic pride in the orchestra.

The Development Manager appointed, Kathy McDowell, was very much of the same mind as her boss in such matters. Among the first things she had to do was to investigate another idea of Ritchie's: a close, working relationship with a composer. Ritchie wanted this to involve more than merely occasional performances of the composer's works and figurehead-cum-occasional-conductor status for the composer. They quickly decided that no one could be more appropriate than Max, with his versatility as a composer, his involvement in music theatre, his pioneering work in musical education and his strong links with Scotland. Accordingly, Max was invited forthwith to accept a newly created position of Associate Composer/Conductor. At the time this was a unique appointment in the musical world. It has been copied elsewhere – Max himself has not one but two identical positions with other orchestras he is especially fond of – but at the time the SCO could congratulate itself on having invented the idea.

Max accepted the post without hesitation, and the relationship very quickly proved to be a fruitful one. The first thing he offered was a symphony, written specially for the SCO. This would, in time, result in the Symphony No. 4; but that would not appear until 1988, by which time an altogether larger scheme was well under away.

It was integral to Ritchie's concept of the relationship between his orchestra and Max that Max, and contemporary music, should be central to the orchestra's work: Ritchie was anxious to get as far away as he could from the notion of contemporary music as a fragile creature that had to be kept in a special ghetto in order to preserve it from death. He felt, and continued to feel throughout his ten-year tenure as MD with the orchestra, that a programme of music for a concert ought to be just that: a programme of music. There ought not to be separate dictionary definitions for 'music' and 'contemporary music' – or, for that matter, for 'early music'. He felt that there was no earthly reason why a concert should not feature a mixture of works from the baroque or pre-baroque period, the classical or romantic mainstream, and the present day.

This meant that from the earliest days of their association, Max's works were to be found on the SCO's programmes side by side with works of Haydn, Mozart, Beethoven and everyone else. Max took his first serious steps as an orchestral conductor, and found that he and the orchestra could get on. They did not, candidly, find him a first-rank conductor, and though he has made enormous strides in the intervening years, they have not changed their view. But they do find him a worthy partner, with whom they can do musical business, so to speak. In particular, many of the players express considerable relief and gratitude for a conductor who, not least because of his own limitations, is bound to trust them to do their part of the work. And of course, even from the earliest days, he always had a great deal to teach them about his own work, irrespective of his conducting talents.

Gradually he began to gain in confidence, and after a while he was invited to start taking whole concerts; the new experience of making microscopically detailed studies of scores of his favourite composers of the classical and romantic periods proved to be a novel and immensely worthwhile experience: he found himself constantly discovering and learning from Mendelssohn, Schumann, Mozart, Beethoven and, in particular, from Haydn. As time went on his conducting became more and more assured, and he found himself with more and more to contribute to rehearsals, with the result that he is now taken entirely seriously as a conductor, and is in considerable demand all over the world as such. This, of course, is by no means an unmixed blessing: he now spends at least six months of the year away from Hoy, living in aircraft and hotels, and, most important of all, not composing. He has declared his intention of cutting down the time he spends conducting, but that looks likely to prove easier said than done.

However, all this was in the future when, one day, apparently out of the blue, Max asked Ian Ritchie, 'What would you say if I suggested that I write a series of, say, ten concertos for you – one for each of the principals of the orchestra?' Ritchie thought fast. It sounded an almost impossibly adventurous and ambitious project, but every instinct told him to jump at it. So he did. They then sat down to discuss the details, not least among them the matter of where the finance for such a huge project would come from.

In due course it turned out to be much easier than they had anticipated. The Scottish Arts Council agreed to put up half the money if the orchestra could find an independent sponsor to produce the other half. Within a couple of months Strathclyde Regional Council had stepped in with an offer of the money, and so the Strathclyde Project, and the sequence of Strathclyde Concertos, came to life.

The hub of the idea was that music was a community resource, a communal activity. Central to it was the belief that children were innately musical, and that their musicality naturally included some ability to create music. Strathclyde Regional Council took the view that the children of its enormous area should have every opportunity to develop this aspect of their musicality as a normal part of their music education. That this met with enthusiastic agreement from Max almost goes without saying – twenty-five years before at Cirencester he had been pigeon-holed a revolutionary for nothing more than this.

Accordingly, the plan was drawn up: there would be ten concertos. As each was written, it would be taken out to the people: a group of professional composers would be recruited, and each would be assigned to one of the regions of the Strathclyde Council's territory. (It was realized that Max could not possibly be involved in this stage in any close personal way: he was far too busy composing the concertos. But it provided very valuable experience – and very handy cash – for a whole clutch of younger composers.) Each composer would then go on the road in his assigned area, visiting all the schools and helping, encouraging, advising and offering theoretical and, more important, practical guidance to the children. They would examine 'their' concerto, look at the mechanics of its composition, and use the knowledge they thus gained to make small compositions of their own – all under the eye of their own composer-in-residence.

In addition to all this, members of the orchestra would also visit the schools, offering additional advice and guidance from their respective points of view. The various soloists went out with the concertos they were to perform, explaining the compositional techniques from the performer's point of view, and in general reinforcing the work of Max at the source and the other composers downstream.

So, for example, when Max had written the first of the Strathclyde Concertos, for oboe and orchestra, the Scottish composer Bill Sweeney was assigned to it, and both he and the work were in turn assigned to the Dumbarton district of the Strathclyde region. Sweeney, and later Robin Miller, the orchestra's principal oboist, duly travelled extensively in this region, offering instruction in the way described. The second concerto, for cello, was given to the Ayr region, and the young Scottish composer James MacMillan, then working for his PhD in Manchester, was offered the assignment. He accepted it with alacrity and since then has gone on to become one of the brightest lights among the next generation of composers. He has worked extensively with Max, at St Magnus Festivals and the more recently founded Hoy Summer Schools for young composers; it is no exaggeration to add as a postscript that it was the chance of involvement in the Strathclyde Project that was largely responsible for bringing him back to live and work permanently in Scotland – in effect, reclaiming him for Scotland. So Ian Ritchie thinks, anyway.

The philosophy behind this approach to children's music education was naturally attuned to Max's own lifelong views. It holds that the musical life of a nation depends equally on three sides of a triangle: the composer, the performer and the listener. All too often in the pre-packaged entertainment world of today, the adherents of this view claim, the three sides are completely separated, never to meet on any level at which they can communicate: so composers compose in a vacuum, blithely ignorant of how their work is viewed by performers or listeners alike; performers are handed wodges of music, told to get on with it and do so; while the audience is left to make what it can of what is offered.

According to the Strathclyde faction, this is all wrong. Composers have no more right to make a living irrespective of their customers' tastes and requirements than anyone else; they may live in ivory towers if they wish, but they cannot expect the public to pay them a living if they divorce themselves too far from what the public wants. The same applies to performers. In a sensible world, all three sides of the triangle will be in contact with both other sides, with a healthy dialogue, a constant exchange of ideas, and a resultant evolutionary leap in the creativity of all of them.

This is what the Strathclyde Project is really all about. To this extent, also, it is concerned with reversing the trend set around the beginning of the twentieth century, in which the artist, in all fields of creativity, withdrew from contact with ordinary people, creating instead art that was solely for, and appreciable only by, highly educated elites, the members of which were equipped with special keys of admission. Those involved with Strathclyde wanted art to come back towards the people. Max himself had wanted the same thing at least since he had been a schoolmaster, and probably before, in other words for three decades.

Finally, underlying the project was a profound concern for the future of music in Scotland as a whole, not only as part of the education system. The Strathclyde pioneers – Max, Ritchie, his development manager Kathy McDowell, the district composers-in-residence, the entire Scottish Chamber Orchestra and not least the Strathclyde Regional Council itself – all took it as axiomatic that children who are encouraged to compose music at school – even if it never gets beyond little tunes in any individual case – who experience the excitement of meeting real, live composers and dealing with them on equal terms, just as if the composers were ordinary human beings, who are made aware that they are sitting in on the actual creative stages of the composition of something extraordinary, by someone extraordinary (and famous: a useful lure for children) are infinitely more likely to grow into adults for whom the concert hall is a normal and natural part of their lives. On the other hand, children whose music education consists of having music rammed down their throats in indigestible slabs and being told to be quiet and appreciate genius when they hear it are more than likely to resent the process, and reject music as a consequence.

And so Max returned, in perhaps the most unexpected way imaginable, to a central involvement in the musical education of his country of adoption. The contribution of an extraordinarily enlightened regional authority can scarcely be overstated: without it, the entire Strathclyde Project would have been inconceivable. If Max had been living in England, Strathclyde simply could not have happened. It was the differences between the Scottish and English educational systems that proved essential, and the ever-strengthening bonds between Max and Scotland were further cemented.

When posterity comes to judge Max's contribution to the world, the answer will undoubtedly be that it was the extraordinary, prolific flow of wonders from his own pen. But if at the same time the question is asked what his greatest contribution to the life of his own country was, the answer may well be different: in that more limited context, it may well be felt that his greatest single contribution was to musical education.

10 ~ *In His Pomp*

While his innovative relationship with the Scottish Chamber Orchestra was being forged, life was still going on as usual for Max. In 1985 he went with the Fires on their last major foreign tour, spending five weeks in early winter in North America. It was the usual combination of bone-racking travel and enthusiastic receptions, culminating in five shows at the Lincoln Center in New York.

On his return home he still managed, despite the increasing calls on his time, to carry on composing, though not as prolifically as usual: 1986 produced six new works, but all but one were of less than fifteen minutes' duration. Not that that in itself is any indication of their inventiveness; but it was certainly something of an anti-climax after the succession of titanic works, especially for full orchestral forces, of recent years. But Max had been working at full stretch for a very long time, and, tireless though he usually seemed, he needed a period of calm to gather his forces for what was to come. More importantly, throughout 1985 and the first half of 1986 he had had to live with the harrowing knowledge of his mother's pitiful condition, at the same time as he was still coming to terms with grief at his father's death.

Most of the pieces from this year were Orcadian-influenced, three of them settings of Mackay Brown. *House of Winter* is a cycle of songs for Christmas, Orkney-style, commissioned by the King's Singers, and given its first performance by them at, rather incongruously, the St Magnus Festival that summer. *Sea Runes* was also commissioned by them, but is much smaller, being a single three-minute song run up from six 'runes' – miniature vocal harmonies for different combinations of the versatile ensemble's six voices. *Winterfold* is perhaps the most substantial piece from this year. It is another Christmas piece: a setting of a lovely, very funny poem, 'The Keeper of the Midnight Gate', in which the Bethlehem town gate-keeper greets all the cast as they arrive to take their places in the crib scene. The title of the piece is taken, not from the title of Mackay Brown's poem, but that of the collection that includes it. It is set for Mary Thomas and an ensemble of seven, the usual Fires line-up plus guitar. It was composed specially for a Fires concert at the Queen Elizabeth Hall in January the following year, 1987.

So was *Dowland: Farewell-a-Fancye*, a realization of an intimate piece for lute now recomposed for the Fires, with a dark, mellow-toned line-up of alto flute, bass clarinet, viola, cello, piano and marimba.

Jimmack the Postie is a lively, at times rumbustious piece for full orchestra. It was commissioned by the Scottish Post Office and dedicated to its Chairman, Ian Barr, a long-standing and vigorous supporter and friend of the St Magnus Festival – it was first performed at the 1986 festival. Max chose to describe in music another of the characters of Hoy, the local postman. According to Michael Tumelty, in the same *Glasgow Herald* column in which he told the stories of Isaac Stern, the borrowed socks and other lighter moments of the festival, the piece fell on at least one pair of deaf ears: alas, those of none other than Jimmack the Postie himself. Fortunately its subject's indifference does nothing to diminish the bright bravura of the piece. In the end, though, the show is stolen by the island of Hoy. The descriptions of its brooding landscape are painted with all the loving poignancy and fidelity that Max always bestows on depictions of the beloved place.

The last piece, *Excuse Me*, is the longest of the year's crop, and is another arrangement of an earlier composer, this time of four parlour songs by Charles Dibdin, who lived from 1740 to 1814. The setting is faithful to its original, and presents a light, amusing portrait of the man through his songs. It was premiered by Mary Thomas and the Fires early in the year.

In terms of simple numbers of new compositions, the following year was a low point: in 1987 there were two new works. Both, however, were landmarks, especially the first of them to be completed. This was the first fruit of the Strathclyde Project: the concerto for oboe and orchestra; and if anyone had felt any momentary misgivings over the previous year or so, any fears that Max was wobbling at all, this should have instantly allayed them. The concerto, written for Robin Miller, at that time principal oboist of the SCO, is scored for a chamber orchestra of classical proportions, minus oboes and bassoons, so that the soloist has naturally increased prominence; and it shows Max back to his quicksilver best. It is based on a plainsong, 'Dum complerentur Dies Pentecostes', which is heard early in the work – rather uncharacteristically of Max, who always had a fondness for leaving such source material to make its first proper appearance towards the end of the works founded on it.

The concerto is dark-toned and elegiac throughout – possibly a further step in Max's working-out of grief for the loss of his parents. The first movement begins with an atmospheric adagio molto in the lower registers of the strings, with the orchestral woodwind gradually joining in before the soloist comes in with a gentle, meandering theme, all suggesting dawn coming up over the sea. A light, skipping solo takes over, followed by a cadenza. The second movement, adagio, and the final allegro are equally sombre, mysterious and wistful. In the adagio there is a long, sinuous, elegiac melody from the soloist over shimmering strings, but then tension builds up, with the timpani given particular prominence. The last movement begins darkly, with tremolando strings. This is followed by a jaunty solo line and a dialogue with the horn, then the clarinet, and the work ends with a high, plaintive melody for the soloist.

It was an impressive start to an extraordinarily ambitious idea, and from this low point (as measured by mere fecundity at least), Max accelerated rapidly towards his normal prolific level of output. Over the next six years, to 1993, he produced Strathclyde concertos at a steady rate of one a year, with two in 1991. It is a remarkable record of sustained invention – just how remarkable is brought home if we remember that the Violin Concerto, composed in 1985, was Max's first venture into the medium. In eight years from that beginning – impressive enough by any standards – he produced the first eight Strathclyde concertos: for cello in 1988; horn and trumpet, 1989; clarinet, 1990; violin and viola, and flute, 1991; double bass, 1992; and bassoon, 1993. Not content with that, he also produced a full-scale trumpet concerto, for full symphony orchestra, in 1988.

Critics, commentators, assorted pundits and interested parties of all kinds have expressed decidedly mixed opinions about the merits of the Strathclyde sequence. One assemblage of passing comments from a single review conveys the general flavour very well. In *The Times* of 26 November 1993, Gerald Larner reviewed the first performance of Strathclyde Concerto No. 8 for Bassoon and Orchestra. The second sentence of his review runs: 'With awesome industry and *chilling* regularity, Sir Peter Maxwell Davies has produced Strathclyde Concertos at a rate which suggests that the whole unlikely project could be over within the next twelve months or so.' The italics are mine, for 'chilling', it is clear, is the crucial word. In the next sentence he goes on: 'The scores he has written for the principals of the Scottish Chamber Orchestra have not been of uniform interest, *of course* . . . ' Once more, the italics are mine: let us examine what, precisely, 'of course' suggests.

Max is by no means the first great composer to fall foul of the critical establishment of his day for the sin of being prolific. On more than one occasion Max has been taken to task for what amounts to over-facility; the implication being that genius and the production of works of genius must necessarily be difficult and arduous. Thus if a composer – or any other creator, for that matter – produces works at a great rate, they simply cannot be great works, or not all of them, anyway. The fact that the most cursory glance at the recent history of artistic creation demonstrates that this judgement flies clean in the face of the facts seems to make no difference to the regularity with which it is levelled.

Gerald Larner's use of the word 'chilling' to describe Max's regularity in producing the Strathclyde Concertos is immediately seen to be loaded, although one hastens to add that Larner himself almost certainly did not intend it to be so at the time. Indeed, it should be stressed that, overall, Larner's review is very favourable, with a sensible and objective description of the bassoon concerto, and some notably kind words about it at the outset. I am not in any sense accusing him of traducing Max; but his possibly unconscious use of certain loaded terms is highly suggestive of the general tenor of critical thinking.

Larner's assumptions, conscious or unconscious, come more sharply into focus when he mentions that the eight Strathclyde Concertos written and heard so far 'have not been of uniform interest'. That would be a fair and legitimate comment for any critic to make: where he gives the game away is in that casual little postscript, 'of course'. There is no 'of course' about it: Larner is trying to pass off an opinion as if it were objective fact.

Larner's article is typical of most of the critical opinion that has been passed by reviewers on the Strathclyde Concertos so far. Even a critic as amicably disposed towards Max as Bayan Northcott, a personal friend of his, who declares freely that in his other persona as a composer he owes Max a great deal – not least for commissioning a work from him for the Fires – has expressed doubts over Max's later work. To be fair to him, he was not singling out the Strathclydes. But they are central to the block of Max's work about which he has reservations, notably on account of their 'long, grey movements' and the elusiveness (for him) of the musical sources on which many of the pieces are founded.

It is a different story when one listens to the players talking about the concertos written for them. One is immediately reminded of the judgement of György Pauk and Isaac Stern, that Max's violin concerto seemed to have been written by a violinist, and a very good one. It is remarkable with what unanimity the soloists for whom Max has written these concertos say words to the effect of 'It's astonishing how well he's written for my instrument – as if he was a (cellist, violinist, double bass player, or whatever) himself. He seems to have gained a perfect understanding of the capabilities and the limitations of the instrument – and its player.' John Steer, the principal double bass player with the SCO, spoke for all when, after hearing the first performance of the double bass concerto (Strathclyde Concerto No. 7) in November 1992, he said excitedly, 'It's exactly what we [double bass players] were all hoping he'd write for us.'

The remaining testimony is that of another side of the eternal triangle, the audience. Of their view there is no doubt: they approve of the Strathclydes wholesale: every one of the eight premieres has been received enthusiastically, some of them frenetically, wherever in the world the concertos have been played.

The second in the Strathclyde sequence was the cello concerto. Like its predecessor for oboe, it is a predominantly lyrical piece, and if it is not quite so overtly dark a work, it is at any rate reflective and sober in tone. Of all the concertos it is the most demanding for the soloist, who is active almost continuously throughout the substantial length of the work – over half an hour. The cellist enters almost immediately, with a slow, sad melody above a growling accompaniment in the low registers of the strings. There follows a long section of writing that is rather unusual for Max: a long, ravishing theme for the entire body of the strings in unison. Indeed, with the exception of No. 5, which is scored for string orchestra alone, this concerto is the most string-dominated of all the Strathclydes. There follows an ominous section with menacing muted brass and palpitating strings, after which the mood becomes alternately lyrical then menacing again, with a full choir of heavy brass and timpani. The movement ends with a cadenza, punctuated by more minatory blasts from the brass and a relentless, railway-train rhythm in the strings.

The second movement, lento, begins with a long, singing melody from the soloist over a soft, subdued background in the strings. Thereafter the movement is generally dark in tone; but it is lit from within by an extraordinary tonal depiction of a wonderful sight Max saw from his cliff-top eyrie at Bunertoon one day, when a vast shoal of mackerel swam into the bay far below. The flashing, swerving iridescence of the shoal is portrayed by high, shimmering figures in the violins, flashing and vanishing and flashing again. The movement ends with a short cadenza for the soloist.

The finale begins with violent outbursts from the brass and timpani, followed by a rolling rhythm and a busy, chattering commentary from the soloist. More blazing brass is followed by a calmer, more reflective theme for the soloist, and finally a dazzling acceleration towards a climax, which never quite comes before all is suddenly stilled and the work ends quietly, with a tender melody from the solo instrument in its lower registers.

The Concerto for Horn and Trumpet is naturally, in view of the solo instruments involved, a much more brilliant affair, scored for classical orchestra but with no orchestral brass. It begins adagio, with a bright series of hunting calls from the trumpet, then a cheerful dialogue takes place between the two soloists above a restrained accompaniment from the woodwind and strings. A grand, spacious, almost Bruckner-like theme from the strings follows, expanding to an excited passage for the full orchestra from which the soloists gradually rise to take part in another bright duologue. The next section begins with a dark orchestral introduction, from which the horn emerges as the dominant of the two soloists, and the movement keeps both of them very active from then on. The slow cadenza is a virtuoso dialogue, and is followed by a darker passage on the woodwind. A solemn trumpet solo is soon counter-pointed by decorations on the horn, which still dominates its naturally brighter-toned partner. After more dark musings from the woodwind a solo for the alto flute leads into the andante. This begins with a calm melody in the strings, very reminiscent of Shostakovich, then proceeds through solo passages for the two brass soloists, including a brief but unmistakable snatch of *The Last Post* on the trumpet.

Menacing interventions from the timpani introduce the final allegro. There is virtuoso work for the soloists throughout the movement, in duet (they are closely integrated throughout the work), ending with a series of stabbing chords – a fiery, dramatic end to a dramatic work.

The Concerto for Clarinet opens with a fathomless, dark rumbling of low strings and bass clarinet. Out of these depths the soloist comes bubbling up to begin the jolly, bouncing allegro moderato, with its constantly shifting metres. The heart of the work is the central adagio, an extended movement of oceanic serenity, with languorous melodies for the soloist coming in one after another above a rocking accompaniment with prominent marimba and strings. The soloist spends most of this movement – and, indeed, most of the work as a whole – in the mellow lower regions of the instrument's range. The movement ends with the soloist more animated than hitherto, and leads straight into a magical cadenza. Here the clarinet begins by babbling softly to itself, like Tennyson's brook, but quickly becomes reflective, exploring the whole of the instrument's register, all above a soft, sustained humming of low strings, producing a deeply restful, almost hypnotic atmosphere of tranquillity; this in turn leads straight into the final adagio, the consummation of the whole concerto, in which the unearthly calm becomes more profound still. In a luminous F sharp major the soloist plays a Scottish folksong ('Cumha craobh nan tend'), fragments of which had been heard earlier in the work, above a soft background of the wind keening in the sparse grasses of Hoy. It is a sound as desolate as the end of the world, but the effect is one of unassailable peace.

The clarinet concerto was notable for one innovation: it was the first of the Strathclydes to include any percussion beside timpani, making modest use of marimba, crotales and a large Japanese temple gong. The part played by the gong is of interest in its own right, in that it offers a revealing sidelight on the extraordinary lengths of ingenuity to which Max will go in search of the exact musical effect he wants – in this case, the soft sound of the wind sighing in the final few bars of the piece. This wind noise is as realistic as it well could be: a truly authentic realization of one of the simplest sounds. To create it, the temple gong is placed flat on the skin of a kettle-drum. Then, while the pressure inside the drum is varied by use of the pedal, the player gently strikes the edges of the gong with the stick. It is a very clever conjuring trick; but the effect is true magic. When asked how he procured it, Max grins shyly. He is clearly rather proud of it, but he makes light of it. One thinks of the exchange between Dr Watson, gasping with admiration, and Sherlock Holmes: 'Excellent', I cried. 'Elementary', said he.

The fifth concerto was written in 1991, the bicentenary of Mozart's death. With interminable commemorations of the anniversary going on everywhere, Max was perhaps offering his own tribute with this, the Concerto for Violin and Viola, in a reference to Mozart's celebrated *Sinfonia Concertante* for the same pairing (K364). Once again Max varied the orchestration: this concerto is for the two soloists and strings alone.

It begins with the soloists singing together (they play as a pair throughout the work) a poignant, yearning melody over a slow, intense accompaniment from the orchestra. The opening adagio soon develops into the main allegro moderato, with the music becoming first animated, then agitated, with a lot of pizzicato and a spectrum of rich, exotic sonorities reminiscent of Debussy. The movement concludes with a driving, pounding theme in the orchestra leading straight into the second movement. This is pastoral with occasional sudden bursts of frenzy, and returns to the driving rhythm, and guitar-like effects from the soloists. It then develops into a noble adagio, almost Elgarian in its broad, expansive themes, with soaring melodies for the soloists, a final, very brief, excitable climax before fading into stillness. The final surging, turbulent allegro rushes headlong into a brief section marked più lento, with the soloists soaring high above throbbing tremolando strings before dissolving, magically, into nothing. Steve Pruslin's description of this work could hardly be improved on: the soloists, he wrote, were 'red highlights in an overall sound picture of rich mahogany'.

The year that brought forth this, the richest in texture and, with the Concerto for Horn and Trumpet, the most closely argued of the eight Strathclydes completed at the time of writing, also produced the lightest and merriest of the series, the Concerto for Flute. Once again the scoring is careful, designed to show off the solo instrument with maximum prominence. To this end, not only flutes are omitted from the orchestra, but also oboes and violins; and the trumpet parts are scored very sparingly – not at all in the central adagio movement. The result is that the soloist plays against a mellow, sonorous background of clarinets (including bass clarinet), bassoons, horns, violas, cellos and double basses, plus a modest platoon of percussion. The glockenspiel is prominent in the outer movements, while in the central slow movement it is replaced by the distinctive sound of claves. These come from South America, and are short pieces of very hard wood: when struck against each other they produce an inimitable resonant clocking or clonking sound which Max uses to great effect.

The opening movement is a lively, dancing allegro moderato, preceded and followed by slow, mellow passages in which the solo instrument is set against a haunting accompaniment from the orchestral woodwind. The slow movement is all mysterious oriental effects, evocative of Japanese gardens, bonsai and fragile-looking pagodas, and distinctly reminiscent in its elegant shaping of the 'Oriental Garden' movement of *Five Klee Pictures* from all the way back in 1959. As well as the novel tones of the claves, the movement includes a lot of highly atmospheric work for the timpanist. The final allegro andante is full of jaunty, bubbling melodies, and it, too, includes a prominent part for timpani.

The Concerto for Double Bass is by some way the shortest of the Strathclydes so far: twenty-one minutes, as against an average of about twenty-eight for the rest. What it lacks in length, however, it more than makes up for in passion and lyricism: the old bull fiddle, very much the Cinderella of the concerto world, is allowed to sing its heart out, and it does so eloquently, indeed with considerable majesty, right from its entry virtually at the beginning of the work.

The piece is of somewhat unusual construction: there are only two movements, moderato and lento, and the solo instrument is rarely silent after its entry. The work begins with a series of broad, sweeping tunes distributed open-handedly between the soloist and the orchestra. It is followed by a section full of spikier, jolting rhythms, interspersed with gentler, rolling passages. The movement finishes with a rather special cadenza. The second movement, lento, has mysterious flute solos, eerie high shimmers in the strings and a sense of dark, intense foreboding. A central section has a background of great brilliance for the brass and woodwind, against a dark commentary from the soloist in the lower registers, followed by some spectacular harmonics from the soloist over a grinding rumble from the low orchestral strings. At the end there is a single enormous climax for the orchestra, followed in rapid succession by soaring flights from the soloist, a great dramatic cry from the horns, a high tremolando from the strings, and the work ends with a series of drawn-out calls from the double bass that can surely be nothing other than the mournful lowings of a ship's foghorn – perhaps feeling its way through mist on the Pentland Firth.

Why is that cadenza rather special? From time to time through this account of Max's life we have seen examples of the kindness which has endeared him to so many people throughout his life, and the cadenza in this concerto represents just such a gesture. The concerto was written to be performed by John Steer, the double bass principal of the SCO. Unfortunately, some years earlier he was injured in an accident that could hardly have been more catastrophic for someone of his profession: travelling in a train in Italy, he was standing at the open window of the coach, with his hands resting on the lowered glass and his fingers on the outside of the door. A train passing in the opposite direction had managed to pick up and somehow trap a heavy joist of wood, in such a way that it was being whisked along beside the train and smashed against Steer's hands as the two trains passed each other. As a result his fingers were mangled beyond any apparent hope of repair. However, he was rushed home, and a surgeon at St Thomas's Hospital worked virtual miracles, with the astonishing result that Steer's hands were not merely mended, but to such effect that he was actually able to resume his occupation: he is still the principal double bass player with the orchestra. There are limits even to miracles such as this, however, so that although he was still able to manage the orchestral repertoire for his instrument, he knew that the soloist's part in any concerto by Max would be beyond him. However, he was still insistent that Max should include a concerto for his instrument in the Strathclyde sequence, and invited the distinguished double bass virtuoso Duncan McTier to play the solo part. But when the new soloist and the SCO got together to look at and rehearse the piece, they discovered that the cadenza, instead of being for the soloist alone, featured a dialogue with a solo double bass in the orchestra. The part for the orchestral partner had been meticulously written to ensure that it was within Steer's capacity to play.

This story demonstrates both Max's thoughtfulness and also his extraordinary understanding of the possibilities and limitations of instruments and their players. To write to the outermost limits of an instrument – especially with a Duncan McTier to cater for – is one thing, but there is probably not one composer in a dozen who would be capable of working out, to a nicety, just how far he could go in writing for a severely injured and only partially restored performer. It is a small point, but it gives a revealing insight into the man.

The eighth in the Strathclyde series, the Concerto for Bassoon, was the last one completed when this book went to press. As with all the other instruments, Max was concerned to allow the solo instrument to sing – which in this case meant getting the bassoon away from its customary role as the funny man of the orchestra, making domestic plumbing noises and animal representations. Once again, he succeeded: the work is another lyrical piece, with more than a little showmanship in it.

This concerto is unusual, however, in two ways: first, whereas most of the Strathclydes begin with a slow introduction, this one begins quickly, with music of great brilliance for the strings. Second, in most of the others he omitted from the orchestra those instruments which were at all close to the solo instrument in timbre and tessitura – as, for example, where he left out the flutes, oboes and violins from the flute concerto. In this one his orchestra is mainly deep-toned, with an alto flute as well as an ordinary flute, a clarinet in A and a bass clarinet, two contra-bassoons and horns but no trumpets.

The bassoon covers most of its range within a few bars of its first entry in the opening presto. This movement develops into a lively, dancing allegro, with big, spacious melodies from the soloist, mainly in the upper registers of the instrument, set against the dark-toned orchestral woodwind. The slow movement begins and ends with a song of simple beauty, with ominous entries from the timpani and much passionate commentary from the soloist in between; and the finale is a recitative followed by another dancing melody, ending with a slow coda.

This completes the Strathclyde sequence to date. Still to come are the last two concertos in the series: No. 9, which will be for a group of soloists in a chamber ensemble, plus orchestra, and No. 10, which is to be a Concerto for Orchestra. It will have been, as everyone, including Max's detractors, has said in one form or another, a remarkable achievement.

Ian Ritchie, who has since left the SCO for another post, remains anything but a detractor, and he says without hesitation that the Strathclyde Project was the most significant event to take place during his entire ten-year stint with the orchestra: it largely achieved all his ambitions for his players. It took them in all kinds of new directions,

into the community, into the schools; in a meaningful sense it put the
future destiny of the orchestra in the hands of the present generation of
players – their handling of the children in the schools they visited would
be highly influential in determining those children's attitudes towards
live orchestral music when they grew up. So in a large sense the present
players were deciding whether their successors ten or fifteen years later
would have full houses to play to or not. It also, incidentally, provided
the players with a lot of fun.

Outside the small world of Strathclyde, 1987 had begun auspiciously:
Max was created a Knight Bachelor in the New Year Honours List. The
award came as a complete surprise to him. Michael Arnold rang him
and said, 'I've had this letter from Downing Street . . . ' At first Max
didn't believe what he was told. When he was finally convinced, he was
in something of a quandary: his political views had always been to the
left of centre, and as the period of Conservative government went on
after 1979 they moved further and further in that direction. So, while he
never for a moment imagined that his award had anything to do
personally with the occupant of No. 10 Downing Street at the time,
Margaret Thatcher, who, he presumed, had never heard of him, he felt
considerable reluctance to accept anything emanating from her abode.
In addition, although he felt no particular personal animosity towards
the Queen or the royal family – indeed, he was on rather friendly terms
with the Queen Mother – he was at least in theory a republican, and felt
a little awkward about accepting the honour from the hands of the
Queen.

In the end, however, he decided to accept, partly because it was
possible to regard it as an honour for the musical profession, and
especially for the composing fraternity, and partly because Judy Arnold
threatened to hit him with her handbag if he so much as contemplated
refusing it. Her arguments were both emotional and practical: first, she
demanded, if his parents were alive, what did he think they would have
said if he turned it down? And second – this proved to be the clinching
argument in the end – how much easier her own job would be in future
with a Sir Peter to promote and talk about. This argument, though it
sounds more than a little frivolous, was in fact a very shrewd one: the
title has, in truth, made it enormously easier for her to approach people,
has got her through doors that would otherwise have remained shut,
and, in general, done exactly what she said it would: made her job a
good deal easier in many small ways.

Even Max himself has found his knighthood of some use from time
to time. For example, among the various minor honours and honorary

positions he had collected along the way was the Presidency of the Composers' Guild of Great Britain. This position entails very little actual work, but occasionally he has to write a letter in support of some composer who has been hard done by at the hands of a record company, a music publisher, a broadcasting organization or whatever; and then, he finds, the title lends no small extra weight to the intervention.

Max is very amusing about his Knighthood, saying that it was one of the funniest things he has ever experienced. There was very little to it, he says: a short rehearsal, being taught how to walk backwards and so on, and then the ceremony. In it, each recipient got a very carefully orchestrated thirty seconds, then it was all over. His recollections of the occasion are blurred, a mixture of horror and hilarity: the thing he remembers most clearly is that when the new knights entered the chamber there was some kind of military band in a gallery, playing selections from the shows, 'out of tune, in hideous arrangements'. It lent a faintly surrealist air to the proceedings.

He does not remember what the Queen said to him, though he remembers that she had been well briefed, and knew who and what he was, and so on. His only other memory of the occasion is when he got back to Judy Arnold and Metin, the man he was living with at the time. Entirely out of character, Judy had gone out and bought a large, rococo and preposterous hat. When Max returned to them they both descended upon him, demanding, naturally enough, 'What did she say? What did she say?' Without thought, and without hesitation, he said, 'Oh, she said she adored Judy's hat and give her love to Metin.' It halted them in mid-charge, two mouths dropped open, and it was half a minute before it dawned on them that it was a mild, sly joke.

This was not, of course, by any means the first honour or award that Max had received – it would have been surprising if he had not picked up a good many in the course of an illustrious career. Since we have not yet looked at any, other than to mention his award of CBE in 1981, this is perhaps an appropriate point to pause and glance briefly at what he had collected along the way.

It was both apt and ironic that the first body to honour him formally was the Royal Northern College of Music, as his old alma mater, the Royal Manchester College, had by then become. In 1978 the College made him a Fellow; and three years later Manchester University followed suit, only they went the whole hog and made him an Honorary Doctor of Music. This was where the irony really comes in: he had not been especially happy in either establishment, but it was at the University that he had really felt stultified; and it was at the University that Professor Humphrey Proctor-Gregg had held the composition classes from which Max had been unceremoniously expelled for being interested in the wrong kinds of music and not being sufficiently ashamed of the fact.

Over the years he gathered a string of similar honours, mostly honorary doctorates of music – though there was one weird exception: the University of Aberdeen chose to make him an honorary Doctor of Law. He also became President of the Schools Music Association, the North of England Education Conference, the National Federation of Music Societies, and then, in 1986, as we have already seen, he became President of the Composers' Guild, a position he has retained to the present day. That year also he resigned his position as joint Artistic Director of the St Magnus Festival, and accepted the Presidency instead. This was not because of any falling-off of affection for 'his' festival, as his ready acceptance of the Presidency shows; it was simply a recognition that he had too many other calls on his time and his energy, boundless as it seemed to those who didn't know him, to do the job justice. Looked at in that light, it is in fact a testimony to his special devotion to the St Magnus: he was not willing to hold the title of Artistic Director and skimp the responsibilities or the work.

Only three weeks after the announcement of Max's knighthood there was another landmark occasion, this time, though, a very sad one. On 20 March the Fires of London gave their twentieth anniversary concert at the Queen Elizabeth Hall. It was also their last. By this time the Fires had metamorphosed into yet another line-up, the second long-lived team having broken up just in time for a third to present a sort of coda to the group's twenty-year existence. So it was Helen Keen on flutes, Madeleine Mitchell on violin and viola and Mark Glentworth on percussion who had the honour of playing the last night, alongside the survivors of the second line-up, David Campbell on clarinets, Jonathan Williams, cello and, almost unnecessary to record, Steve Pruslin on keyboards. Guesting on guitar was, as usual, Timothy Walker.

The programme they played was, fittingly, made up almost entirely of works by Max. The concert opened with two works written the previous year with this concert in mind: *Farewell-a-Fancye*, based on Dowland, and the song cycle *Winterfold*, sung, needless to say, by Mary Thomas. These two were separated by the only item in the programme not by Max, the world premiere of Concerto for Six Players by Ronald Caltabiano – and so the Fires kept up their outstanding record of commissioning new pieces from unknown composers right to the last. The first half ended on a lighter note, with Max's hilarious realizations of a *Fantasia and Two Pavans* of Purcell. The second half was devoted to a dramatic performance of the work that even in 1987 still had some claim as Max's most famous piece – or his most notorious: the *Eight Songs for a Mad King*, with the versatile bass-baritone David Wilson-Johnson as soloist.

So ended twenty years at the forefront of British musical life. The Fires could look back with immense pride on their record: as one of the most innovative and versatile ensembles in modern musical history; as the vehicle for the works of a composer who now, by widespread consent, was one of the greatest anywhere in the world, and one of the greatest ever produced by Britain, with over fifty works specially written for them; as the most influential group in the country in the fostering of young composers at the start of their careers by taking the risk of commissioning works from them (over forty composers had cause to be grateful to the Fires in this way); and, overall, simply as one of the finest chamber ensembles of their time.

It was always going to be an occasion of profound sorrow when they finally broke up, and so, in the event, it proved: there was hardly a dry eye in the house. As things turned out, it was compounded by two extraneous factors which both struck jarring notes. First, a number of people were deeply offended by the style of the announcement that the group was to disband. The complaint was in every case that the announcement had been peremptory, with almost no warning. The aggrieved parties describe the closure in terms that suggest that they were telephoned one day to be told virtually that they were to lose their jobs the next. This was the cause of yet more criticism of Judy Arnold's style of management. In her defence she says that it was essential that no member of the group should learn of the impending disbandment from any source other than herself: the last thing she wanted was for anyone to learn of it by way of an excited telephone call from one of the other members or, worse, some outsider. No announcement at all could be made, therefore, until she knew that she was going to be able to get in touch with every member of the group in the same round of telephone calls. This seems quite reasonable; and to it may be added the justification put forward elsewhere, that she would assuredly not have done anything so drastic without Max's own approval; and that is adequately supported by his unequivocal support for her position when questioned about it since. But however sad the occasion may have been, the more sensible way of looking at it must surely be the one suggested by Steve Pruslin: that in reality the Fires were lucky, first of all to have lasted as long as they did, and second, to have had the benefit of working in close concert with one of the finest musical minds of the time.

The second discordant note was struck after the concert. After taking curtain calls at the close, Max called for silence, got it, and proceeded to make a speech. It was anything but the kind of anodyne, fond reminiscences that might have been expected on such an occasion. Instead, Max chose to deliver a savage harangue on the pitiful state of arts subsidy in Great Britain, citing as the most immediate example the inadequate support received by the Fires from the Arts Council over the years, pointing out that he had sunk large sums of his own money into the group without any hope of recovering it, and adding that numerous other individual supporters had done the same. Later on, at the party afterwards he got up, stood on a chair, and said the same thing all over again.

This unexpectedly acrimonious way of ending an epoch of his life that he had described in the programme notes for the concert as 'the most important musical experience in my life to date' was received with feelings that were more polarized than merely mixed. Many people thought his words were the most ill-chosen possible, the speech as a whole in the worst taste, and that it had thoroughly spoiled what should have been a sad but sentimental, bittersweet occasion. Others, notably including Louise Honeyman, who had managed the Fires for three years in the early 1970s before going on to run the London Mozart Players, felt that, on the contrary, it had been high time someone spoke out against the derisory funding of the arts in Britain as compared with other prosperous countries, and were silently roaring Max on and wishing him more power to his elbow. It was really a matter of temperament: those who shared Max's own ever-increasing hatred and contempt for the Conservative government, and did not find the idea of standing up and raging against it offensively un-British, tended to support him vigorously; others who, irrespective of their own views on such matters, felt that the occasion should not have been spoiled by the uncompromising introduction of such unpleasant topics, disapproved strongly.

It was in the same year as this farewell performance by the Fires of *Eight Songs for a Mad King* that another, utterly different production of the work brought Max a great deal of undeserved opprobrium. The production was a joint venture between the London Sinfonietta and Opera Factory. The same director had staged the work with the Ensemble Intercontemporain a couple of years earlier, at the Châtelet Theatre in Paris. Judy Arnold had seen it and been horrified by it, and was profoundly relieved that Max had not seen it. Now, in August 1987, she was a great deal more horrified to learn not only that they were going to repeat the production at the Queen Elizabeth Hall, but that it was going to be broadcast on television as well.

Briefly, the production centred on a naked man sitting on a lavatory, periodically reaching down into the bowl, fetching up a handful of realistic-looking excreta from within, and throwing or smearing it about. Judy urged Michael Vyner, the Artistic Director of the London Sinfonietta, to try to persuade the director of the production, David Freeman, to amend this, but Vyner refused, saying it was out of the question, and that it was up to Max to fall in with their plans. He was in any case deeply incensed with Max for not having attended the Paris production, or the rehearsals for his own production – Max had refused to go – and considered that he could not possibly have any conception of what Freeman was trying to do or say. In point of fact, all Max was interested in was blocking the production, at least from going out on television, if he could. Vyner, however, exerted mild moral blackmail by declaring that if the television production was halted everyone concerned – including the London Sinfonietta – would lose their funding and go broke. In the end Max had to be satisfied with a disclaimer on his behalf at the beginning of the television programme, when it was eventually broadcast on Channel 4 over two years later, at the end of 1989. In the meantime his only mild satisfaction was that when the first live performance of the production was staged at the Queen Elizabeth Hall, he sent the Director a beautifully and elaborately wrapped gift, consisting of a large plastic pooper-scooper.

It did him little good. The result was predictable enough: the television station's switchboard was blocked within minutes of the start of the programme by nauseated and outraged viewers, the press suffered one of its periodic fits of morality, and, of course, Max got all the blame. All the energy he had expended in doing his utmost to sabotage the production, to secure agreement to an alternative production, getting the disclaimer added to the programme, went unnoticed, unreported and uncredited.

This is always a potential problem for composers of music theatre works because, according to Max, and other composers interviewed, the composer has no right or control over how his work is produced. In the rogue production of *Eight Songs*, the director merely dismissed Max out of hand as someone who had no understanding of the medium in which his work was being produced. The situation was further complicated by Michael Vyner's moral blackmail.

Among the numerous composers and performers, both musical and theatrical, whom I asked about this problem, opinions were divided. The composers, not surprisingly, were unanimous: the composer was the author of the work, it was his baby entirely, and he was entitled to what he wanted from it. He should include stage directions as elaborate as he needed, and his agent should stipulate in every individual contract that the directions were to be obeyed.

They all also recognized that unfortunately this was a counsel of perfection in an imperfect world, and that such scrupulous and strict adherence to the composer's original intentions was impossible for a wide variety of practical reasons. Without exception, however, they all sympathized strongly with Max. Most of them had suffered something of the kind themselves, usually at the hands of television people.

The theatrical people tended to take the opposite view, declaring that composers as a breed were altogether too fond of keeping dogs and barking themselves. They felt that theatrical work was one speciality and writing music another, and the practitioners of both should have enough trust in the other side to leave them to get on with their work. The musical performers, generally speaking, were less pre-committed and more thoughtful about it than the other two groups, but on reflection they generally declared for Max.

The dilemma was best stated, perhaps, by David Wilson-Johnson, who includes much of Max's work in his wide-ranging repertoire, and is an experienced and accomplished performer of *Eight Songs*. 'In general', he says,

> the composer gave birth to the work, so he has rights in it. In the operas, for instance, Max is quite entitled to say how he wants the piece to be staged, and – if it's practicable – that's how the production company ought to do it. But that said, probably the composer oughtn't to hang on too long, or too grimly. After a while he should perhaps let go a bit. So with a work as well known as the *Eight Songs*, for instance, which has had hundreds of performances, well, if we wanted a truly authentic performance, we'd have to bring back Roy Hart from the dead.

In the end, he felt, if a piece is strong enough to be worth doing after a long period of time, it will be strong enough to carry a few bad performances, or even a few rogue performances; and that is probably an appropriate place to leave the discussion.

The only other work that Max completed in 1987, alongside the Strathclyde oboe concerto, was also a large one, and of major importance in Max's eyes if in few others'. It was an opera, *Resurrection*, which offers a parallel with the Symphony No. 3. Just as the symphony has its origins in Max's work with the young architect, Jonathan Mansfield, while they were on Harkness Fellowships at Princeton together, so *Resurrection* can be traced back to the same period, when Max wrote excitedly to Donald Mitchell to say that he was planning an opera set in an operating theatre, and that he was arranging to watch brain surgery and heart-lung operations as part of the necessary research. This opera now appeared, but it has never been performed in Britain – or, after its opening run, on the Continent or anywhere else – and most people either know nothing of it or dislike what they have heard. Max, on the other hand, insists that it is among his most powerful, profound and important works. This is very likely to be at least partly the kind of protectiveness that takes the form of defiant affection for and loyalty to those of his works that do not have many friends, and makes him defend, say, *The No. 11 Bus* against all comers.

On the other hand, the reason for its unpopularity may have something to do with that first production, in Darmstadt. Judy Arnold, who was present at some of the performances in this run, describes the occasion quite vividly. 'It was an utter catastrophe. Max was totally excluded from all stages of the discussions about the production until just before the premiere, by which time of course it was far too late to do anything about it. There was no consultation whatsoever. The director to whom Max had entrusted the work had done several excellent productions previously of *The Lighthouse* and *The Martyrdom*, so Max was confident that he would deliver the goods. However, despite the fact that the director knew the libretto and what it demanded, virtually none of Max's stage directions were adhered to . . . the rock band was hopeless. The rock singer was worse than hopeless. The amplification for the rock band was handled by a novice of eighteen who was reading the instruction book on how to handle the machinery while she did it. The tap dancers couldn't tap . . .

'*Resurrection* is a black comedy. Without the laughter the whole thing is unbearable. One should be cracking up with laughter the whole time – gallows humour – at the awfulness of it all. *Resurrection* is a mighty piece . . .

'The critics, who more or less universally loathed it, were quite right: there was nothing to admire or to like. It looked hideous. Nothing spoke. All Max's allusions were totally lost in costumes which had nothing to do with anything. It was one of the most supremely disheartening and disagreeable experiences I have ever had, and I can't even begin to imagine what Max must have suffered . . .'

However bungled the solitary production may have been, it is not at all difficult, from a glance at the libretto, to see which of Max's concerns it deals with.

The central 'character' is actually not a character at all, but a larger-than-life-size dummy. In the first part of the opera various members of the dummy's family and other characters, each representing some form of authority figure – a headmaster, a vicar, a doctor – all take turns to indoctrinate the dummy with their different contemporary orthodoxies until his head explodes. This section, the Prologue, is broken periodically by 'alchemical dances' in which a cat (represented by a rock band in the score) is transformed into a dragon, and the action throughout by a series of mocking parodies of commercial advertisements, which become increasingly blurred into reality until the two are synonymous. These are performed on stage by dancers and broadcast via a giant television screen, and clearly express Max's view that commercialism unrestrained, gone mad and running amok, may one day reduce reality to its own debased and false values.

In the main act the dummy is transported to an operating theatre, where he is operated on to 'cure' him of various 'anti-social' tendencies, in the form of individualistic – therefore unorthodox, therefore anti-social – social, political, intellectual, religious and sexual attitudes, in contrast to the bland, safe conformism fostered by the state. These anti-social attitudes are conjured up on stage by means of fantasies involving further stock figures: a capitalist, a trade union functionary, a party apparatchik, more religious ministers, a rabbi, a hot gospeller and others, each spouting his own debased form of the language, and the operating team rids him of them by operating to remove his brain, heart and genitals, replacing each with a sanitized, 'safe' substitute.

The reluctant clone, all individuality surgically removed and replaced by the state's ideas of what are correct values, rises up and turns on its creators, machine-gunning the operating team and the audience. As a twist in the tail, as the dummy disappears, who should appear but Max's old friend from *Taverner*, the Antichrist, rising from its tomb amid a stroboscopic disco light-show.

Here, then, once again we have Max as the essentially moral composer, demanding that we face the issues about humanity and contemporary life that he regards as the most dismal and depressing, and asking us what we should do about them. Here are the excesses of unfettered capitalism, authority and the ease with which, given the slightest lapse from vigilance, it can slip unobtrusively over the line dividing it from its evil twin, authoritarianism – indoctrination by both unfettered laissez-faire commercialism and unfettered state authority. Here also are rock bands, television, advertising, disco music and light-shows, and, in short, anything and everything in the modern world used to bombard us with its endless trivia, plastic dustbin-bait, kitsch, lies and distortions – all, in short, that make it such an uninhabitable desolation.

One cannot fail to notice that while Max asks these questions, he does not make any attempt to answer them. He would, I have no doubt, contend that the composition of his opera is his answer. In this moral dimension of his work, then, he has clearly not shifted his position in the slightest from the time of *Taverner*; in other words, from when he was a schoolboy of eighteen.

One is immediately reminded of a close parallel with *Resurrection* in Anthony Burgess's *A Clockwork Orange*, in which the same kind of monkeying by a totalitarian state with a human being's individuality produces a similarly inhuman monster, which also rises up to threaten its creating power. It is a grim irony that *Resurrection* is among Max's least liked works in Britain, and has not been performed there. Stanley Kubrick's film of Burgess's parable, austere, highly moral and very closely faithful to the original novel, was withdrawn by Kubrick himself from all public performance in Britain, partly in frustration at a conspiracy by a confederation of dunces in Parliament and the press wilfully to misunderstand and misrepresent it.

11 ~ *Con Fuoco*

Over the next couple of years life proceeded a little more restfully for Max. Apart from the first performance of *Resurrection* in the Stadts-theater at Darmstadt, the city which had commissioned it, Max spent more time on Hoy, composing and consolidating his life there.

One very sad incident serves to indicate how strong Max's ties to Hoy had become. The headmaster of Hoy School, John Eccles, suffered a tragedy when his eleven-year-old son, Jan, fell from the roof of the family house and was killed. Max was in London when it happened, but someone told him. He promptly cancelled his business in London and hurried home for the funeral, at which he played the harmonium in the draughty Victorian church. He had already, incidentally, written *Songs of Hoy* for the children of the island's junior school, at the suggestion of his near neighbours, Jeff and Avril Clark. He had also dedicated *Kinloche His Fantassie* to the Clarks when they finished building their house.

Max was also increasingly enjoying the company and support of his closest neighbour, friend and ally on Hoy, David Hutchinson, known to the world as Hutch. Hutch lives in a croft, much like Bunertoon, at the bottom of a steep, almost vertical cliff, and Max lives at the top. They get on extremely well, not least because Hutch is one of very few people with a mind capable of keeping up with Max's. In addition he is one of those rare people who seldom open their mouths except to say something sardonic out of the corner of it, and he has a superb, almost French contempt for authority, officialdom and, especially, for any sort of pomposity, so the two of them thoroughly enjoy each other's company.

Max has never lost his horror of telephones, and does not have one in Bunertoon. Until recently, if he had to make a call, he had to tramp a mile across the mountainside to the nearest phone box, at Jack Rendall's. He now has a mobile phone, of which no one except Judy Arnold knows the number. However, Hutch often helps Max out with errands of one kind or another, so they have rigged up an intercom line between their two crofts, up the vertical cliff. This way Max can give Hutch a ring and ask him if he'll help him out by doing odd bits of shopping and so forth, if he happens to be going to the village or to

Stromness. (The short score of *An Orkney Wedding* bears amusing testimony to this arrangement: on the back of one page of manuscript score are the words 'David: bog roll, salt, loaf'.)

Max and Hutch have also invested in an enormous, shared deep-freeze, which was the main casualty one summer when Max loaned Bunertoon to a friend who needed solitude to work for a short while. When she left she followed instructions and locked everything up; unfortunately, not knowing about the existence of the freezer and thinking she was doing the right thing, she also obligingly switched off the electricity at the mains. Some time later Max duly returned, laden down with food and wine, which he and Hutch then had to lug up the cliff to Bunertoon. In Hutch's graphic words, 'The maggots were coming down the mountain to meet us.'

Now that he was spending a little more time in his retreat, Max was able to compose more. In 1988 he produced a set of *Six Songs for St Andrew's*, for the children of St Andrew's Primary School, Orkney. They are for children of six to nine, accompanied by recorders, tuned percussion, cymbals and a big drum, and were first performed at the St Magnus Festival that year under Glenys Hughes's direction.

The same year saw also two other minor works, and one major one: the Concerto for Trumpet and Orchestra. This was commissioned by the Philharmonia Orchestra, with their virtuoso principal trumpeter, John Wallace, in mind for the solo part, and was premiered by them in Hiroshima in September that year, as part of their tour. Like almost all Max's concertos, this work begins quietly; but this is not the serene quiet of dawn that often opens Max's works since his entrenchment on Hoy. This is a dark, uneasy quiet, with ominous chords in the lower registers of the strings – and, indeed, the mood of grim foreboding remains throughout the movement, and the work. One cannot help speculating whether the intended venue for the first performance of the work was on Max's mind while he composed it.

At all events, once the soloist has entered, he has all the usual fireworks that Max provides for this instrument, a favourite of his from as far back as his opus 1, the celebrated sonata that electrified the musical world at the New Music Group Manchester concert at the Arts Council in 1956. The second movement continues without a break from the first, and again opens quietly and ominously. It is mainly a spacious virtuoso cantilena for the solo instrument, ending in a great erupting chorus of birdsong. The final movement, presto, is then introduced by one of the dialogues between trumpet and horn that Max likes – looking forward to the third Strathclyde concerto. It has a brilliant part for the soloist, soaring over a dark, muttering orchestral accompaniment led by subdued brass, and there is a great deal of highly dramatic work for the timpanist, and many shimmering arpeggios for the chinese bell tree. The piece finally reaches a sort of calm, and ends quietly, but still on a dark, disturbed note, as it began.

There is more to this concerto than that, however. It is not an accident that the piece is based on the plainchant 'Franciscus pauper et humilis'; for Max had been planning for many years to write an opera on the life of St Francis of Assisi, and this concerto stands in the same relationship to the opera as the fantasias to *Taverner* – a kind of instrumental chewing over of the musical material of the opera. In the opera, if it ever finds a sponsor and materializes, St Francis himself will be closely identified with the trumpet. The concerto tracks the plot of the opera roughly like this: the first movement deals with Francis's early life, up to his conversion on the steps of the cathedral, his fight with his father, and his public embracing of the life of a hermit, living in kinship with nature in the woods. The second is the sermon to the birds with which this saint is always especially associated, with the great shower of birdsong at the end of the movement their response to him; and the finale shows him exorcizing demons and taming the wolf of Gubbio.

The theme of kinship with nature does not come as a surprise in Max's music. Nor is it any kind of a surprise to find that St Francis has apparently migrated north from his usual haunts to chilly, windy Orkney – jerked out of the sun rather as the guitar was jerked from sunny Spain to play *Hill Runes*. This is made clear by the fact that in the great shout of birdsong at the end of the second movement, all the cries are of northern sea-birds. There is no anomaly about this: anything that interests Max is likely to find itself being Orkneyized, and St Francis would have liked the Orkneys: they are full of birds.

As for the concerto itself, the great Swedish trumpeter, Håkan Hardenberger, who has taken the piece enthusiastically into his repertoire and plays it often, says of it that it is an intensely spiritual piece. He detects, as perhaps only a virtuoso of the instrument could do, great similarities between the writing for the solo instrument in this concerto and that in the sonata, opus 1, written thirty-two years earlier. There are certain gestures in both, though particularly in the concerto, he says, that are almost romantic in quality. It is the work, he feels, of a composer who cares deeply about his listeners. But then, he adds modestly, 'It's not for me to make judgements like that about him or his standing. I'm just a thirty-year-old trumpet-player!' He concedes that even for a performer of his extraordinary gifts the work is difficult; but he immediately adds the comment that we have become accustomed to hear from people for whose instruments Max has written: it is exceptionally well written for the trumpet, as if Max himself was an accomplished trumpeter.

In the next couple of years Max wrote several small works, including three short but interesting choral pieces: a motet, *Hallelujah! The Lord God Almightie*, to a Scottish text, and *Hymn to the Word of God*, to a Byzantine one, and a carol, 'Apple Basket, Apple Blossom', to a poem by George Mackay Brown. He also composed a short pavan *Threnody In Memoriam Michael Vyner*. Vyner had been a very popular figure as artistic Director of the London Sinfonietta, and Max was only one of numerous composers who honoured his memory with a piece of music.

Then, in a sudden rush, came four music-dramas for children, *The Great Bank Robbery*, for eleven-to-fourteen-year-olds, *Jupiter Landing* and *Dinosaur at Large* for eight to eleven-year-olds, and *Dangerous Errand*, for six to eight-year-olds. These pieces are unique in Max's output: they sprang up, four of them in a row, like mushrooms, in 1989–90, and he has never produced anything remotely like them before or since. They were published by Longman, who had never published anything of Max's until this sudden flurry of children's music theatre.

Finally, this period produced four major works: the third and fourth Strathclyde concertos, a full-length ballet and his Symphony No. 4.

The ballet was commissioned by the Kongelige Theater of Copenhagen, choreographed by Flemming Flindt, who had commissioned and choreographed Max's earlier ballet, *Salome*. It concerns the unhappy life of the eighteenth-century British princess Caroline Mathilde, trapped in holy deadlock with the epileptic and mad King Christian VII of Denmark. She has a passionate affair with the King's physician, Doctor Struensee, who heals the King first. The couple are mocked by the people, then a trap is set for them at a masked ball where they dance voluptuously together before being arrested. Struensee is executed, and Caroline Mathilde goes into exile.

It is a passionate, hot-blooded ballet; and it receives throughout passionate, hot-blooded music. There is nothing difficult or complicated about it: the music is bold, vigorous and tuneful, always sympathetic to the hapless young princess, trapped, because of her station in life, in a loveless marriage and doing the only thing that she can see to be done about it. It has so far generated no fewer than three spin-offs for the concert-hall: matching *Concert Suites* from Acts I and II of the ballet, and *Two Dances from Caroline Mathilde*, arranged for flute and harp, first performed at Thurso in September 1993. As for the ballet itself, it has been an instant and continuing success in Copenhagen, being performed in front of consistently sold-out houses for three consecutive seasons.

The true giant among the pieces composed in these years, however, was without doubt the fourth symphony. Composed, as we have seen, for the Scottish Chamber Orchestra, it is necessarily on a somewhat smaller scale than the three previous symphonies. It had two independent sources of inspiration. One was the plainchant 'Adorna thalamum tuum, Sion' (Adorn your bridal chamber, daughter of Sion). Max himself has described the second source:

> I came out of the house one morning very early, to be confronted by a golden eagle, perched on the fence a few yards from the door. He took off, slowly unfolding a huge wingspan, floating upwards with an overwhelming grace-in-strength – the while regarding me with icy disdain – and moved slowly out to sea, against the rising sun. This vision has haunted me, and although the music does not attempt to portray the flight literally, I hope something of the reverberations of that extraordinary moment come through.

There are those who have regularly carped at Max since his move to Orkney and the increasing influence of Orcadian sights, sounds and scenes in his music. He has been accused of joining the cow-pat school, of becoming just another English pastoralist, and so on. But the above description alone ought to be sufficient answer to those critics: he has allowed Orkney into his music, quite simply, because Orkney has shown him such extraordinary things. If one thinks of his vision of the golden eagle – a sight that scarcely any inhabitant of the British Isles is privileged to see nowadays – and of the shoal of mackerel that swam into the bay below Bunertoon and provided the ever-shifting play of silvery light in the slow movement of the Strathclyde Concerto No. 2, for Cello, he would have had to be more than human *not* to feel the need to turn them to account in his music somehow.

The symphony is very different from its three predecessors. It is much more strident in colouring, louder, more discordant and brighter in tone. Like the third symphony, it has a very prominent part for the timpani, but no additional percussion at all; and although it is scored for unaugmented chamber orchestra – that is, with no trombones or tuba – the two horns and two trumpets have a tremendous amount to do, and make enough noise for a whole arsenal of heavy brass.

It is a work of contrasts: the first movement is a tremendous affair, all brass and timpani. It starts with brass fanfares followed by dark, low strings, more fanfares, then dark, low woodwind. There is a series of climaxes, each giving the brass a little more to do, before the movement ends with a series of eerie, poignant melodies for oboe and flute over string tremolandi. A timpani solo dramatically announces the scherzo, but the movement itself is generally more restful, though with a good deal of anguished music for the strings, ending with another oboe solo, taken up by the flute before fading into silence. The slow movement starts with slow, spacious melodies for the woodwinds, then the brass and timpani enter to bring a big climax, but we are soon back with the woodwind, over a rocking figure in the strings. The movement grows gradually more agitated, with cries from the brass and dark mutterings from the strings. The final movement is much closer in sound to the first two symphonies, with murmuring sea sounds. The work ends with a series of crashing chords, each followed and resolved by a short statement on the woodwind.

Meanwhile Max was busy picking up three further honours: in 1988 he was made Officier dans l'Ordre des Arts et des Lettres – a comparatively rare example of a British musician being honoured by the French, who generally pay little attention to British music. The following year he became President of the National Federation of Music Societies, and was awarded the Cobbett Medal for services to chamber music.

In early 1990 he was pitched into a major retrospective, the 'Max' Festival at the South Bank. This was a considerable honour – there are few living composers for whom it could have been laid on without a fair certainty of embarrassment. The festival ran from 27 March to 10 April and included thirteen concerts. Eight of them were orchestral, with three orchestras appearing: the Royal Philharmonic presented three programmes, in which Max's first three symphonies were performed in sequence; the BBC Symphony Orchestra – the Londoners, for a change, not his friends from Manchester – gave one, with *Worldes Blis* alongside works by Stravinsky and Alexander Goehr; and the Scottish Chamber Orchestra gave the other four. William Conway played the solo part in the Strathclyde Concerto No. 2, for Cello, which had been written for him; Robert Cook and Peter Franks did the same in their Strathclyde Concerto, No. 4 for Horn and Trumpet. Neil Mackie performed *Into the Labyrinth* – once again the performers being those for whom the work was written – on an evening which also featured *An Orkney Wedding, with Sunrise*, with the Highland piper, George McIlwham, who has made a worldwide reputation for himself with his performances of the bagpipe part in the work.

The SCO also accompanied Music Theatre Wales, which put on a performance of *The Martyrdom of St Magnus*, following their very successful CD recording of the opera. The final four concerts were sources of special pleasure to Max. The first was a full-scale reunion of the Fires of London, in which the full second line-up reassembled to perform a variety of works: *Antechrist*, *Leopardi Fragments* and *Ave Maris Stella* made up an afternoon concert for Part One. The same evening they put on *Image, Reflection, Shadow* and *Vesalii Icones* for Part Two. Tom Yang, the Chinese dancer who had given many early performances of *Vesalii*, came to dance the work at the reunion.

The last three concerts all took place on the same day, and formed three sessions of 'Children's Day'. Each session made up a complete and generous concert, and each had the assistance, for one major work on the programme, of a group of players from the SCO, fulfilling their now customary role bringing music to the community, and particularly to children. Each programme was different, and the central one was of special interest, in that it included the world premiere of *Jupiter Landing*, one of the spate of children's music theatre works Max had produced so suddenly for Longman the previous year. In all, twenty-eight of Max's works were performed in the course of the fortnight.

The following year he gathered two especially prestigious awards, and the year after that he took on two equally prestigious positions. He also found time to do some composing. The two honours that came his way in 1991 were the First Award of the Association of British Orchestras. It was presented to the person considered by the Association to have contributed most, during the past year, to the benefit of orchestras and the promotion of orchestral life in the United Kingdom. The other was the Gulliver Award for the Performing Arts in Scotland, given annually to the person who has made an outstanding contribution to the performing arts in Scotland.

The new posts he took on were not semi-figurehead ones like the various presidencies he had already accepted. Both had the effect of cementing especially close relationships that had gradually grown up between Max and two other orchestras: the Royal Philharmonic in London and the BBC Philharmonic in Manchester.

The association with the RPO came about at a time of change for the orchestra. The General Manager, Ian Maclay, had done a long tour of duty with the RPO, and had been instrumental in changing the fortunes of the orchestra – by methods which had occasioned a good deal of lip-curling on the part of the musical establishment. It is true to say, however, that without his efforts the orchestra would probably have turned turtle. The funding of the four independent London orchestras – the London Symphony, the London Philharmonic, the Royal Philharmonic and the Philharmonia – had been both chaotic and parsimonious over many years. There had always been a noisy school of thought that held that it was absurd for London to have so many full-blown symphony orchestras, while Berlin, Vienna and many other great cities had one or at the most two. There was an equally large and vociferous faction, on the other hand, which felt that four such orchestras constituted a national treasure-house of talent, and ought to be recognized as such. The result was that the four orchestras struggled along, competing for the same audience, often playing the same core repertoire, with none of them receiving anything like an adequate government subsidy, measured by the standards of European and American orchestras of similar ability and standing.

It has been a standing reproach to the philistinism of successive British governments that our orchestral players are by common consent the fastest and most accurate sight-readers in the world, not because of any innately greater genius, but simply because they are always so strapped for cash that they have to perform on a fraction of the rehearsal time available to their continental and American brethren. We should recall Max's comment after the superlative performance of *Worldes Blis* by the RPO at the Festival Hall in March 1993: 'For them to produce a performance like that after two rehearsals – well, that's a bit of history in the making.' No other orchestra of such calibre in the world would have been required to perform such a difficult piece on such comparatively scanty rehearsal time – apart, of course, from the other three London orchestras. The Berlin or Vienna Philharmonic would have had two weeks, not two rehearsals of three hours each. Similarly, it has become one of the best-known and most shameful facts in contemporary music that the Berlin Philharmonic, for example, receives more than three times as much money from the German government as the four London independents receive together from the British government.

Over recent years the Royal Philharmonic has generally been the least favoured of the four by the Arts Council, to such an extent that by 1993 only 7 per cent of the orchestra's total income was money directly contributed as grant by the Arts Council. The rest was made up by a variety of schemes, all unashamedly aimed at raising money. They issued a series of records of popular classics with a disco beat, under titles such as *Hooked on Classics* and the like; they spent a great deal more of their year than their three rivals touring the provinces with a core popular repertoire. And their reward for such enterprise, forced on them though it had been by sheer financial necessity, was that they were openly regarded by the lofty patrons of the arts in the Arts Council as less serious, less hard-line 'classical' and, therefore, less deserving of government support than their competitors. An interesting ploy: you force your orchestra to go populist by making it the only way open to them of getting money; they do it, and then you use that as a rod to beat their back with, accusing them of being plebeian. Comparing this with the response of the Strathclyde Regional Council when faced with an improbable but fascinating and unbeatable-value musical offer is a useful exercise, and, from an English perspective, depressing.

The long and the short of all this was that just about when Ian Maclay was calling it a day after many years with the RPO and giving way to Paul Findlay, from the Royal Opera House, Covent Garden, Max accepted a position identical to that which he already held with the SCO: Associate Composer and Conductor. It was, moreover, a clearly defined position, with firm commitments on both sides. Paul Findlay is emphatic about this: it was no figurehead post, with either side gaining reflected glory from mere association with the other. On the contrary, it was a direct development of the work Max had done for so many years with the Fires, but with the full resources of a symphony orchestra at his disposal.

Max's brief was to produce two commissions a year for the orchestra, one for a large work, on the scale of a symphony, perhaps, the other for something smaller, of concert-overture size. More significant in the long term, though, is an altogether more innovative responsibility: Max was to be solely responsible for all commissioning of new music for the orchestra; in particular in the RPO's fiftieth anniversary year, in 1996, it will be Max's task to look at all the music written during the five decades of the orchestra's life, and work the best of them into that year's programming. This is passing power to the composer with a vengeance.

It is very noticeable that when Paul Findlay of the RPO speaks of Max, it is often in the identical words used by Ian Ritchie of the SCO: Max got this job, with its exceptionally challenging and wide-ranging brief, for two reasons. First, he was instantly accepted by the players, who liked him for his easy, direct manner, and for his total lack of airs and graces. And second, he was an administrator's dream to work with: in Findlay's words, 'feet firmly on the ground, recognizing that the administrative people had their part to play, utterly pragmatic'. Once again, he was taken to by musicians because he was above all else a musician's musician. Not for the first time, his North country working-class roots stood him in good stead: the people at the RPO recognized immediately that in him they had found a musician who inhabited no ivory towers, who did not plan the jamboree concert without bothering to cost it first. The old-fashioned ethic of giving value for money was what got him this post, as it had got him the same at the SCO and was about to get him again with the BBC Philharmonic.

About the similar post with his own old favourites at the BBC in Manchester little needs to be said. There too the orchestral players took to him at once, recognizing the same virtues as the other two had seen and jumped at. Trevor Green, the Head of Music at the BBC in Manchester, is as unequivocal as Ritchie and Findlay, and says substantially the same things. The fact that a provincial BBC orchestra has recently been signed up for an extensive, high-prestige tour of the United States, Green says, owes more to the orchestra's association with Max than to any other single factor.

Several new pieces were added to Max's already extensive list of works in 1991. It was, as we have seen, the bonus year in which he produced not the usual one but two Strathclyde concertos, those for violin and viola and for flute. The two concert suites from the ballet *Caroline Mathilde* appeared this year. So did another children's music theatre piece, *The Spiders' Revenge*, this time for very young children, a short piece for solo oboe, *First Grace of Light*, and finally, a commission from the Ojai Festival in California resulted in the *Ojai Festival Overture*, a brilliant, straightforward piece of fun – Max with his cowboy hat on, as Steve Pruslin wrote of it, although actually it would have been more proper to talk of Max with his feathered headdress on, since the word *Ojai* (pronounced something like the 'och, aye' of a music-hall Scotsman) is of American Indian origin.

He was back to his customary prolific output, moderated as it had unavoidably been by his growing commitments as a conductor; and this continued through 1992 and 1993. The first of these two years saw the double bass Strathclyde concerto written and premiered; it also saw the death of the fine English conductor, Sir Charles Groves. Max had a special affection for Sir Charles, who had been a lifelong champion, in a very quiet, English-gentlemanly fashion, of new music. He had also been the Principal Conductor of Max's pet orchestra, the BBC Northern, back in Max's childhood, when he would listen to it at every opportunity. On one occasion, when Max was about twelve years old, he had been taken to meet Groves and had shown him a small composition for piano. Max has very little recollection of what Groves said at the time – he had been too overwhelmed by awe and shyness – but he remembers being given a benevolent pat on the head as they parted. Since then they had become good friends.

In memoriam, Max wrote a short, affectionate tribute: *Sir Charles, his Pavan* is a beautiful piece of about four minutes' duration. It is slow, as its title indicates, dignified and sad, but with a very distinct twinkle, entirely befitting its genial subject, and not at all funereal. Two small things about the little piece make it noteworthy, apart from its commemoration of a musician very much in Max's mould and after Max's own heart. First, it is based on the very theme for piano that Max had taken to show him, no less than forty-six years before – perhaps the most extreme case of things brewing long inside Max before bursting into the world. Second, although Max had not had anything published by the firm of Schott & Co. since the early *Sinfonia* in 1962, Sir Charles's daughter, Sally Groves, was a senior employee of the company, and it was to Schott's that he gave the little piece for publication. It was a small but typically thoughtful kindness.

The other two works from 1992 were both for children. One was a half-hour piece of music theatre, *A Selkie Tale*, selkies being seals, which live in great numbers in the sea round Hoy. The other piece was a very different affair, and once again brought Max into the forefront of musical education in Britain.

The piece was titled *The Turn of the Tide* and, like the Strathclyde concertos, was the final result of a large and very adventurous project. It had its origins in a speech made by Max as far back as 12 November 1985, just before Ian Ritchie took on Kathy McDowell as Development Manager for the SCO. Max was giving a pre-concert talk before the premiere of his *First Ferry to Hoy*, given by the London Sinfonietta and ILEA children's and youth performers at the Queen Elizabeth Hall, in which he claimed that 'Children must get their hands dirty with music.' As anyone who has traced Max's career this far will know, this has been the underpinning theme of his ideas about music education right from the start, from his time as Director of Music at Cirencester Grammar School and before. It flowed naturally from his disgust at the path his own musical education had followed, and his determination that future generations of children should have the option of something better. But even as late as 1985 his ideas were still thought of in many places, including most high places, as verging on the revolutionary; and those words at the pre-concert talk blazed into life in the mind of one member of the audience: Kathy McDowell. They were a crucial part of the inspiration behind the Strathclyde Project, which she had done so much to turn into a reality; and they were the moving spirit behind her next big venture, the Turn of the Tide project.

After some years working for Ian Ritchie and the SCO, Kathy McDowell went to work in her native Northern Ireland, as Deputy General Manager of the Ulster Orchestra. During her time there the Association of British Orchestras decided to strike out in a completely new direction. Until then it had been purely a negotiating body, to represent the orchestras in salary negotiations with the Musicians' Union, and so forth. It now decided to expand its activities to embrace training and planning for the future of the orchestral life of the country as well. (It is almost certainly no coincidence that the Chairman of the ABO at this time happened to be Ian Ritchie.) The result was a pilot national education scheme, to involve many of the country's orchestras, and it had twin objectives: to help as many children as possible to gain some musical education of the 'hands-on' kind advocated so strenuously by Max, Ritchie, McDowell and other far-sighted people, and to offer some experience in this kind of working in the community to those member orchestras that as yet had none.

By chance, the government at this time was in the throes of installing the new National Curriculum. One of the working parties set up to handle this was devoted to the musical curriculum, and it produced the conclusion, among others, that musical education should be creative, with children composing – in effect, the working party ended up publicly proclaiming much the same ideas as Max had been implementing at Cirencester almost thirty years before. Any satisfaction this decision brought was short-lived, however: the Secretary of State for Education of the day, Kenneth Clarke, promptly overruled the working party and decreed that music would continue to be taught by the traditional methods of listening to music, appreciating it if that happened to flow from the listening, and a limited amount of performance by singing and learning to play individual instruments. Cirencester and Strathclyde might as well never have happened.

Max and the ABO fought fiercely on the side of the working party, and the ABO decided to do something about it on its own initiative. All four Arts Councils – for England, Wales, Scotland and Northern Ireland – were to be involved, and a major work was to be commissioned from a front-rank composer as an integral part of the project. (As a postscript, the working party and its lobby eventually won the argument, under a new, somewhat less intransigent Education Secretary, and the children will now duly 'dirty their hands with music' under the National Curriculum.)

The front-rank composer more or less chose himself: assuming only that he would be able to spare the time, it was a case of *aut Max aut nullus*. Kathy McDowell, fearing that the answer would be that he was too heavily committed, nevertheless approached him and rather diffidently asked him if he would consider the idea. Not very surprisingly, he said he would be delighted.

The resulting scheme was in many ways much like a bigger version of the Strathclyde Project. Sixteen orchestras agreed to take part. Each of them was assigned a region of Britain, and its members were to go out into all the participating schools in their region, helping, advising and generally working closely with the children, at their own level, to fulfil their role in the composition of the Turn of the Tide music. The way this was done entailed a full-scale partnership between Max, the children and the orchestral-players-cum-part-time-teachers, and it was managed without putting an insupportable strain on Max's limited time.

It worked like this. Max devised a work of six sections. It was on his favourite theme of man's destructiveness towards the environment, and his responsibility to take care of it. In this he was, without doubt, much motivated by the ecological vulnerability of his own island home, with the periodically renewed threats of possible uranium mining on land and the ever-present peril of oil slicks from the sea. He composed, in full, parts 1 and 2, which deal with the creation of life and its first flourishing. The next two sections are to be composed by the children who, very importantly, also play the parts they have composed, joining the orchestra assigned to their region for concert performances of the complete work. These two sections develop the life-flourishing theme in section 3 and, in section 4, initiate the next main theme, the onset of pollution into the natural creation. This is completed in the apocalyptic section 5, in which Max takes over again, on total toxic overload – planetary death, when the biosphere can no longer absorb any more pollution. The sixth and final section is a nine-minute hymn of thanksgiving for a last-minute reprieve: Man, at the fifty-ninth minute of the eleventh hour, at last listens to the message of nature, that he cannot live outside nature and play merry hell with the natural creation, and the tide, which is ready to sweep us all to destruction, turns.

It is – in the parts written by Max, which form the concert version of the work – a predominantly simple, lyrical piece (the fifth, apocalyptic section apart), highly approachable, all soft, autumnal colours and restrained volume, and comes fully into bloom only in the final hymn. We have seen all along that Max's repudiation of religion has run parallel to a compelling need to probe and understand mankind's religious imperatives. It is clear that his urge to explore this murky region of the human spirit has been one of the constant driving forces behind his creativity. At one point I suggested that he has spent much of his life writing religious music in search of a religion. The closing hymn in this work is a typical example, illustrating Gerard McBurney's notion of Max as the entirely moral composer, par excellence. Sung by large choirs with the distinctive sweetness of young voices, it is by turns wistful and jaunty, and almost unbearably moving.

The piece was jointly commissioned by the four Arts Councils and the ABO. The sixteen orchestras that then took it out to the schools were: the Ulster Orchestra, the SCO, the Northern Sinfonia, the English Northern Philharmonic (the orchestra of Opera North in civvies), the Hallé, the Manchester Camerata, the BBC Welsh

Symphony Orchestra, the BBC Philharmonic, the City of Birmingham Symphony Orchestra, the Bournemouth Sinfonietta, the Orchestra da Camera, the Docklands Sinfonietta, the City of London Sinfonia, the London Sinfonietta, the Academy of St Martin-in-the-Fields, and the London Symphony Orchestra. The money to fund the ambitious project came partly from the Foundation for Sport and the Arts, which is largely bankrolled by the football pools promoters, and by money provided by Shell UK, a traditional supporter of the ABO.

By the beginning of 1993 Max was accepting conducting assignments from orchestras in America, Leipzig, Lausanne and elsewhere, as well as his regular work at home and on tour with his own three orchestras, and was by now spending a full half of his year conducting. All the living on planes, in hotels and out of suitcases that this entailed meant that he was also getting pretty sick of it, and was making determined New Year resolutions to cut it down. On the other hand he was greatly enjoying the close study it necessitated his making of scores from the classical repertoire, especially of Haydn, whom Max regards, interestingly, as the most seriously under-rated composer of truly great stature.

Haydn, in fact, is not only a composer of whom Max is particularly fond, but also one to whom he acknowledges a great debt in his own work. He was introduced to his work, in particular the string quartets, by Hans Keller way back in the 1960s, when, as he confesses, he was not greatly familiar with Haydn. But since he has been conducting more and more of the classical repertoire and therefore making intensive studies of many of Haydn's symphonies, he has come to admire and embrace many features of the older composer's style. 'You realize', he says, 'that in many things in music, Haydn was there first. Not just monothematic last movements in the symphonies, and double varia- tions, both of which are little trademarks of his, but in very small things – such as making bridge passages interesting by foreshadowing what is to come and echoing what had gone, and development sections where the material is chopped up in the most irregular phrasings you could imagine, cross-phrasing and so forth: these have got into my own pieces; especially in the fourth symphony . . . '

He also enjoys Mozart, and once again acknowledges a great debt to the earlier master. He spent one season, in 1989, on tour with the Glyndebourne Opera Company, conducting *The Marriage of Figaro*. 'After doing a *lot* of performances of that, it got into me, right deep down. *Caroline Mathilde*, for instance, would never have been the same without that. Mozart's ability to portray someone in a very quick line, and make it absolutely clear, and being able to hold three or four strands together throughout and make those people's identities perfectly clear, just from the music they sing – that's quite miraculous. I learned a lot from that, and it got into the ballet very strongly.'

Max is also especially fond of Mendelssohn – 'a great hero' – Debussy and his perennial favourite, to whom he always returns with his reverence undimmed, Beethoven. Among his earliest influences, Bartók has persisted. One of the pieces he broadcast on *Children's Hour* when he was about fourteen was a dark, discordant, troubled piano piece in which the influence of Bartók was clearly audible; now, almost fifty years later, he is rediscovering him. Other great loves are Vaughan Williams, in particular the symphonies 3, 4, 5 and, most of all, no. 6, which he vividly remembers hearing as a boy and being bowled over by it; and of course the influence of medieval and Renaissance music is as powerful as ever.

On the other side, Brahms is a composer he has never been able to get on with, though unhesitatingly conceding his greatness (an attitude that was shared by Benjamin Britten); and as for Richard Strauss, Liszt and especially Wagner, he dislikes the nature of their musical statements and dismisses them very amusingly. Though he ought not to be mentioned on the same page as the others, the composer he execrates above all others is Carl Orff, partly on extra-musical grounds – his collaboration with the Nazis – but mostly because of what Max regards as his utter musical vacuity.

Despite Max's increasing conducting commitments in 1993, he still found time to compose: Strathclyde Concerto No. 8, for Bassoon, *Seven Summer Songs*, a delightful set of songs on texts by Max about a visit to Granny's farm somewhere in Orkney, for performance by primary school children, the *Two Dances from Caroline Mathilde*, arranged for flute and harp, and a big piece, *Corpus Christi, with Cat and Mouse*, for the choir of Balliol College, Oxford. This last is a hilarious piece, taken from manuscript texts in the college's celebrated library. Some of the material was in code, including the punch-line, which is wonderful, and must on no account be spoiled by disclosure here. Nor must the secret in *Six Secret Songs*, another set for children. There was also a carol for children, 'Shepherds of Hoy', commissioned by *The Times* jointly from Max and George Mackay Brown, and *A Spell for Green Corn: The MacDonald Dances*, a substantial and delightful piece commissioned by Donald MacDonald, the genial businessman who is also the very capable and go-ahead Chairman of the SCO.

In the course of 1993 he also gathered more honours: Honorary Doctor of Music, Glasgow University, Member of the Royal Swedish Academy of Music; and he was announced as the next President, from 1994, of the Cheltenham Arts Festival, with which he has had a long and mostly happy association since his Cirencester days. He also had the immense satisfaction of clinching a deal with the British Library, which bought his entire archive of autographed manuscripts and sketches, including everything available up to the end of 1991, thus ensuring that a national treasure beyond price will remain for the benefit of the nation in the future.

His composing schedules are already full to overflowing for the next few years, not to mention his conducting commitments. The latter, however, will be eased a little in the year between summer 1995 to summer 1996 when he has flatly declared he will be taking a year off from all international commitments, to spend a full, blissful year on Hoy, drinking wine with Hutch, enjoying the company of all his friends, relaxing, reading, walking the beetling brows and crags of his beloved island, and indulging his greatest passion of all, writing music.

Also during 1993 he was working on the score of his Symphony No. 5, commissioned by the Philharmonia Orchestra and due to be premiered at the 1994 Promenade Concerts, thus continuing what Paul Griffiths has called 'the most important symphonic cycle since Shostakovich'. And as soon as he has finished that he will have to begin work on Symphony No. 6, again already commissioned, this time for the Royal Philharmonic, for their fiftieth birthday celebrations in 1996.

The summer of 1993 saw the fifth successful year of the Hoy Summer School for young composers. This was Max's own brainchild, and achieved with help from the industrious and *sympathique* Kathy McDowell while she was still at the SCO. It may be remembered that during his less than happy five-year tenure as Artistic Director of the Dartington Summer School, Max had been of the view that it should be altered radically, to cater solely for aspiring professional composers. This had been baulked, but the concept continued to haunt Max until he had the idea of running his own composers' course. He decided on the spot that it should be held in the Kirk on Hoy. Kathy McDowell raised money from various sources, and in July 1989 the first Summer School was held, on Hoy, and was an immense success. Max recruited James MacMillan as his deputy instructor and between them they applied the direct, hands-on methods that Max has advocated so strenuously all his life.

Since then it has been a regular event, now under the care of Eona Craig, McDowell's successor as Development Manager. Every July, nine or ten young hopefuls of known talent assemble from all corners of Britain, with an occasional visitor from Europe or the United States, paying £350 to be driven fiendishly hard by Max and his chosen sidekick – a role Judith Weir has often taken with some glee. They rough it on

Hoy, too, clumping about in large boots, eating simple, steaming stews and kipping in sleeping bags in the youth hostel. The first week of the two-week course is devoted to composing their own pieces and working on technical skills; it is in the second that it really becomes fun, when four or five selected players from the SCO arrive by Stevie's ferry to perform the students' compositions. The fortnight is rounded off with a free concert in the Kirk, at which the fledgling composers' works are tried out on the local population – who always turn up, which can only be encouraging.

All agree that having the chance to *hear* their works is of invaluable assistance to them in their development – especially hearing it performed by real, live professionals. 'Max for his part was a welcome source of pragmatic and professional advice as well as a creative input. He is also a consummate entertainer, as anyone lucky enough to be invited to dinner at his home on Hoy will attest,' said pupil Harry London. 'Max and Judith were excellent tutors,' said Michael Mullen. 'I felt instantly at ease with them both, and found their observations and remarks very stimulating. It was also a great experience to be confronted with the task of conducting my own piece!' And all the others say much the same. This is the final aspect of Max's lifelong commitment to the education of the nation's future composers, musicians and music-lovers, as mentioned earlier, but it bears being said again: while it is certain that his great gift to posterity internationally will undoubtedly be his compositions, it may well come to be adjudged that his greatest contribution to the musical life of his own country was his work in education.

And so we come to the most recent event of great significance in Max's life at the time of writing. We saw earlier that there had for a long time been considerable disagreement about whether four independent orchestras were too many for London. In mid-1993 the Arts Council was told by the government that for the first time in its history its funding was to be cut. The Council might have dug its toes in, refused to implement such a policy, and defied the government to abolish it. For whatever reasons, it decided instead to act as the government's mouthpiece, and dutifully announced that it was going to save money in one direction by funding two of the four London orchestras a little more generously – or rather, a little less parsimoniously – by cutting off the grant altogether to the other two. It was an odd conclusion to come to, as, given a conductor who knows his business and a half-way decent allocation of rehearsal time, any one of them is as good as any professional symphony orchestra in the world.

The London Symphony Orchestra was declared exempt from all that followed, on grounds of artistic excellence. The other three orchestras – the London Philharmonic, the Royal Philharmonic and the Philharmonia – were invited to submit applications for the second of the two grants on offer. One of them would get it. The other two would be unlucky, and would, in all probability, go out of business. It is almost certain that the Arts Council hoped that the orchestras would save it embarrassment by coming to some private agreement beforehand, whereby two of them would merge, leaving just one out in the cold, or perhaps even that all three would merge, thus solving the Council's problems for it. The orchestras declined to assist at their own dissolution, however, and all three most unhelpfully applied for the remaining subsidy.

That these orchestras were being made to go through an appallingly undignified, indeed humiliating procedure does not seem to have occurred to anyone on the government or Arts Council side. At all events, the next step was the government's appointment of a committee, headed by a recently promoted Lord Justice of Appeal, Lord Justice Hoffmann, to decide which of the three contenders for the grant would be successful.

By the end of the affair, however, more than one member of the committee were undoubtedly wishing they had never agreed to sit on it, and they undoubtedly included Lord Justice Hoffmann himself. He felt driven to take a step that must surely be unprecedented in the entire annals of government committees of inquiry, when he told the Musicians' Union (which, needless to say, was ferociously opposing the whole business) that of all the possible results of his committee's deliberations, the one he hoped the government would adopt would be to ignore its findings altogether and re-think the whole question.

Lord Justice Hoffmann was not the only one to be embarrassed. Reports were filtering out towards the end of the committee's deliberations that another member of the committee, Henry Fogel, executive director of the Chicago Symphony Orchestra, was not only acutely embarrassed, but thoroughly sick of his self-imposed albatross.

Meanwhile, the rest of the musical and cultural world sat and watched, dumbfounded and profoundly though helplessly sympathetic towards our superlative orchestral musicians. Dr Helga Grünevelt of the Berlin Philharmonic Orchestra – one of the very orchestras which the Arts Council had held up to the hapless London orchestras as a model to be emulated by the 'super-orchestra' that was expected to emerge from the battle – sent open messages, expressing sympathy for the orchestras, with a good deal of blank incomprehension plainly visible between the lines. There was a great deal of hand-wringing; but nobody actually *did* anything at all – mainly, one feels fairly confident, because nobody could think of anything constructive to do.

This led to a certain amount of paralysis among the horrified opponents of the proposed measures. Among the first to act, however, was Max, with a strongly worded letter to *The Times* on 9 August. It was a passionate plea that glorious orchestras that had taken decades to build should not be destroyed by a stroke of a bureaucrat's pen.

Eloquent as the letter was, it produced nothing in the way of action from the government, predictably enough. But Max's next move did have an effect – and a decisive one.

He had been present at a private dinner where the conversation turned to the orchestral affair, as it was bound to: in any gathering where any musician was present, it was the only topic of conversation at the time. Max commented that if any of the orchestras went under as a result of the government's actions, he would have to think very seriously about returning his knighthood and leaving Britain for ever. He did not intend this for public consumption, but, as was virtually inevitable, news of his outraged declaration got out. The following day not only was Michael and Judy Arnold's telephone ringing till it was red-hot with journalists trying to get the full facts, but the *Evening Standard* carried a report of Max's words on the Diary page. The next development was surprising: the *Daily Mail*, normally regarded more or less as the Conservative Party's house journal, contacted Max, asking him if he had really said what he had allegedly said, if he was serious, and, if so, if he would write a full-page article for the paper on the same theme.

Yes, he had; yes, he was; and yes, he certainly would, he replied, and the article appeared on Friday, 12 November, under a headline extracted from the text of his piece: 'I cannot live in a country that grants me a knighthood, but so scorns its people it would deny them music'.

The article beneath this headline repeated substantially the arguments Max had deployed in his letter to *The Times* three months earlier. He added details such as that he had just returned from conducting the RPO in Munich, where the programme of Holst and Vaughan Williams had been broadcast over forty European radio networks, and the audience stood cheering them for so long afterwards that the players actually had to leave the stage to bring the applause to a close. At the reception afterwards he was asked about the reported switching-off of the orchestra's grant (the RPO knew before they ever thought about asking for the remaining grant that they would not be the successful applicants, given the views of the musical establishment on their fund-raising methods discussed earlier). Max had replied that yes, it was more than probable that the orchestra would have its subsidy withdrawn, and that it would go out of business as a consequence. This was greeted, he said, by a mixture of hilarity and general disbelief from their German hosts, both at the paltriness of the sums made available by the British government and at the threat to cut even that pittance.

He ended his article by claiming that musicians still found Britain 'despite its officials' an attractive and worthwhile place to live. He asserted that it was time to declare that that would change utterly if any of our orchestras were lost. No decent musician from abroad would consider setting foot in the place, he said; and as for himself, 'who was born here, bred here, live here and love this land – I could not remain in a country that so scorns its people that it would deny them music. In 1987 I was proud to receive a knighthood for services to the music of Britain. I now have no option but seriously to consider returning that knighthood.'

The effect was immediate, and dramatic. No one knows quite what went on behind the scenes, or to what effect and extent the Hoffmann Committee, the government or the Arts Council were influenced by Max's quiet but deadly serious declaration. What is certain is that the outcry rapidly turned into a tumult of ferocious criticism of the government's attitude. Very soon after it, the committee produced its verdict: divided, with a majority abstaining, it came down on the side of the Philharmonia as most worthy to receive the second grant; and almost immediately the government, through the Arts Council, announced that the whole sorry business was to be shelved, and that all four orchestras would receive at least some grant – enough to scrape by on it appears – for the present.

So in the end the result was a fudge, acceptable to no one but better than sudden death for one of the orchestras. The whole affair was a sickening piece of skulduggery, typical of the philistinism and incompetence of successive Conservative governments. One thing is clear: the London orchestras owe their survival *pro tem* to Max as much as to anyone. It may turn out that this was his finest hour.

It was an impassioned and brave stand. Impassioned because it clearly came straight from the heart, and was unarguably sincere, brave because, as one commentator remarked, 'it risked the ridicule of failure'. Well, that's as maybe; but in the event, it worked. For myself, it also generated a fit of the shivers on Max's behalf. I could not imagine the idea of his leaving his home on the crag on the Hoy coast, or his friends there and in the Orkneys generally.

I talked to Max about the affair shortly after his stand, and just before the final verdict on the orchestras' fate, and naturally I asked him first if he had really meant what he said about leaving the country. This brought a wry smile, and an oblique answer. He had had many letters and personal comments, he said, and without a solitary exception they had all been to the effect of – in his own words – 'OK, chuck your knighthood back, that doesn't matter, but for God's sake don't go.' I asked next where he would go to live, and he answered that promptly enough: to the south of France or to Italy. But my own feeling was that he would not, almost certainly could not, conceive of leaving Hoy.

This leaves the distinct possibility that he might at any rate remain on Hoy, continue his increasingly deep-rooting experience in Scotland, and, if he eschewed anything, eschew England. This leads us to one final aspect of his recent life. In 1983 he had made the last of his numerous moves within London, selling his flat in Judd Street and taking a much larger, penthouse apartment in Kingsley House, near Olympia.

In January 1992, however, he made one more move, and this one was different, in that it represented a decisive shift of his centre of gravity north of the border; for in May of the same year he bought a new flat in a very smart part of Edinburgh. In addition to being in the best part of the city, it was within spitting distance of the SCO's offices; and it meant that for the first time in his life he had no home, not even a pied-à-terre, in London, or in England at all. This was only a part of a general Scotticizing process that had begun, it is fair to say, at the precise moment when he fell in love with Hoy back in 1970. If further evidence of this is needed, the following story, which comes from his own mouth, provides it.

In 1992 *An Orkney Wedding, with Sunrise* achieved the relatively uncommon distinction, for a work by a living composer, of being performed at the last night of the Proms. To add to the distinction, it was in the second half, too, among all the sea-shanties and union-jack-waving, and to be broadcast to half the world's televisions. It was a great success, too, with a generous ration of the usual horseplay from Andrew Davis and a large bottle of Scotch, the latter generously partaken of by, among others, George McIlwham, the piper, his usual magnificent self in full Highland rig, and thirsty after performing his part with all his customary panache. There was one awkward moment, however, when Andrew Davis called on Max to take a bow. The camera panned round to where, not long before, it had clearly discerned Max in the audience, and there, starkly revealed was . . . a very empty Albert Hall seat.

Once again, having the chance to ask him, I did so: had he stormed off in high dudgeon, I asked, because Andrew Davis temporarily forgot his duty, so that the call for Max to take his bow was a little late? Or had he disapproved of the horseplay with the whisky bottle?

Neither, said Max. No. The reason was that 'I'd disappeared to the bar with the bagpiper. Obviously, as someone who lives in Scotland, I couldn't be seen among people singing "Land of Hope and Glory", so one simply had to get out. It really is the most frightful piece of English imperialism, and the Scots are deeply concerned about England, and democracy, so it was simply something one couldn't be a part of . . .'

This demonstrates Max's essential attitude, which is that he is very glad to be of Scotland, but does not consider himself Scottish, even by adoption. He is extraordinarily sensitive about this distinction, feels acutely conscious of his status as a guest of the Scottish people in their country; and he will do nothing to put in jeopardy the special relationship he has spent the last twenty-odd years constructing with the Scottish. He has, I think it is fair to say, been so successful that it would be possible for him to retain his Scottish and Orcadian homes, and his happy, comfortable relationship with the Scots, if he did ever decide to abandon England in despair.

If, then, he sees himself as being of Scotland but not Scottish, does he still think of himself as essentially English? No, he said; and he went on to say something rather astonishing, and rather sad: 'I think I shall always be an outsider wherever I go, simply because of being a composer. This is largely the result of the arts revolutions in the early part of the twentieth century, which alienated the creator from the rest of society. However, I have put down roots in Orkney, more than anywhere else I've ever been except Manchester, which is not somewhere I want to live. But I'm always conscious of having an English accent; and I'm conscious of not wanting to trespass on Scottish composers' ground. Not that I think I've done so, but I don't want to risk being resented by seeming to declare myself a Scottish composer. I see myself as a citizen of Europe, based in Scotland, influenced by Scottish music, and by the people I've got to know there.'

As a summing-up it is entirely typical of the man that Max has become, in many ways a parallel of the music – or, more likely, the music has faithfully reflected its creator's state of mind. So, just as the late music has been possessed of an inner tranquillity unlike anything underlying the music of his earlier phases, so this statement of how he perceives his own position in the world is that of a man considerably at ease with himself, confident in his powers. It's a long way from Salford. Yet the repose to which it testifies perhaps represents a return to the stability of his childhood after a spiritual journey embracing many decades, many phases and much internal strife. Possibly – his friends will all hope so – it is the declaration of a man who has found peace.

Postlude

In October 1993 Max conducted a concert of his own works in Oslo, which was received with a standing ovation lasting no less than ten minutes – which, standing after a long period of paying proper attention to music, is a fair definition of eternity. The following day's press reports were as rhapsodic as the concert audience had been – with one exception. The general tenor of the dissenting judgement was that the programme, which had included the concert suite from *Caroline Mathilde*, the Trumpet Concerto and the *Orkney Wedding*, had been far too cosy, far too comfortable; the audience, wrote the dissenter, had clearly been enjoying themselves far too much for a programme of contemporary music . . . which exemplifies the pretentiousness and snobbery of much talk about contemporary music. Much more importantly, however, it goes to show that at a time when most people still shun contemporary music, Max's has been an exception. Over many years he has received a generally good press; and nowadays full houses and standing ovations are quite common at his concerts. It is clear that he is among a small (though growing) minority of contemporary composers who are actually *liked* by a fair proportion of the musical public.

Further confirmation of this comes from his record company, Collins Classics. He has, most unusually for a living composer, an exclusive contract with them, and they are running an imaginative programme of recordings, taking major new works into the studio as they appear and interspersing them with what in the company's judgement are the most significant of the older pieces. In a highly adventurous scheme Collins are continuing and expanding on good work begun many years before by another of the brighter spirits among the recording companies, Unicorn-Kanchana – also a small independent company, which says much about the British recording industry. They had already got a very respectable amount of Max's work, mostly from his middle period, on to LP and then on to CD. Within a year or two of publication of this book Collins will have issued recordings of most of the Strathclyde concertos, most of the symphonies, two more of the operas, the enormously popular *The Lighthouse* and, perhaps bravest and most enterprising of all, *Resurrection*, giving that maligned and – in Max's firm opinion at least – unjustly neglected work a chance of a fair hearing, and a good deal more. Meanwhile, their CD of two masterpieces from the 1970s, *Black Pentecost* and *A Stone Litany*, has already been an enormous success, and their next venture, with *Worldes Blis* and *Turn of the Tide*, an even bigger one.

So far as the record catalogues are concerned, then, Max has already joined the highly select band of living composers with a fair and just representation of their work, and that is set to improve; and this must be owing principally to the fact that there are sufficient people who like his music enough to spend money on recordings. So he is not without honour in his own time and his own country.

Not without honour. And not without notoriety, either, at times. What is to be our final assessment at the end of this account, as Max approaches his sixtieth birthday?

From the late 1950s and early 1960s when his teaching methods at Cirencester not only attracted nationwide attention from the educational establishment but became matter for general news programmes and articles in national radio, television and press, to his pivotal intervention in the orchestra-funding crisis of the nineties, he has been at the centre of British musical life for over three decades. They span the austere early works drawing on medieval and Renaissance music, through the lurid expressionism of the 1960s, of which his friend James Murdoch could say, 'You have to remember that in those days Max was utterly rejected by the Establishment: gay, mad, a witch.' The decisive move to Orkney in the seventies brought ever-deepening roots and security, with an array of symphonies, concertos, tone poems and song cycles, a rich harvest of consummately crafted works, inventive, entertaining, often searching.

Yet there has for some time been a gathering school of thought that seems to feel he is slipping from a high position in the musical life of the nation. One commentator went so far as to put it in precisely those terms, during the row over orchestral funding in late 1993: writing in the *Independent on Sunday*, Michael White voted Max his 'Musician of the Year' for his part in that sorry débâcle, saying in passing, ' . . . Sir Peter Maxwell Davies, who has reclaimed the central position in British musical life that he seemed, not so long ago, to have surrendered . . . ' This feeling is closely bound up with a strong groundswell of feeling that he is also becoming conservative musically: less adventurous, more accessible, more tonal, more tuneful, certainly not the angry young man of the 1960s and early 1970s.

Most of this is nonsense: he *isn't* an angry young man any more, not least because he isn't a young man any more, though he isn't exactly doddering either. But he is certainly still angry, as anyone can testify who has heard him speak at any time in the recent past of the government or the Arts Council, to offer only a couple of examples. But no one in his right senses would expect a composer of any genuine calibre *not* to have moved on from the heady days of his twenties and thirties when he was turning out screeching, harrowing expressionist works. Since then he has grown two decades older, travelled the world, put down roots on Hoy deeper than anywhere he has known apart from the city of his childhood, found steadfast and beloved friends there and, most crucial of all, found in great measure the serenity that he had, in a sense, been seeking all his life. He has made most of the Great Statements About Life that he had felt impelled to make, and since then he has, to put it in a couple of words, grown up.

None of this has deterred a lot of people from saying things like 'You know, old Max is becoming a romantic in his old age . . . ' or 'Max is becoming a part of the musical establishment . . . ' Others cite the 'long grey movements he writes all the time these days.' One commentator, musically very learned, a friend of Max's and very sympathetic towards him, says that he often finds nowadays that he is unable to hear the musical sources that Max claims underlie his recent works. Max, he says, will say that such-and-such a work is based on such-and-such a plainchant. But when he, the friend, comes to hear the work, he can hear nothing whatever of the plainchant. I asked him whether this could possibly matter, and he went on to say he felt that it suggested strongly that Max is unsure of himself musically, and is trying to erect imaginary compositional supports to cover his uncertainty.

Max himself provided the most effective riposte to those who would seek to turn the act of creation into some arcane black art, the preserve of a few initiates only, when he pointed out that the mathematical equations that had gone into the second symphony were of great interest to composers but of none to listeners. To return to our metaphor of the scaffolding, if the builder was scared of heights and took a parachute when he worked on the roof, there is no more reason why we should know that than about the nature and quantity of scaffolding, once the house is built. So, provided that Max is happy with the piece of music and the use he has made of the plainchant within it, it doesn't matter a damn whether we can hear it distinctly or whether it has been comprehensively subsumed into the fabric of the new piece.

As for the notion that his music is somehow of less interest, or of less intrinsic value now that it is more tuneful, less discordant and less obviously 'difficult', that is purely a matter of individual taste. Personally, I find all his music interesting, from all the phases of his career; and I have favourites from all periods, from the Trumpet Sonata of his university days, through the *Five Klee Pictures* from Cirencester, *Worldes Blis* from the works of angry expressionism, right up to the more lyrical, more tonal symphonies and Strathclydes of the present day. But the music he is writing today is if anything *more* adventurous than anything he has done before, more interesting. This is not least because as it becomes more accessible it loses the protection that comes from being of an avant-garde movement, with the passionate support of a coterie assured, no matter what the rest of the world think. The great works of the late 1980s and the 1990s go into the world quite naked, with nothing to depend on but themselves. The clinching argument for me is that whatever else may be said about Max's most recent work, it still sounds like no one else's but his. That is perhaps the sternest test one can apply of all.

Max has given more than one definition of what he is about and what he hopes he is achieving. 'I'm determined', he said on one occasion, 'to overturn the notion that classical music is elitist. Music is for everyone and they deserve the best. If it is presented in the very best way, then everyone will enjoy it.' He has, most will agree, been faithful to that ideal in his own work and conduct. From his days at Cirencester to the taking of music out into the community in the Strathclyde and Turn of the Tide projects, from his generous purchase by stealth of the clavichord for the schoolboy while he was at Princeton to his head-on confrontation with the forces of philistinism over the orchestra-funding row, he has never failed to try to live up to his sworn object of bringing music to everyone who wants it. There has always been opposition, and when he has overcome it, as he usually has, he has done so mainly by the use of a blunt, uncompromising honesty and integrity: he is not a man who could ever be blackmailed.

Another form of words he found to express what he was trying to do was in answer to a question from me when I interviewed him at Bunertoon, while a screaming tempest howled round the little croft outside. 'The composer's function is to give insight into experience in a way that can't be expressed through words or visual imagery,' he said. That he has done that much, at least, will surely not be disputed. For many, he has done a great deal more.

He has achieved the distinction, still uncommon, of becoming popular well within his own lifetime, and he has done so without in any way compromising his own artistic standards: he has always been his own man, he has never condescended, never composed down to any audience – on the contrary, the principle of never composing down to people, including young people, has been central to his creative ethic since his time at Cirencester and before.

He has written not merely good music, but a lot of good music: his bestowal of his gifts has been prodigious; but no one has ever successfully accused him of being *merely* prolific, of being prolific for its own sake. His music has been of a remarkably consistent quality throughout his composing life right up to the present day; children's pieces, pop jingles for film scores or light-hearted pieces for Pops orchestras are as scrupulously crafted as the great symphonic, chamber and music theatre works.

There are several important hallmarks of Max's work. First, his versatility, unmatched by any contemporary British composer. To see this at its most extreme we have only to set the high jinks of *An Orkney Wedding* beside the bleakness of *Ecce Manus Tradentis*, the ferocity of *St Thomas Wake* beside the simplicity and sweetness of *Lullaby for Lucy*, or the anguished dementia of *Eight Songs* beside the tranquil serenity of the close of the fourth Strathclyde Concerto. And the eight Strathclyde concertos so far written are a lecture course in versatility of mood and texture.

Then there is the high moral tone that runs through so much of his work. This, in turn, is balanced by his humour, sometimes boyish, sometimes mordant, often black. It is obvious enough in works such as *Orkney Wedding* or *Winterfold*; it is the moving spirit behind much of the opera *The Lighthouse* and (at its blackest) all of *Resurrection*, and has its part in most of the music theatre pieces, wry and poignant in *Eight Songs* and *Miss Donnithorne*, alternately gentle and ferocious in *The No. 11 Bus*. But it has never been far beneath the foxtrots, the creative force beneath many of the little dances and realizations and enlivening many an otherwise sombre or reflective piece, from the *Five Klee Pictures* of 1960 onwards.

But perhaps Max's most recognizable signature is his passionate portrayal of landscapes and, especially, seascapes. It is arguable that no composer has evoked the spirit of a place as variously and hauntingly as has Max in his continuing portrayal of the Orkneys – the sea eagle, his golden cousin, the vast skies, the beetling bluffs and scarps, the keening wind and the tanned, tough, humorous people, but most of all and always, the roar of the sea . . . it is in his depiction of the islands and the eternal, unresting ocean that thunders on their shores that we see Max at his most personal, his most committed and his most solitary. In the end it may well turn out that the city boy will be remembered as the greatest British creator of musical seascapes.

In an Article in *The Sunday Times* of 16 January 1994, the composer Steve Martland attempted to find some way of calibrating the merit of a composer. He identified a primary difficulty in doing so, because 'the cultural imperative of our so-called post-modern world denies art any meaningful criticism because it insists that all creative endeavour is of equal significance. There is no commonly held consensus against which "good" and "bad" can be measured.' However, Martland goes on to suggest various possible ways of assessing composers' relative worth. Some composers, he says first, 'like pop stars . . . are defined by their popularity with the CD-buying public'. He lists several composers, many of them minimalists, to whom this criterion might apply, and says that despite the fact that their music is cordially loathed, mostly by hard-line modernist critics, it can't be a bad thing that so much contemporary music is so popular.

This seems quite unarguable whatever you think of the composers he lists (Reich, Glass, Pärt, Gorecki, Tavener, John Adams and Michael Nyman). Even if you think their music is worthless, if the public are buying their music in large quantities there is reason to hope that the same public will, eventually, graduate to better music – or, at any rate, to what you regard as better music; and if you think the listed composers are fine anyway, the problem doesn't arise in the first place.

By this rather wobbly criterion of popularity with the CD-buying public, Max need not worry. There are very few living composers with more CDs in the catalogue than he has, and he is rapidly overhauling those few.

Having opined that the popularity of these composers couldn't be a bad thing, Martland went on to quote Gerald Larner as a high priest of modernism, denouncing the growing popularity of the composers mentioned as 'the triumph of market forces over a previous philosophy that had composers "taking pride in their impenetrability"'. If this is really something Gerald Larner relishes, he is clearly the spiritual equivalent of the Norwegian reviewer with whom this Postlude began. His attitude contrasts pointedly with Max's comment on what he had learned from his generally miserable time at university: 'I learned that composing is only ten per cent. You've got to give 90 per cent to the struggle to get heard.' This cuts the heart out of the whole ethic of composers revelling in their own impenetrability. But none of this is needed: by definition, art is creativity shared with other people.

Fortunately, there have always been sufficient people – young ones significantly more than old ones – who have found Max's music relatively easy to share. This fact sets him aside both from people like Larner on the one hand, and from those who claim that he's getting conservative and romantic as he gets older, on the other. And if it doesn't take us any farther along the road of deciding how he stands in relation to other composers, that is ultimately because the attempt to do that is fatuous in the first place.

That Max is among a handful of great composers of his day is, however, pretty generally conceded in the musical world. It is still vigorously denied, of course, by detractors, both those who simply damn all new music with blanket condemnation and those who profess to like some of it but don't like Max's. Some, fairer-minded, concede his stature while not finding his music to their own taste. In the end none of this matters much. History will make its own judgement and it won't care what we think.

Not least among the ways in which Max's music has always been unmistakably his own is that he has never sought to separate his creation from his own attitudes. On the contrary, he imports them quite openly into his music. Here is the 'intensely moral composer' that McBurney called him, with his horror at cruelty, philistinism, and anti-intellectualism, his detestation of the cheap and nasty, the bogus and the kitsch, his distaste for religion, especially in its authoritarian, thought-policing aspects, his concern for the environment, his hatred of commercialism run amok, all written plainly in his music. McBurney contrasted Max's music with that of Harrison Birtwistle, which, he said, was 'as moral as the rock in a hillside – it's not moral at all, it's just there.' I find all these attitudes of Max's profoundly sympathetic, and I get an inspiring feeling of relief to find such concerns embedded as an integral part of a composer's musical being.

But I also love his music, as Beecham put it, for the noise it makes. The giant seascapes in the first two symphonies, the shoal of mackerel in the second Strathclyde, the golden eagle in the fourth symphony and his sea-going cousin in his own little horn piece; George Mackay Brown's limpid poetry and prose, worked together with Max's music like gemstone and precious metal worked into something greater than the sum of its parts – here, surely, is a partnership straight from Heaven; all the pastel colours of Orkney, all the liquid metals of the Pentland Firth, the revellers at Jack and Dorothy's wedding and the sudden glory of the piper piping the sun up the sky, and the ravishing simplicity of the little lullaby for their child – all of these, and many more, come high among the things that, for me, make life worth living.

Max is a man of contrasts. Some of these we have seen, such as the rejection of religion coupled with the fascination for religious forms and attitudes; the co-existence within him of an immense capacity for pity for the suffering and injustice in the world and an equal capacity for anger and violence of his own in response to it, often expressed in his music; the instant spiritual and creative rapport with the Roman

Catholic poet Mackay Brown working in the Calvinist setting of Orkney, and so forth. He is intensely intellectual: all his tastes tend towards the highbrow or the heavyweight; his musical and literary tastes leave no room for the occasional Stephen King paperback, or a sneaking soft spot for Led Zeppelin, Glenn Miller or even Thelonious Monk. Yet he is at the same time an intensely emotional man, given to making emotional responses to events or people. The tension thus set up within him and around him, like an electro-magnetic field, is integral to his creation. Meanwhile, like many people with much to be assuming about, he is the most unassuming of men, genuinely modest, uncondescending.

In the last resort, of course, any judgement must be personal. James Murdoch spoke for many when he remarked once that 'He has joined the ranks of the saints: immortal through his music.' That may well prove to be true; but how history judges him is for history to say. What is undeniable is that his music, so unambiguously his own, is suffused with the essence of the man: his quick wit and humour, his anger and outrage in the face of injustice and, above all, his profound humanity. For his own time, we may adapt the words of the poet of his adopted homeland, and say that his rank, whatever it may turn out to be, will be but the guinea's stamp, but the man's a man for a' that.

LIST OF PUBLISHED WORKS
INDEX OF WORKS
GENERAL INDEX

List of Published Works

This list includes works commissioned but not completed at time of going to press. The year given is the date of composition. Where a compact disc recording is available, details are given at the end of the entry for the work concerned.

1952   *Quartet Movement*, string quartet
1955   Sonata for Trumpet and Piano, opus 1. CDs: 1) BIS RECORDS (SWEDEN) CD 287 trumpet Håkan Hardenberger, piano Roland Pontinen; 2) CRYSTAL (USA) CD 665 trumpet Thomas Stevens, piano Zia Carno
1956   *Five Pieces for Piano*, opus 2
1956   *Stedman Doubles*, for clarinet and percussion
1956   Clarinet Sonata
1957   *Alma Redemptoris Mater*, for ensemble
      St Michael Sonata, for seventeen wind instruments
1958   *Prolation*, for orchestra
1959   *Ricercar And Doubles on 'To Many a Well'*, for ensemble
      Five Motets, for SATB soli, SATB chorus and ensemble
      Five Klee Pictures, for school orchestra (rev. 1979)
      William Byrd: Three Dances, arranged for school orchestra
1960   *O Magnum Mysterium*, for SATB chorus, with two instrumental sonatas and organ fantasia. CDs: 1) COLLINS CLASSICS CD 12702/COLLINS CLASSICS CD 30032 (excerpt) The Sixteen Choir and Orchestra cond. Harry Christophers, organ Margaret Phillips; 2) CHESKY (USA) CD83 (excerpt) Westminster Choir cond. Joseph Flummerfelt
      Five Voluntaries, arranged for school orchestra
1961   String Quartet
      'Ave Maria – Hail, Blessed Flower', carol for SATB chorus
      Te Lucis Ante Terminum, for SATB chorus and ensemble
1962   *First Fantasia on an 'In Nomine' of John Taverner*, for orchestra
      'Carol on St Steven', for SATB chorus
      'Jesus Autem Hodie', carol for SATB chorus
      'Nowell', carol for SATB chorus. CD: DEUTSCHE GRAMMOPHON CD 410 590 2GH Choir of Westminster Abbey cond. Simon Preston
      Alma Redemptoris, for chorus of four equal voices
      Leopardi Fragments, for soprano, contralto and ensemble
      The Lord's Prayer, for SATB chorus
      Sinfonia, for orchestra. CD: UNICORN-KANCHANA CD UKCD 2026 Scottish Chamber Orchestra cond. Peter Maxwell Davies
1963   *Veni, Sancte Spiritus*, for SATB soli, SATB chorus and orchestra
1964   *Second Fantasia on an 'In Nomine' of John Taverner*, for orchestra
      Shakespeare Music, for ensemble

Ave, Plena Gracia, for SATB chorus with optional organ
Five Little Pieces for Piano

1965 *Seven 'In Nomine',* for ensemble. CDs: COLLINS CLASSICS CD
10952/COLLINS CLASSICS CD 30032 (excerpt) Aquarius cond. Nicholas
Cleobury
Ecce Manus Tradentis, for SATB soli, SATB chorus and ensemble
Revelation and Fall, for soprano and ensemble (rev. 1980)
'Shall I Die for Mannis Sake?', carol for SA chorus with piano
The Shepherd's Calendar, for youth chorus (SATB) and ensemble

1966 *Notre Dame des Fleurs,* for soprano, mezzo-soprano, counter-tenor and
ensemble
Five Carols, for SA chorus. CD: DECCA ARGO CD 436 119 1 ZH Choir of
King's College Cambridge cond. Stephen Cleobury

1967 *Antechrist,* for ensemble
Hymnos, for clarinet and piano

1968 *Missa Super l'Homme Armé,* for speaker or singer (male or female) and
ensemble (rev. 1971)
Stedman Caters, for ensemble
Fantasia and Two Pavans after Henry Purcell, realization for ensemble. CD:
UNICORN-KANCHANA CD UKCD 2044 The Fires of London cond. Peter
Maxwell Davies
St Thomas Wake – Foxtrot for Orchestra, on a pavan by John Bull. CDs:
COLLINS CLASSICS CD 13082/COLLINS CLASSICS CD 30032 (excerpt) BBC
Philharmonic cond. Peter Maxwell Davies

1969 *Worldes Blis,* for orchestra. CD: COLLINS CLASSICS CD 13902 Royal
Philharmonic Orchestra cond. Peter Maxwell Davies
Eight Songs for a Mad King, music theatre work for baritone and
ensemble. CD: UNICORN-KANCHANA DKPG CD 9052 The Fires of
London cond. Peter Maxwell Davies, singer Julius Eastman
Solita, flute solo
Gabrieli: Canzona, realization for chamber orchestra
Vesalii Icones, music theatre work for dancer, solo cello and ensemble
Sub Tuam Protectionem, for piano

1970 *Taverner,* opera in two acts
Points and Dances from 'Taverner', instrumental dances and keyboard
pieces from the opera *Ut Re Mi,* for piano
Buxtehude: Also hat Gott die Welt geliebet, cantata for soprano and
ensemble; realization including 'original' interpretation

1971 *From Stone to Thorn,* for mezzo-soprano and ensemble
Suite from 'The Devils', for instrumental ensemble with soprano
obbligato, drawn from the sound track of Ken Russell's film. CD:
COLLINS CLASSICS CD 10952 Aquarius cond. Nicholas Cleobury
Suite from 'The Boy Friend', for orchestra or instrumental ensemble,
drawn from the sound track of Ken Russell's film based on the musical
by Sandy Wilson

1972 *Blind Man's Buff,* masque for soprano (or treble), mezzo-soprano, mime
and small orchestra
Fool's Fanfare, for speaker and ensemble

Hymn to St Magnus, for ensemble with mezzo-soprano obbligato

Tenebrae Super Gesualdo, for mezzo-soprano, guitar and instrumental ensemble. CD: UNICORN-KANCHANA CD UKCD 2044 The Fires of London cond. Peter Maxwell Davies

Canon in Memoriam Igor Stravinsky, puzzle canon for instrumental ensemble

Lullaby for Ilian Rainbow, for guitar. CD: PAULA (DENMARK) CD Per Dybro Sorensen

J. S. Bach: Prelude and Fugue in C sharp minor, 'The 48' Book 1, realization for ensemble. CD: UNICORN-KANCHANA UKCD 2044 The Fires of London cond. Peter Maxwell Davies

Dunstable: Veni Sancte Spiritus, Veni Creator Spiritus, realization plus original work, for ensemble

1973 *Stone Litany – Runes from the House of the Dead*, for mezzo-soprano and orchestra. CD: COLLINS CLASSICS CD 13662 BBC Philharmonic cond. Peter Maxwell Davies, mezzo-soprano Della Jones

Renaissance Scottish Dances, for ensemble (anon. arranged Maxwell Davies). CD: UNICORN-KANCHANA DKP CD 9070 Scottish Chamber Orchestra Ensemble cond. Peter Maxwell Davies

Si Quis Diligit Me, motet for ensemble (Peebles and Heagy, arranged Maxwell Davies). CD: UNICORN-KANCHANA UKCD 2044 The Fires of London cond. Peter Maxwell Davies

Purcell: Fantasia on One Note, realization for ensemble. CD: UNICORN-KANCHANA CD UKCD 2044 The Fires of London cond. Peter Maxwell Davies

Fiddlers at the Wedding, for soprano and ensemble

1974 *Dark Angels*, for voice and guitar

Miss Donnithorne's Maggot, music theatre work for soprano and ensemble. CD: UNICORN-KANCHANA CD DKPG 9052 The Fires of London cond. Peter Maxwell Davies, soprano Mary Thomas

All Sons of Adam, motet for ensemble (anon. Scottish 16th century arranged Maxwell Davies). CD: UNICORN-KANCHANA UKCD 2044 The Fires of London cond. Peter Maxwell Davies

Psalm 124, motet for ensemble (Peebles, Fethy, anon. arranged Maxwell Davies)

J. S. Bach: Prelude and Fugue in C♯ major, 'The 48' Book 1, realization for ensemble. CD: UNICORN-KANCHANA UKCD 2044 The Fires of London cond. Peter Maxwell Davies

1975 *Ave Maris Stella*, for ensemble. CD: UNICORN-KANCHANA UKCD 2038 The Fires of London

The Door of the Sun, for viola

The Kestrel Paced Round the Sun, for flute

The Seven Brightnesses, for clarinet

Three Studies for Percussion, for eleven percussionists

My Lady Lothian's Lilte, realization for ensemble and mezzo-soprano obbligato

Stevie's Ferry to Hoy, for piano (beginners)

1976 *Three Organ Voluntaries*. CD: (*O God Abufe* and *Psalm 124*) ECM

(GERMANY) CD 849655-2 Christopher Bowers-Broadbent

Kinloche His Fantassie, realization for ensemble. CDs: 1) UNICORN-KANCHANA CD UKCD 2044 The Fires of London cond. Peter Maxwell Davies; 2) UNICORN-KANCHANA DKP CD 9070 Scottish Chamber Orchestra Ensemble cond. Peter Maxwell Davies

Anakreontika, Greek songs for mezzo-soprano and ensemble

The Blind Fiddler, song cycle for soprano and ensemble

Symphony No. 1, for orchestra. CD: COLLINS CLASSICS (to be released 1995) BBC Philharmonic cond. Peter Maxwell Davies

The Martyrdom of St Magnus, chamber opera in nine scenes without interval for mezzo-soprano, tenor, two baritones, bass and instrumental ensemble. CD: UNICORN-KANCHANA KDP CD 9100 Music Theatre Wales, Scottish Chamber Opera Ensemble cond. Michael Rafferty

1977 'Norn Pater Noster', prayer for SATB chorus and organ

Westerlings, for SATB chorus and orchestra

Runes from a Holy Island, for ensemble. CD: UNICORN-KANCHANA CD UKCD 2038 The Fires of London cond. Peter Maxwell Davies

A Mirror of Whitening Light, for ensemble

'Ave Rex Angelorum', for SATB chorus. CD: CONTINUUM CCD 1043 Elysian Singers cond. Matthew Greenall

Our Father Whiche In Heaven Art, motet for ensemble (Angus, arranged Maxwell Davies). CD: UNICORN-KANCHANA UKCD 2044 The Fires of London cond. Peter Maxwell Davies

1978 *The Two Fiddlers*, opera in two acts for children to play and sing

Le Jongleur de Notre Dame, masque for baritone, mime/juggler, ensemble and children's band

Salome, ballet in two acts

Four Lessons, for two clavichords

Dances from 'The Two Fiddlers', for ensemble. CD: UNICORN-KANCHANA DKP CD 9052 Scottish Chamber Orchestra Ensemble cond. Peter Maxwell Davies

1979 *Black Pentecost*, for mezzo-soprano, baritone and orchestra. CD: COLLINS CLASSICS CD 13662 BBC Philharmonic, mezzo-soprano Della Jones, baritone David Wilson-Johnson

Solstice of Light, for tenor, SATB chorus and organ. CD: DECCA ARGO 436 119 2 ZH Choir of King's College Cambridge cond. Stephen Cleobury, tenor Neil Mackie, organ Christopher Hughes

Nocturne, for alto flute

Kirkwall Shopping Songs, for young children to sing and play

The Lighthouse, chamber opera in one act with prologue for tenor, baritone, bass and ensemble. CD: COLLINS CLASSICS CD (to be released autumn 1994) BBC Philharmonic Ensemble cond. Peter Maxwell Davies, tenor Neil Mackie, baritone Christopher Keyte, bass Ian Comboy

Cinderella, pantomime opera in two acts for young children to play and sing

1980 *The Yellow Cake Revue*, anti-nuclear cabaret for voice and piano

Farewell to Stromness, piano interlude from 'The Yellow Cake Revue'. CDs: 1) UNICORN-KANCHANA DKP CD 9070 Peter Maxwell Davies; 2) COLLINS CLASSICS CD 30332 Seta Tanyel; 3) CENTAUR (USA) CD CRC 2102 David Holzman

Yesnaby Ground, piano interlude from 'The Yellow Cake Revue'. CDs: 1) UNICORN-KANCHANA DKP CD 9070 Peter Maxwell Davies; 2) COLLINS CLASSICS CD 30032 Seta Tanyel; 3) CENTAUR (USA) CD CRC 2102 David Holzman

A Welcome to Orkney, for ensemble

Little Quartet No. 1, string quartet

Symphony No. 2, for orchestra. CD: COLLINS CLASSICS (to be released 1994) BBC Philharmonic cond. Peter Maxwell Davies

1981 *The Medium*, monodrama for mezzo-soprano

Piano Sonata. CD: CENTAUR (USA) CD CRC 2102 David Holzman

The Rainbow, music theatre work for young children to sing and play

Hill Runes, for guitar. CD: PAULA (DENMARK) CD Per Dybro Sorensen

The Bairns of Brugh, for ensemble. CD: UNICORN-KANCHANA CD UKCD 2044 The Fires of London cond. Peter Maxwell Davies

Little Quartet No. 2, string quartet

Sonatina for Trumpet

Lullaby for Lucy, for SATB chorus. CDs: 1) COLLINS CLASSICS CD 30032 The Sixteen cond. Harry Christophers; 2) UNICORN-KANCHANA DKP CD 9070 Choir of St Mary's School Edinburgh cond. Peter Maxwell Davies

Brass Quintet

Seven Songs Home, for children's voices. CD: UNICORN-KANCHANA DKP CD 9070 Choir of St Mary's School Edinburgh cond. Peter Maxwell Davies

Songs of Hoy, for children to play and sing

1982 *Sea Eagle*, for horn. CD: EMI CD CDC 7 54420 2 Michael Thompson

Image, Reflection, Shadow, for ensemble. CD: UNICORN-KANCHANA CD UKCD 2038 The Fires of London

Sinfonia Concertante, for orchestra. CD: UNICORN-KANCHANA CD UKCD 2026 Scottish Chamber Orchestra cond. Peter Maxwell Davies

Organ Sonata

Gesualdo: Two Motets, arranged for brass quintet

Tallis: Four Motets, arranged for brass quintet

March: Pole Star, for brass quintet

1983 *Birthday Music for John*, trio for flute, viola and cello

Into the Labyrinth, cantata for tenor and orchestra. CD: UNICORN-KANCHANA CD UKCD 2022 Scottish Chamber Orchestra cond. Peter Maxwell Davies, tenor Neil Mackie

Sinfonietta Accademica, for orchestra. CD: UNICORN-KANCHANA CD UKCD 2022 Scottish Chamber Orchestra cond. Peter Maxwell Davies

1984 *Agnus Dei*, for two solo sopranos, viol and cello

Sonatina for Violin and Cimbalom

Unbroken Circle, for ensemble

The No. 11 Bus, music theatre work for tenor, mezzo-soprano, baritone, two dancers, mime and ensemble

Guitar Sonata. CDs: 1) PAULA (DENMARK) Per Dybro Sorensen; 2) NEW ALBION RECORDS (USA) CD NA 032 David Tanenbaum

'One Star, at Last', carol for SATB chorus

1985   Symphony No. 3, for orchestra. CDs: 1) COLLINS CLASSICS (to be released 1994) BBC Philharmonic cond. Peter Maxwell Davies; 2) BBC RECORDS CD 560x BBC Philharmonic cond. Edward Downes

An Orkney Wedding, with Sunrise, for orchestra. CDs: 1) UNICORN-KANCHANA DKP CD 9070 Scottish Chamber Orchestra cond. Peter Maxwell Davies, highland bagpipes George MacIlwham; 2) COLLINS CLASSICS CD 30032 Royal Philharmonic Orchestra cond. Peter Maxwell Davies, highland bagpipes George MacIlwham; 3) PHILIPS CD 420–946-2 Boston Pops Orchestra cond. John Williams, highland bagpipes Nancy Tunnicliffe

First Ferry to Hoy, for junior SATB chorus, junior percussion and recorder band, and ensemble

The Peat Cutters, for brass band, SATB youth chorus, and children's chorus

Violin Concerto, for violin and orchestra. CD: SONY CLASSICAL CD SMK 58928 CBS CD MK 42449 Royal Philharmonic Orchestra cond. André Previn, violin Isaac Stern

1986   *Jimmack the Postie*, for orchestra. CD: UNICORN-KANCHANA CD DKP 9070 Scottish Chamber Orchestra cond. Peter Maxwell Davies

House of Winter, for vocal sextet or AATBBB chorus

Sea Runes, for vocal sextet or AATBBB chorus

Excuse Me, for voice and ensemble

Dowland: Farewell-a-Fancye, realization for ensemble

Winterfold, for mezzo-soprano and ensemble

1987   Strathclyde Concerto No. 1 for Oboe and Orchestra. CD: UNICORN-KANCHANA DKP CD 9085 Scottish Chamber Orchestra cond. Peter Maxwell Davies, oboe Robin Miller

Resurrection, opera in one act with prologue. CD: COLLINS CLASSICS (to be released spring 1995) BBC Philharmonic, The Steve Martland Band, Electronic Vocal Quartet, Marching Band cond. Peter Maxwell Davies

1988   *Mishkenot*, for ensemble

Strathclyde Concerto No. 2 for Cello and Orchestra. CD: UNICORN-KANCHANA DKP CD 9085 Scottish Chamber Orchestra cond. Peter Maxwell Davies, cello William Conway

Concerto for Trumpet and Orchestra. CDs: 1) COLLINS CLASSICS CD 11812 Scottish National Orchestra cond. Peter Maxwell Davies, trumpet John Wallace; 2) PHILIPS CD 4320752 BBC Philharmonic cond. Elgar Howarth, trumpet Håkan Hardenberger

Dances from 'The Two Fiddlers', arranged for violin and piano

Six Songs for St Andrew's, song cycle for young children to play and sing

1989   *The Great Bank Robbery*, music theatre work for children to play and sing

Symphony No. 4, for orchestra. CD: COLLINS CLASSICS CD 11812 Scottish Chamber Orchestra cond. Peter Maxwell Davies

Hallelujah! The Lord God Almightie, for SATB chorus and organ
Jupiter Landing, music theatre work for children to play and sing
Strathclyde Concerto No. 3 for Horn, Trumpet and Orchestra. CD:
   COLLINS CLASSICS CD 12392 Scottish Chamber Orchestra cond. Peter
   Maxwell Davies, horn Robert Cook, trumpet Peter Franks
Dinosaur at Large, music theatre work for children to play and sing
Threnody in Memoriam Michael Vyner, for orchestra. CD: COLLINS
   CLASSICS CD 13082/COLLINS CLASSICS CD 30032 BBC Philharmonic
   cond. Peter Maxwell Davies.

1990   Strathclyde Concerto No. 4 for Clarinet and Orchestra. CD: COLLINS
   CLASSICS CD 12392 Scottish Chamber Orchestra cond. Peter Maxwell
   Davies, clarinet Lewis Morrison
Dangerous Errand, music theatre work for very young children to sing
   and play
Caroline Mathilde, ballet in two acts
Apple Basket, Apple Blossom, for SATB chorus
Hymn to the Word of God, for tenor soli and SATB chorus. CD: DECCA
   ARGO CD 436 119 1ZH Choir of King's College Cambridge cond.
   Stephen Cleobury

1991   *The Spiders' Revenge*, music theatre work for young children to play and
   sing
Ojai Festival Overture, for orchestra. CD: COLLINS CLASSICS
   CD 13082/COLLINS CLASSICS CD 30032 BBC Philharmonic cond. Peter
   Maxwell Davies
Caroline Mathilde, Concert Suite from Act I of the ballet. CD: COLLINS
   CLASSICS CD 13082/COLLINS CLASSICS CD 20022 (CD single)/COLLINS
   CLASSICS CD 30032 (excerpt) BBC Philharmonic cond. Peter Maxwell
   Davies
Strathclyde Concerto No. 5 for Violin, Viola and String Orchestra. CD:
   COLLINS CLASSICS CD 13032 Scottish Chamber Orchestra cond. Peter
   Maxwell Davies, violin James Clark, viola Catherine Marwood
First Grace of Light, oboe solo
Strathclyde Concerto No. 6 for Flute and Orchestra. CD: COLLINS
   CLASSICS CD 13032 Scottish Chamber Orchestra cond. Peter Maxwell
   Davies, flute David Nicholson
Caroline Mathilde, Concert Suite from Act II of the ballet

1992   *A Selkie Tale*, music theatre work for children to play and sing
The Turn of the Tide, for orchestra, children's chorus, and children's
   instrumental groups. CD: COLLINS CLASSICS CD 13902 BBC
   Philharmonic cond. Peter Maxwell Davies
Strathclyde Concerto No. 7 for Double Bass and Orchestra. CD:
   COLLINS CLASSICS CD 139628 Scottish Chamber Orchestra cond. Peter
   Maxwell Davies, double bass Duncan McTier
Sir Charles, his Pavan, for orchestra. CD: COLLINS CLASSICS CD 13902
   BBC Philharmonic cond. Peter Maxwell Davies

1993   *Seven Summer Songs*, for young children to sing and play
Strathclyde Concerto No. 8 for Bassoon and Orchestra. CD: COLLINS
   CLASSICS CD 139628 Scottish Chamber Orchestra cond. Peter Maxwell

Davies, bassoon Ursula Leveaux

Two Dances from Caroline Mathilde, arranged for flute and harp

Corpus Christi, with Cat and Mouse, for SATB chorus

A Spell for Green Corn: The MacDonald Dances, for orchestra. CD: COLLINS CLASSICS CD 139628 Scottish Chamber Orchestra cond. Peter Maxwell Davies, violin James Clark

Six Secret Songs, for voices and piano

'Shepherds of Hoy', carol for children

Chat Moss, for orchestra

A Hoy Calendar, for SATB chorus

1994 Symphony No. 5, for orchestra

Strathclyde Concerto No. 9: Chamber Concerto. CD: COLLINS CLASSICS (to be released 1995) Scottish Chamber Orchestra cond. Peter Maxwell Davies

1995 Strathclyde Concerto No. 10: Concerto for Orchestra. CD: COLLINS CLASSICS (to be released 1995) Scottish Chamber Orchestra cond. Peter Maxwell Davies

Index of Works

General Index